EMILY MORRIS has an MA in Writing Studies from Edge Hill University. As well as memoir, she loves writing scripts, young adult fiction and short stories. *My Shitty Twenties* is her first book, based on her award-winning blog of the same name. Emily teaches writing workshops to both adults and teenagers. She lives in Manchester with her son and her cat and is no longer in her twenties.

EMILY MORRIS

MY SHITTY TWENTIES

A Memoir

SALT

LONDON

PUBLISHED BY SALT PUBLISHING 2017

2 4 6 8 10 9 7 5 3 1

First published in Great Britain in 2017 by
Salt Publishing Ltd
International House, 24 Holborn Viaduct, London EC1A 2BN United Kingdom

www.saltpublishing.com

Salt Publishing Limited Reg. No. 5293401

A CIP catalogue record for this book is available from the British Library

ISBN 978 1 78463 091 1 (Paperback edition)
ISBN 978 1 78463 092 8 (Electronic edition)

Typeset in Neacademia by Salt Publishing

Printed and bound in Great Britain by Clays Ltd, St Ives plc

*For my son and my mum, both of whom made this
book possible in various, wonderful ways.*

One

SEPTEMBER BROUGHT THE students back. They clogged the aisles of the Magic Bus, grubby festival wristbands ringing their arms, unsullied trainers on their feet, skin tanned by the Thai sun. Everything they said came out in a question: they'd all had *amazing* summers, they were all like, totally skint, man, and some complained of being *blatantly* on the worst comedown in the history of the entire universe?

I'd never understood why people were nasty about students. Suddenly I did. It's easy to dislike people when you're not part of what seems to be their fun and privileged club, even more so when you *were* a member but are no longer because of your own stupidity.

Being a student had afforded me more than my insular village upbringing ever could have done: an endless supply of knowledge, freedom of the city with which I had become besotted, friends who didn't think I was weird for liking techno; even a few who liked it too. And parties, so very many parties. Nights in warehouses out of town, in basements where sweat rained down from the ceiling, evenings venturing out with keys and a tenner and nothing much else, knowing I'd see the gloaming before home.

In the end, the freedom and the hedonism led me to the very opposite.

The Magic Bus was the cheapest one to get from the student suburbs, south of Manchester, into the city centre.

Apart from the massive wizards painted on the sides, there was nothing magic about that bus. I still needed to catch it most days; not because I was going to university, but because I was going to work. My part-time student job was in a call centre, selling package holidays to members of the British public who needed their regular spells in the sun. It was alright, as far as part-time student jobs go: we enjoyed our own heavily-subsidised holidays, plentiful rewards and trips called 'educationals' that were basically all-expenses-paid tours of sunny places. It was before the credit crunch and the travel industry was booming, which is why my company was happy to oblige when I'd asked if I could switch to full-time. Five days a week, I didn't disembark the bus when it stopped outside the universities and the students jostled off, bags full of books bobbing on their backs. Instead, I rested my head against the filthy window, gazing out of it, feeling my skull rattle and my teeth chatter with the thrum of the stationary bus. Each time, at All Saints Park, I craned my neck towards my building, unable to see it but wishing I was there, rushing through the wide, bright atrium with its abundant green plants, on my way to a lecture about architecture or photography or feminism. As the bus nosed its way back into the Oxford Road traffic and soared under the Mancunian Way, I'd look forwards and get out of my seat, ready for another day hooked up to the telephone, feigning cheer.

I was intercalating, a word I had only just discovered that meant taking a year out of university. Despite the feeling that my life had just come to a very sudden and jarring halt, I was very busy doing lots of alien verbs. I was intercalating, gestating and abstaining. Before long, I would be lactating.

I wished my neighbours had complained to the police and

the *Manchester Evening News* about my epic house party. I wished my student loan was, like, not even in my account. I wished my friend had burnt a pothole in my awesome vintage dress. I wished my library fine had hit three figures. I wished my housemate had pissed in the oven. I wished I had missed my connecting flight from Koh Pan Ngan to Bangkok. I wished my tent had been washed away on a wave of sewage in the famous Glastonbury floods.

Mostly, I wished I was one of them.

On this particular morning, I didn't get off the bus after the students, but before them. It was raining and the moisture drew all the bad smells out of everyone's clothes: stale smoke, sour laundry that had been left in the washer too long, patchouli joss sticks and skunk. Around that time, weird smells made me want to puke (bananas in the supermarket especially), so I spent most of the journey trying not to breathe. I'd managed to get myself a seat, a small triumph I regretted as soon as I realised I was going to have to squeeze my way through the smelly crowds before I missed my stop. "Sorry, excuse me, thank you, sorry excuse me, thank you," I said, holding my breath and sidling through. "I'm one of you, you know," I wanted to add, pointlessly.

I stepped off on to the wet pavement and took a deep breath of freshish air (diesel fumes mixed with wet grass). The Magic Bus hissed off through the puddles, spraying me with silt. In front of me, the brick of the Whitworth Art Gallery (my favourite gallery in Manchester and the world) shone glossy like red marble. Rain slapped down from the top of the grand trees in Whitworth Park, their branches sagging under the weight of the downpour. It was autumn, but few of the leaves had begun to turn. It wouldn't truly be autumn until they were golden, I told myself, or until they were shrivelled and skeletal and stamped into the ground. Autumn was my favourite time of year, but that year, I didn't want it to come. I was frightened of it, because autumn meant the definite end of the summer in which it had all begun, and would carry me closer to the thing that was inevitably next.

The last time I'd walked down Hathersage Road had been in the summer, for an exam. It was on architecture, if I remember rightly, and it was on the (now demolished) Elizabeth Gaskell Campus. I'd just got back from India (courtesy of the job) and was sporting a pair of leather flip-flops and a precarious skirt made of bits of old saris sewn to a tie-on waistband. I was terrified, of failing my exam and of the skirt slipping clean off in the middle of the street. Now, four months later, I was schlepping down the same stretch, wearing scuffed Converse All Stars and jeans that were way too long, the rain darkening the denim, a water line that edged ever closer to my knees. For as long as possible, I stayed on the same side of the road as the Elizabeth Gaskell Campus, trying to remember what it was like to only have things like exams and potential wardrobe malfunctions to worry about. When I knew I couldn't go any further without missing my appointment, I looked up at the hospital and crossed the road.

I wished I hadn't believed him when he said he couldn't get me pregnant.

But I did, and he could, and I was.

I wished I was on the worst comedown in the history of the entire universe.

In a funny way, I was.

Two

THIS IS THE still.

Everything could change in this moment, but it won't.

I'm only doing it for peace of mind. And because I needed a break from the bloody phones. I wish I could press a button that said, "August is peak season, so I'm afraid you really won't be able to find a week in Spain for £99. Not even on a last minute deal. Not even if it's allocation on arrival. Not even a cancellation."

The Pound Shop do two tests in a packet for a quid. I should have gone there, really, but I didn't have time to go anywhere except the chemist across the road. Plus I wanted to be sure. I don't know how reliable the Pound Shop ones are and this feels like the sort of thing I shouldn't scrimp on, like bras and sun cream and earrings that won't make my earlobes itch and swell up and explode.

It'll be over soon. When I've finished, I will put everything in the tampon bin, kick myself for wasting seven quid and go and sell some holidays.

Outside, the matted pigeons are cooing on their crusty sill. The air is hot and static; there's a storm on its way. London was bombed this morning. It's on the TV screens that are screwed to every wall in the office, ticker tape constantly crawling in front of images of flashing lights and people in uniform, and a bus with its top blown off.

My bus crashed on the way to work today. It was after the

news had come through about London, so everybody knew. For one tiny second after the impact, the other passengers and I looked at each other and thought the same thing. It wasn't serious, but the driver wanted us to stick around until the police arrived and be witnesses. The car had pulled out in front of him, he said, effing and blinding at its driver. I hadn't noticed; my head had been full of the familiar morning swill that kept telling me to stop going out in the week.

"Oi, come back!" the driver shouted at me, as I stepped over thick chunks of glass, gems scattered on the grubby pavement.

I couldn't though; I was going to be late for work.

Anna thinks that's why I am feeling weird: a delayed reaction to the shock of the bus crashing on a day of such horrible news. I emailed her as soon as I got to work, typing the words slowly as the voice in my headset asked me if I thought it was still safe to travel to Majorca, given the news about London.

'I think I might be pregnant,' I wrote. 'I feel dazed and like I can't function.'

'You're hungover,' she replied, "and probably a bit shaken. Mainly hungover, though.'

Maybe she was right, but once the idea had entered my head, it wouldn't go away. I switched my status to COMFORT BREAK, marched to the chemist, bought the test, came back to the toilets and locked myself into the end cubicle, the one with the most reliable lock.

I get the stuff out of the box. This is stupid. I am only a day late and I can't actually be pregnant. I just need to make sure, then I can go and carry on with the rest of my shift and the rest of my life.

I'm about to begin the final year of my degree. I'm supposed to be going on a work placement at a New York art magazine. I've just put a deposit on a flight to visit my friend Alex in Sydney for new year. When the fireworks pop over the Opera House, I will think back to this ridiculous moment and silently thank the sky that I didn't turn out to be pregnant.

The second line appears immediately. There's already one and if a second one appears, crossing through it vertically, it means you're pregnant. It's alright though; the instructions, on translucent, Bible-like paper, tell me I have to wait two minutes for a result to appear. It will therefore take two minutes for the line to disappear and for everything to return to normal.

I wait ten minutes, just to be sure. I lay the stick on a piece of tissue on top of the sanitary bin. I close my eyes and press my thumbs into the sockets, watching pixels and fractals fizz and twist against the black. I listen to someone lock herself in the next cubicle, wee, not wash her hands, blast them under the drier for a second, and leave.

When I open my eyes, I blink away the colours. The line is still there: blue, unmistakable, bold. I am furious: it was supposed to be the best test in the shop and it is wrong. I want my seven quid back.

"You can't argue with me," the stick seems to gloat, resplendent atop the tampon bin, "I am 99% correct."

I clutch the broken toilet-roll holder and hold on tight. I close my eyes and gasp and open them again and the line is still there, of course it is: the negative has become a positive, the minus a plus.

Three

I DECIDED TO keep my baby at Queen Victoria's feet. She was staring down at me, pigeon shit streaking her cheeks and dripping off the end of her nose. She was not amused.

It was the second time I'd sat there, on the steps beneath the statue in Piccadilly Gardens. The first time had been four days after I had found out I was pregnant, the soonest I could get a consultation at a clinic. I hadn't cried since I'd found out, but it all came out then, when the male doctor who wouldn't look me in the eye was giving me an internal examination to determine precisely how pregnant I was. Afterwards, I told the nurse I'd need more time to think and I walked out on to the hot pavement and pulled my big plastic sunglasses down over my eyes and walked and wept and walked and wept until I reached Piccadilly Gardens and collapsed beneath Victoria.

The sobs were all-consuming, humungous, grief-shaped. No oversized sunglasses were ever going to disguise them. Four days of tears and snot had been dammed by the shock and now they were flooding out all over me and the steps of Queen Victoria in the city's biggest square. Several passers-by stopped to ask me if I was OK and stood awkwardly over me for a few seconds as I lied to them that I was. I often wish I could thank those people. Most of them were men, a fact that touched me and set me off crying even more. Eventually, Anna, who I'd phoned, came and yanked me up like an old lady out of a low-down chair and dragged me to the pub for lunch.

"It doesn't have to be the end of the world," she said, sliding an orange juice to me across the soggy, mahogany table.

"It is."

"It's not. People are in way worse situations than you are now. You're alive, you're healthy."

I knew all this, and I felt bad about it. I also knew that there were women out there who'd do anything to piss on a stick and see two lines instead of one.

"You're going to have to make a decision and stick with it."

"I know. But I'm shit at decisions, you know I am: it took two years and two false starts for me to figure out what I wanted to study at university. I can't even decide what to buy for tea without flipping a coin or doing ip-dip-do in the middle of the shop."

"OK, so you need longer to think. Maybe it's not a disaster, that's all I'm saying. I actually think you'd make an amazing mum."

I laughed, for the first time in days.

"Don't be ridiculous."

Yet as soon as Anna left me to go back to work, I went to Waterstones. Instead of seeking out new fiction, or leafing through mighty books about art theory, I looked for a department I'd never even been to before. Someone asked me if I needed any help and I told them I didn't because I didn't want to say the name of the section I was looking for out loud. When I found the right shelf, I checked over both my shoulders to make sure I was alone, like someone sneaking a look at a top-shelf magazine. It didn't take long to find the part I was looking for: shrimps floating in black space, eyes like seeds in a watermelon, creepy-looking things. WEEK SIX, it said, *Your baby is about the size of a daisy petal, its heart has started to beat.*

I slammed the book shut, shoved it back on the shelf and walked and wept, walked and wept all my way to the bus stop.

What followed was a torturous few weeks of copious puking and very little sleep. It was like pregnant purgatory. I was sleep-deprived, hormonal, alone: no state to be in when you've got a big decision to make. There were two counsellors, one through the family planning clinic and one at university. In the night, when I was wide awake, I regularly called the Samaritans and begged them to tell me what to do. They all listened, and were brilliant, but they couldn't give me the answer. I went to my GP and there was nothing she could say or do to make me feel better (I think I wanted her to prescribe me the right answer). I tried the father a few times, but he'd been elusive ever since the day I told him and I knew I couldn't rely on him for help or advice or anything else. I spoke to Mum, who made me weep when she told me she'd support me whatever I decided to do; I spoke to several friends who were as horrified and confused by the situation as I was. At my very lowest ebb, I consulted a Stockport psychic.

I would have saved a lot of time and utter despair (and money) had I admitted to myself sooner that I did not want to have an abortion. I think I knew it really, when I was on my own in my room at night, between the calls to The Samaritans and Alex in Australia, listening to the mice scurrying around in the stuff strewn all over my bedroom floor. Had I wanted to end my pregnancy, I would have just got on and done it as soon as I could, but instead I was mulling it over, driving myself mad, venturing into the dark section of maternity books in Waterstones. I wanted to drink barrels of alcohol and forget, but I didn't, because I felt I shouldn't. I wanted to smoke all the cigarettes, but despite the half-full packet of Marlboro Lights and the lighter at the bottom of my handbag, I held off. My head ached constantly with the stress of it all, but I avoided painkillers. I felt I had to end the pregnancy because I was two-thirds of the way through my degree, single, skint, knew nothing about children apart from the fact they hurt, screamed and smelled, and what about all the women who didn't have the option of a free, safe, legal abortion? And yet it was still there: that overwhelming and terrifying urge to protect the daisy-petal-sized thing that had taken root in my womb.

The final realisation came on a journey into town for a counselling appointment. A lot of this story is set on the Magic Bus, but that's the generally the life of a Manchester student (or it was back then, anyway). My bus stopped for longer than normal in Rusholme, where a heady mix of diesel fumes and lunchtime curries stirred my stomach. There were a lot of horns beeping outside and crackly, staccato messages bursting through the driver's radio. Word soon came from the upper deck that the traffic in front was jammed for as far as the eye could see. Eventually, the bus driver yanked open his cabin and announced that we weren't going anywhere because there'd been a bomb scare in town. It was a feasible threat, given what had happened in London just a few weeks earlier. And the first thing I did was worry about the baby; I looked down and my hand was on my tummy. I stumbled off the bus and called the clinic to cancel my appointment, watching strings of cars sizzle in hot mirages, wondering if anything was real.

I called Anna, who worked in town, for an update on the situation. The city centre had just been given the all-clear, she told me, it was a hoax, but buses were probably still going to take ages to get to Piccadilly.

"You've not missed your counselling appointment, have you?" she said, always trying to keep my lateness in check.

"Yeah, I have, but I don't think it matters."

"What?"

"I'll call you back."

I found myself strolling quickly in the direction of town, the soles of my flip-flops slapping my heels. There was no way I was going to have an abortion, I realised. Pro-choice means pro-choice, which is a belief in a woman having the freedom to make up her own mind. Without the option of an abortion, I would have felt completely trapped and desperate. As it happened, the knowledge that there was a way out if I needed it had kept me from plummeting into despair. Choosing to keep my baby wouldn't mean I was pro-life, it would mean me doing what felt right for me. And it did feel right, even though the timing was terrible and the whole thing was totally surreal. I was lucky enough to have a mother who'd promised to support me, something that not everyone who finds themselves in that situation has. But that wasn't to say becoming a single mother was going to be easy, definitely not.

I went to Superdrug and bought a bottle of water and a box of folic acid. I wasn't even sure what folic acid did, but I knew that pregnant women were supposed to take it. If I was going to do this thing, which it seemed I was, I might as well go about it properly. I plonked myself down on the steps beneath Queen Vic again. I looked up at her stern, crapped-on face. At least I didn't live in Victorian times, I thought, when

I'd have been labelled a 'fallen woman' and my baby would have been a foundling and taken away. I thought of my nan, a child of Victorian parents, who'd carried their values into the 21st century. When I went on holiday with a boyfriend, aged nineteen, she took me to one side: "Now here's your ice-cream money," she whispered, pressing the traditional holiday fiver in my hand, giving it the name it had had since I was three. "We all know why you're going on this trip but please, don't come back pregnant."

The last time I'd seen Nan had been the day before I did get pregnant. Her Alzheimer's had got worse and my uncle, determined to care for her himself, had guiltily admitted defeat and moved her into a nursing home. Mum, my sister Hannah and I had found her waltzing round the living room, her inhibitions and her teeth lost.

"Look at this," she'd said, tutting and grabbing the ring of tummy that peeped over the brim of my skirt. She turned to Mum and said, "Your grandson's in there, you just don't know it yet."

Oh, how we laughed.

Maybe Nan wouldn't realise I was pregnant, or maybe she somehow already knew, but I hoped that the horrible fact of her dementia, the brief flashes of lucidity mixed with stretches of confusion, would in a way make it easier for her to deal with. I realised that, despite the fact I wasn't living in Victorian England, the idea of shame had haunted me since I'd discovered I was pregnant. It wasn't because I'd 'fallen' out of wedlock, that was fine, but because I had been idiotic enough to let my guard down and believe what I did. When I was a teenager and I read the problem page letters in magazines from girls who wondered whether they could get pregnant if they did it standing up/they were on their period/it was their first time, I smirked, smug in the knowledge that I would never be daft enough to believe such nonsense myself. Then, at twenty-two, on no basis other than the fact he was thirty, which seemed to me like a mature and reliable age, and I had known him for nearly two years, I believed something so ridiculous and dangerous that I ended up in the position I thought I would never get in.

That was what had made me thoroughly ashamed and, in the beginning, angrier with myself than I was with the man who had lied.

I'd had enough time to kick myself though, to punish myself, to come to terms with the fact I couldn't go back and reset my foolishness levels to zero. I was just going to have to get on with it. The adulthood I'd imagined (lots of travelling, a stint living in London, a writing career) looked very different, but I decided to look upon having a baby as a sort of non-exotic adventure, like embarking on a night out with hardly any money and no sense of direction. For at least eighteen years.

Queen Victoria was still making me uncomfortable, so I shuffled round the steps and dropped the folic acid behind her back. In front of me, normality carried on. Trams tooted and snaked through the streets, commuters dashed past, chatting into their hands-free headsets, and Piccadilly Gardens was full of children. There were loads of them, dancing in the spray of the fountains, cooling off in the rare afternoon sun, tiny hands splayed out like flowers. It seemed to me like a strange place to play, but their parents seemed relaxed as they looked on, eating picnics and guarding buggies. Children probably played in Piccadilly Gardens all the time, I'd just never noticed them before. Now, they were everywhere, splashing each other and squealing. On the smaller ones, nappies sagged with the weight of the fountain water. I wondered how old they were, or how old any child is when they stop wearing nappies, or walk, for that matter, or talk, or eat solid food.

I threw the thick tablet to the back of my mouth and washed it down with a good slug of the water, tipping the bottle towards the sky, toasting the unknown.

Four

I SUPPOSE YOU'RE wondering who and where the father of my child was; I know I was. I knew *who* he was, in the literal sense, but he'd turned out not to be the friend I had him down as, which was disorientating to say the least. As for *where* he was, at that point, it was still Manchester, but he'd let me know that he planned to vanish as soon as he possibly could. The day after deciding to go ahead with the pregnancy, I emailed him to tell him. His reply gutted me, not just because of its offensiveness, but because I believed it to be accurately prophetic:

Enjoy your impending shitty, snotty, vomitty twenties. Goodbye.

People's reactions when you tell them you're expecting an unexpected baby vary. Mum rang me when I was on my way to buy my pregnancy test, to talk about what had happened in London.

"I'm at work, Mum, you've caught me on a break."

"Oh, lovely, are you getting some lunch?"

"No, I'm getting a pregnancy test," I said, probably because I hadn't fully grown out of the teenage desire to shock her.

"Why?!"

"Just for peace of mind."

"Well you must think you *could* be pregnant to be doing it in the first place."

"Maybe," I said, "but it's highly unlikely. Anyway, I've got to go."

She sent me a text message when I was in the toilets with the stick.

RU OK?

YEH FINE.

Over the next few days, Mum tried to call me many times, but I never answered. Until three days later, when I couldn't keep it in any longer and I really needed to talk to her. I didn't have to tell her because she already knew. I sat on the edge of my bed, whimpered that I was sorry and adopted the brace position, ready for the bollocking of my life.

"It's alright," she said, "I will support you whatever you decide to do."

"Oh my God, she can't even look after herself, how can she look after a baby?" my sister, Hannah, reportedly screamed when Mum broke the news. I think that's the first time the two of us have ever had the same opinion on anything.

Friends weren't sure how to take it. One said she thought I was mad to bring a child who I knew would be fatherless into the world, and I never saw her again. Another told me she didn't think I was very child-friendly, which made me sound like a pub without a play area. Ellen, who I'd only met about a week earlier, asked me if I'd like a cup of tea. She was going out with my housemate and happened to be the only person at home when I got in from finding out.

"Are you OK?" she asked. "I thought you were working the late shift today."

"I was, but I'm ill."

"Oh no, what's wrong?"

"Actually, I'm not ill, I'm pregnant."

The words fell out of my mouth like pebbles and landed, bouncing, on the laminate floor.

"Shit. Do you want a cup of tea?"

I hate tea and the notion that it cures everything, but I accepted that cup because I didn't know Ellen well enough to be honest with her about that (even though she was the first person after my boss with whom I'd shared the fact I was knocked up). As I took small, reluctant sips, Ellen and I talked about my options. Even then, she said that it might not be a disaster, that maybe there was another way of looking at it.

Most of my friends were as confused as I was and said things like "good luck" and "cool, a baby!" through gritted teeth, giving me feeble hugs. Alex was practical: the circumstances were far from ideal, but I'd just have to get on with it and women had been having babies and surviving for quite a while. Anna, bless her, just kept telling me I'd be an excellent mother until I almost began to believe her. Stu, my best friend who was a man, wasn't sure how to take it.

"I told my mum and she feels really sorry for you," he said.

"That's nice."

We were walking along the Curry Mile in the warm aftermath of a downpour. The sky was daubed with streaks of grey and cream, the tarmac sparkling. Stu is tactless, a good cook and knows loads about Detroit techno. We met at college when we were eighteen and I swapped him a bag of twelve free family-planning-clinic condoms (oh, the irony, etc.) for a lift home with my unwieldy art portfolio. He's one of the best friends I have. Five months earlier, he had accompanied me on a dirt-cheap holiday to Goa.

"How long have we got before we have to stop being seen

together in public, then?"

"What are you on about?"

We carried on along Wilmslow Road, past the sari shops and the fruit stalls and the restaurants that smelt like 3am.

"You know, before you look properly preggers and people can see and they think it's mine."

"Oh yeah. A few weeks, maybe. I don't know. Those taxi drivers in India would say they told us so."

The most popular mode of transport in Goa is the Bedford minivan, which is at odds with the dusty, uneven terrain. Tiny wheels on bumpy tracks make for an undignified ride, especially when everything under your kaftan's being held together with an ill-advised string bikini.

"She is your wife?" the drivers would say to Stu, looking at my reflection in the rear-view mirror.

"No, she bloody isn't."

"Your girlfriend?"

"No."

"But no jiggy jiggy?"

"No, no jiggy jiggy!"

"Definitely not any jiggy jiggy!"

"Then she is your sister?"

"No. We're just friends."

"Here you will come next for your honeymoon!"

After a few days, we realised it was easier to feign romantic unity than face the inquisition.

"She is your wife?"

"Yes," I said.

"Fuck's sake," said Stu, giving me a sharp kick in the mosquito-bitten shin.

"I wish I'd have known," I said.

We were outside the restaurant where we'd eaten on our first ever weekend in Manchester, star-struck by the big city. (Imagine, an entire neighbourhood just for the curries!) We had both been ecstatic about our first move out of home, from Southport to the same huge halls of residence, just off Oxford Road.

"Wish you'd have known what?"

"That within a year of us going to India, I'd have a child."

"What would be the point in knowing? Would you have done anything differently?"

"Maybe been less of an idiot."

"You should have stayed away from that thing in the temple, what was it called?"

"The bull of fertility."

"Yeah, the bull of bloody fertility. Should have kept well away from that sleazy bastard."

The rain was starting up again, lit by the sun, falling like flour through a sieve.

"Shall we have a curry?"

"Go on, then," I said. "Just like Goa."

And we ducked into the restaurant, ordering hot food in metal dishes, talking about elephants, but not the one in the room.

Whilst my friends and I didn't really know how to handle the concept of a baby, the older generation didn't judge me, as I half-expected them to, but seemed to think it was all completely fine. I emailed my tutor at university and tentatively, apologetically, explained my situation (pregnant, single, in need of at least a year out). *Congratulations!* she replied, *What very exciting news!*

Mum, meanwhile, was way too excited by the prospect of

her first grandchild to worry about minor details like the fact its mother was single, useless at getting up in the morning and devoid of common sense. Jane, the older woman who sat opposite me at work on the late shifts and often gave me a lift home, was equally thrilled.

"Aren't you going out tonight?" she said, as I finished one of the last calls of the evening.

"Out?!"

"Well, it is a Tuesday."

Tuesday: the night when I traditionally ignored the last few calls, sneaked into the loos to do my eyeliner and headed straight to the sticky dance floor and predictable, indie soundtrack of 42nd Street.

"No," I said, pulling off my headset and yawning, "too tired."

"You do look worn out. Let me give you a lift."

Jane spent a lot of time looking after her grandchildren, so her car was always full of booster seats, sweet wrappers and gaudy toys.

"Just chuck it all in the back," she said, as I sat on Barbie's sharp feet.

"Not like you not to go out on a Tuesday," Jane said. "You writing an essay or something?"

"Oh no, I'm not at university at the moment."

"Of course, it's still summer. You wouldn't think it with this bloody weather, mind."

"No, I mean I'm not at university for now. I'm taking a year out."

"Oh. You've not given up, have you?"

"No. I hope not, anyway."

"What's up?"

I wondered whether to tell this kind woman, who was old enough to be my mum, who gave me lifts home from work and always made me feel safe, how spectacularly I'd messed up. I must have wanted to, though, because I did.

"Oh, congratulations!"

Jane was beaming; genuinely ecstatic. She'd had no time to forge that face, no time to consider her reaction. She took her left hand off the steering wheel and rubbed my arm.

"Wonderful!"

"I'm not with the father, you know. He doesn't want anything to do with it."

"Silly man! He'll regret that, I can tell you."

"Mum says that."

"Your mum's right. When are you due?"

"March."

"Oh, how lovely! I'm thrilled for you, really thrilled. It'll be the best thing that ever happened to you, you know."

I watched the cardboard Eric Cantona, the Magic Tree and the rosary swinging from the rear-view mirror. And all I could do was hope that Jane was right.

Five

ON THE DRAWERS next to my bed, there were two tickets for The Cribs at the Bierkeller. They'd been sitting there for a few weeks, calling to me from inside their envelope. One was for me and one was a gift for the father of my child. I didn't know what to do with them. Now the date had come around and going to the gig on my own felt like a kind of rebellion.

I ordered red wine, because I had read somewhere that it was good for pregnant women, in moderation.

A friend I'd met in my first year was working behind the bar. I could tell from her face that someone had told her the gossip about me.

"Are you alright?" she shouted over her shoulder, filling a cup at the vodka optic.

"Yeah," I said. "I'm having a baby."

"Sorry, what was that?"

The music was really loud, but I couldn't bring myself to shout what I wanted to say, so I shook my head.

"If I get a break, I'll come and see you."

She didn't, though, not because she didn't want to, but because she was busy. Maybe I'd have stuck around for a bit longer if I hadn't been on my own. After a few vinegary sips of wine, I felt tipsy and guilty. When The Cribs came onstage, the crowd surged forward and I retreated to the back, sustaining several cigarette burns along the way. It felt like

I was a spectator of the audience as much as the band. Ryan Jarman bloodied his mouth on the mic and kept going, his hair plastered to his face in black straggles. People were crashing into each other, sloshing warm drinks over the tops of plastic cups and hitting their heads on the low ceiling. The air was thick with smoke and it was starting to knock me sick. It was filthy, frenetic, spectacular; it was no place for a Woman in My Condition.

The band had only played three songs when I put down my crap wine and stomped up the staircase. As I emerged on to Piccadilly, the smell of doorway urine was like perfume.

When I got home, I lay on my bed, exhausted, stinking, sad. It was almost daylight again when I woke, still in my clothes, contact lenses suckered on to my eyeballs like limpets.

"Jesus, they don't tell you it affects your voice box, do they?"

Calling Alex seemed like a good idea. There was nothing to say to The Samaritans anymore, and I knew she would be awake. I dragged my duvet into the coolness of the hallway and sat on the bottom step.

"Sorry," I whispered, "my housemates are in bed."

"No worries," she said, in what I was sure was an Australian accent. "How are you going?"

I'd met Alex in Freshers' Week; she was my housemate in student halls. She was from the countryside, posh compared to me, but incredibly down-to-earth and practical, thanks to her farm upbringing. A design student, she'd extended the desk in her bedroom with the aid of a stack of plastic crates and a long plank of wood. When I trod on my hair straighteners and was convinced they were broken beyond repair, Alex quickly fixed them with duct tape (and they were still going strong, three years later). When John, the man she loved, moved to Australia, Alex simply took on the breakfast shift at a local hotel, getting up at 4:30 every morning and saving up enough money to book the peak season flight to go and visit him that Christmas. She was also totally cool with kids: the first time she went home to visit her family, I called her on the landline there and was surprised to hear very young children shrieking in the background.

"Just a minute," her mum said. "Alex is helping me out today."

It turned out that Alex's home was not just a farm but a day nursery, and that she was well versed in the care of babies and toddlers.

Alex was blessed with a calm practicality that I severely lacked. She was also very honest, and I knew that if anyone we knew was knocked up and single and not me, she'd have plenty to say about it. Instead, though, she accepted the fact it was happening and acted like it was totally fine. Babies were normal in her world, after all.

"I feel weird," I said. "I cancelled my flight to Sydney yesterday."

"That's probably for the best."

"Yeah. Not really, though. New Year's Eve!"

"New Year's Eve in Sydney is overrated. It's hell even trying to find a place to sit and you can't see the fireworks for people. Even worse for you, being as short as you are. Like standing at the back of a gig."

"The fireworks are in the sky."

"OK, well you wouldn't have been able to see them anyway, you'd have been too intoxicated. And the next day you'd wake up and think 'I can't believe I just spent hundreds of pounds on a New Year's Eve night out and I can't even remember any of it.'"

"Thanks."

"And hangovers are hell in the heat. A horrible business."

We'd been through our fair share of hangovers, Alex and I. She didn't drink often, so hangovers were a big event for her. We'd spent days together in pyjama-clad recovery. She was good at rustling up posh food with filo pastry and pesto; I was good at sticking the previous night's photographs to the 'wall of shame' and doing her make-up before we went out again. Before the call centre, I somehow managed to get a job on a designer make-up counter at a department store in town. They flew me down to London for my training course – in which I got a surprise 100%. Alex, with her immaculate, countryside complexion, was terrified of make-up. I used to sit her down and give her flicks of eyeliner or plum lip stain or lime-green eyelids to match my own.

"I wish you were here, you know."

"I don't wish I was there, sorry, but I don't."

Alex never fell in love with Manchester like I did and I envied her for that. To her, it was fun, but it served a purpose because the art courses were good. Yes, there were parties, but now she was done with them. It was time to marry John and move on. To a different hemisphere.

After crackly goodbyes, I went for a walk. The birds were making a right racket, announcing the dawn. I perched on the road sign at the end of our street, remembering how it felt to be awake at the turn of the day. I thought back to the student halls days: constant company, parties, laughs, loads of free eyeshadow. And I couldn't equate it with wandering the streets in the twilight, pregnant and alone.

The freedom of not knowing, the lightness of no worries, dark clubs that led to after-parties in cool light. I longed to go back, to look at the city through those perfectly made-up eyes.

Back home, I sloped upstairs and ran the feeble shower until it stuttered into a lukewarm dribble, then I stepped under it and scrubbed the stubborn club stamp off the back of my hand. As I clawed the beer and smoke smells out of my soapy hair, I couldn't imagine ever going to a gig again.

Six

THE KNOWLEDGE THAT you're pregnant follows you everywhere, whatever you're doing, whether you like it or not. There's a tiny patch of respite in the mornings, before you're fully awake, when you're stirring and stretching your feet over to the cool side of the bed. I remember those moments, gazing with sleep-misty eyes at the ugly chintz curtains that hung in the bay window of my room. I hated those curtains. On my first night in that house, I flopped down on the bare mattress and told my mum, who had made at least six car journeys ferrying my belongings from my old house to the new one, that the curtains had to go.

"Don't be ridiculous," Mum said, "there's nothing wrong with them."

"They're gross."

"They're perfectly good curtains. Have you any idea how much it would cost you to buy a big pair for a bay window like that?"

"I'll check the charity shops," I said, staring up at the bare light bulb overheard, rolling my eyes to make light trace circles. "They're going. And the nicotine-stained nets behind them. I'll hang a sheet if I have to."

"What's up with you?" Mum asked. "Period due?"

It certainly was, but it never arrived.

And the curtains stayed, greeting me every morning. As I blinked and clawed at the cool sheet with my toes, I began to recognise a heaviness somewhere in my sternum; a feeling that all was not well. It was a bit like the hungover dread, the sort that makes you terrified to look at your photographs, sent messages or recently-dialled numbers for fear of evidence of what you might have done the night before. Only it was more serious than that, I knew, as I grew more conscious. This was something to really worry about. By the time I realised that my bladder was full and I needed to leg it upstairs to the avocado bathroom and hope that no one was in there, I knew: I was pregnant and petrified and I wished I still cared about the curtains.

Once you're awake, that's it: everything is connected to the pregnancy. The more mundane the task, the more patent the fact of the pregnancy. My life had been divided by the blue line of the pregnancy test, everything before it so very different to everything on the other side. I viewed everything through a lens of before and after: this used to feel like that before, I will have to do that differently when the baby is here.

Several weeks in, the knowledge followed me to the supermarket. It stalked me down every aisle and all the way home and it didn't even offer to help me carry my shopping. I realised quickly that few places make pregnancy more apparent than the supermarket. Everywhere you look, you see things that can be linked, however tenuously, to the existence of the imminent child. My route around Somerfield had changed forever: no frozen pizzas, no litres of cheap vodka, definitely no cigarettes. The only section I was relieved to swerve was Feminine Hygiene. I filled my basket with more leafy green vegetables than I could possibly consume before they went off. I had bought fruit and veg in the past, but it had almost always transformed into rancid liquid in the bottom drawer of the fridge (a guaranteed ticket to animosity when your kitchen is shared).

With the booze section out of bounds, I made the bold/ stupid decision to take a short-cut to the checkout down the gauntlet that was the Baby and Child aisle. Having a baby involved so many things, it appeared, and you were supposed to know exactly which ones you'd need and how to use them. I have always been amazed by birds collecting twigs in spring. How do they *just know* how to weave a nest? They don't even have *hands*. Meanwhile, human beings are supposed to figure out what and how much to feed their babies, whether or not to introduce a dummy and exactly how much of the stuff being sold to them is actually necessary. I was confronted with potties, pull-up pants, powdered milks, nappy sacks, scented wipes, sensitive wipes, dummies, endless rows of jars of autumnal-coloured foods, rubber ducks, rattles, teething rings, bottles, anti-colic teats, rusks. And of course, the emblem of all that is shit about parenthood, the things that people kept bringing up: nappies.

"I can't imagine you changing a nappy."

"Do you really want to spend the next few years changing nappies?"

"Have you any idea how much nappies cost?"

Actually, I didn't, so I looked, except it wasn't clear which size or brand or absorbency I was supposed to buy, nor how many the average baby gets through in a normal day, nor for how many months or years after its birth my baby would be wearing nappies. It was difficult to calculate without knowing all this, but I did know that I was about to spend a lot of money on a lot of things that were destined for defecation and the bin.

I was queuing at the checkout when I heard a familiar rasping sound coming from over near the cigarette kiosk. The sound was recorded in my psyche from the part-time job in a Spar I'd had before moving to Manchester. There were a couple of hours to go before the draw, and the queues were long. I hadn't done the lottery since my sixteenth birthday, when I did it just because I could, emerging from the local newsagent's with my ticket and a packet of Lambert & Butler, feeling invincible. The novelty quickly wore off; I knew that, statistically, I was highly unlikely to win, and after the initial rush of getting served for a ticket, the excitement was over. And yet, that day in Somerfield, I joined the queue. It was Saturday night, after all, and gambling is a vice.

While I was queuing at the kiosk, I found myself staring right at a moon-faced baby on the front of a magazine. It had two peg teeth, a sheen on its tiny nose and a tuft of hair that had been arranged in a half-quiff. I think I was supposed to find it cute, but I didn't. Then I read the headlines:

Cracked Nipples: How to Cope
The Complete Potty Training Survival Guide
Real Experience: I Broke My Coccyx Giving Birth!
Jesus.

"Lucky dip for tonight, please," I said when I got to the front of the queue, "and this."

I slid the magazine, rolled-up, on to the counter. Might as well have some idea of what I was letting myself in for, I decided.

"You expecting?"

According to her badge, the shop assistant was called Moira. She unfurled the magazine and waved it in the air for everyone in the queue to see.

"Err . . . yeah."

"Ha. You'll need to win the bloody lottery, love!" Moira's laugh was a raspy cackle, not all that different to the sound of the lottery machine. She sounded like she'd smoked all the tobacco in the kiosk.

"Thanks," I said, plonking a family-sized chocolate bar on the counter. "I'll have that too."

The walk home took longer than normal because I'd bought way too many vegetables. I had to keep stopping for a rest, putting the carrier bags down and flexing my fingers. In an attempt to distract myself from the plastic handles cutting into my palms, I thought about what I would buy if my lottery ticket was a winner. There'd be things like a pram and a cot and whichever of the things I'd seen in Somerfield I was actually going to need. The main thing would be a house, because as it stood, I had no idea where I was going to live. I couldn't keep the baby in the corner of my damp bedroom and I didn't know how I'd afford to rent somewhere, even a cheap council or housing association place. Mum had told me I was welcome to move in with her, but, as kind an offer as that was, it would have to be a last resort. I loved Manchester far too much to end up back in Southport. If I won the lottery, I would be able to afford a house. I wouldn't want a mansion or a place with a swimming pool, just a little terraced house with enough space for me and my kid. I didn't even need the jackpot, just a hundred grand or so.

When I got home, the landline was ringing. I dumped my bags inside the door and picked up the phone.

"Hello?"

"Is that Emily?" a male voice asked.

"Yeah."

"It's your Uncle Paul."

"Oh, hi."

I hadn't spoken to him for weeks and didn't really want to; I loved him, but the idea of him knowing I'd got knocked up made me mortified.

"Your mum told me your news."

"Right."

"How are you feeling?"

"The same, really. Tired, I suppose, but generally—"

"I mean how are you feeling about it all? About the . . . baby, I mean."

He mumbled 'baby' like it was a dirty word.

"Scared," I sighed, "intrigued. It depends on the moment."

"How did this happen, Emily?"

"Well—"

"No, don't answer that. I mean how did it happen to *you*?"

"He told me he couldn't have kids."

There it was again, the excruciating truth.

"What were you doing with a no-mark like that?"

"I don't know."

"I can't believe you've let some absolute—" he sighed, censoring himself. "I can't believe you've ruined your life because of someone like him."

"I know," I said, slumping down the wall and sitting on the hallway floor.

"Have you thought about where you'll live? What you'll do for money? Babies are expensive, you know."

I resisted the urge to tell him it was all under control because I was sure I was about to win the lottery. Instead, I stayed silent, wrapping the curly phone wire around my finger until it started to throb.

"I'm going to work loads of extra shifts at the call centre," I said. "Mum says I can move in with her if I need to."

I unwound the cable from my finger, tracing the yellowed dents it had impressed in my skin. It felt like my heart was beating in the tip of my index finger.

"You're the last person I would have expected to get into this situation: you're clever, you're talented, I thought you were going to be a writer."

Maybe I should have hung up on him, told him to mind his own business, but I felt like he was right, so I just said I was sorry, my voice wobbling as I did.

"Look, I didn't mean to upset you. I'm just worried about you, that's all. It's done now. You've always been resourceful, if anyone can make this work, you can."

I really didn't know how it was going to work, but I thanked him nonetheless.

"I can't give you money, but if there's anything I can do to help, just let me know."

"Thank you."

"It's only a baby. We can't be scared of a *baby*!"

The word was fully-formed now, not a shameful mutter.

"You're right," I said, dragging myself up, "it's just a little baby."

In the kitchen, I stuffed the new vegetables into the fridge and got ready for the lottery results. All my housemates were either away for the weekend or out, so I had the TV and the living room to myself. I wondered if I'd shout when my numbers came up, whether the shock would be OK for the baby. I closed the fridge door and went to grab my lottery ticket out of my jacket pocket. It wasn't there. Nor was it in my purse. Frantically, I yanked all of the carrier bags out of the plastic dispenser like handkerchiefs from a magician's hat and shook them out on to the lino. All I got were flakes of onion skin and crumpled receipts. I pulled the veg out of the fridge and sifted between every curl of kale and every spear of asparagus. I got down on my hands and knees next to the fridge and peered underneath at clods of dust and spider skeletons and the humane mousetrap. My winning lottery ticket was nowhere to be seen, because, I realised, I had left it on the counter at Somerfield. Distracted by the chocolate and the horror of the magazine, I had forgotten my reason for visiting the kiosk in the first place. I imagined Moira, somewhere not-too-far-away, jumping up and down as she celebrated her massive win, courtesy of the customer who was too dozy to take her ticket home with her. I sat on my own on the sofa, watching the ping pong balls ricocheting around Guinevere or Lancelot or whatever the lottery machine was called, and I cried. Then I picked up the chocolate and cracked it into squares inside its smooth wrapper. I tore it open and devoured it all, one square at a time, each square replacing a drag on the cigarette I was craving. Sod it, I thought, I'll eat the kale another day.

Seven

I SIGNED UP to Motherboard, a parenting forum, before I even knew I was sticking with the pregnancy. If the counsellors, the Samaritans and the doctor couldn't give me the answer, maybe some strangers on the internet could. (Among the scant replies I received, I'll never forget an amazing, reassuring and knowledgeable email from a woman in New Zealand who'd found herself in the same position, had the baby and turned out happy.)

Once I got into the swing of being pregnant, or at least tried to, I decided to log in again. The forums were arranged by the month babies were due, so that women at the same stages of pregnancy could talk to each other about all the weird stuff that was happening to their bodies. I signed up to 'Due in March' and quickly realised that most of the threads were indecipherable. On Motherboard, it turned out, people spoke in a strange code, whereby abbreviating every other word for the sake of a few letters was preferable to just writing it. I knew that mothers were busy people, but it was ridiculous. PG was not the rating of a film that might have the odd rude word, but the abbreviation for 'pregnant'. After my first visit to the board, I found it necessary to consult the glossary, which left me a little wiser but no less irritated. When reading the posts about morning sickness and which maternity jeans to buy, my internal voice spoke the acronyms and never the full-blown words. It was like virtually conversing with robots.

DS was not the name of a popular handheld games console, but the shortened version of that well-known, often spoken phrase: 'darling son'. Similarly, DD was not a bra cup size but stood for 'darling daughter'. Things got really confusing when people had multiple numbers of offspring, which is when numbers came into play and people started going on about DS2, DD25 etc. What was wrong with just writing 'daughter' or 'son' was beyond me.

"I am PG with DD2. DS1 and DD1 are going to MIL when I go to hospital."

Oh yeah, MIL stood for 'mother-in-law' and was too close for comfort to 'MILF' if you asked me.

Most irritating of all the jargon though, probably because of the lone boat I was in, were the abbreviations for the men of the pregnant women. A 'DP' was a 'Darling Partner', a 'DH' a 'Darling Husband' and 'OH' (OH!) translated as 'Other Half'.

The worst thing about Motherboard for me was the general air of hysterical excitability. Every page was peppered with far too many smiley faces and exclamation marks and many members had set it so that a gaudy, glittering, animated countdown to their due date sparkled beneath everything they wrote. People posted weekly 'bump photos' of their burgeoning bellies, often taken in the mirror, with wedding photos mounted above luxuriously-furnished beds or smart mantelpieces just visible in the background. All of it felt totally foreign, not just because I wasn't married and I lived in a mouldy shared house, but because I was not as excited as they were and I felt guilty and envious about that. I had established that I loved my baby and that my instinct was to look after it, but I was still reeling from the shock of its existence and petrified about the future. I began to resent the other mothers like I used to the other children in my class in the run-up to sports day. To me, sports day was the stuff of nightmares, yet for everyone else it seemed to be the peak of the academic calendar.

Still, Motherboard had its uses, so I stuck around, rarely writing posts myself, gleaning information where I could. I regularly skipped my 'own' forum and trawled the one for the current month, checking on how things were for those who'd actually had their babies. Graphic 'birth stories' terrified me, yet I kept reading until I got to the endings, which invariably involved reports of ecstasy and it all being worth the pain. I carefully studied images of wrinkled, waxy newborns, sure that they all looked the same. I marvelled at photos of radiant new mothers who didn't look like they'd just nearly died.

Motherboard was both friend and enemy to me: a useful tool for communicating with others, and a hotbed of dangerous self-comparison. Just like Facebook that came after it, most members were only willing to project a perfect version of themselves. In the world of baby-making, that means being slim, wholesome, wealthy and romantically happy, none of which applied to me.

According to the other Motherboarders, I should have been really looking forward to my first appointment with my MW (midwife), which was called 'booking in', and sounded a lot like it had something to do with travel. I was about to book into a pretty shoddy hotel, with bodily-fluids spattered on the walls and horrible noises in the night.

"Come in, come in!"

I'd never been in upstairs at the doctor's before. The new room was cold and clinical, but Margaret the midwife was quite the opposite. I took a deep breath of latex and disinfectant-scented air, mustering a flimsy smile.

"Now, before you get comfy, do you think you can fill this for me?" Margaret grinned and held up a clear plastic pot.

"Probably."

One thing I had already learnt about being pregnant was that you need to wee a lot. It was inconvenient most of the time, but useful when you needed to do it on demand. Except when you couldn't. I took the pot downstairs to the toilet, took my best guess at an aim and . . . nothing. *Think of waterfalls*, I told myself. I thought about the waterfalls Stu and I saw in India, then about the nervous excitement I'd felt when I'd come to the doctor's for my travel jabs. It had only been weeks ago and now I was back, pissing in a pot for a midwife. Waterfalls didn't work, so I switched on the tap in the hand basin. It twisted quickly into full blast and water ricocheted against the porcelain and on to the crotch of my jeans. Consequently, I spent some time with my crotch angled under the hand dryer, thrusting my pelvis forward every time the hot air stopped. Thankfully, by the time I was done with all this, I actually needed to wee, but my ordeal was far from over. If you are a woman who is not accustomed to peeing in pots, it is almost impossible to do without getting it all over your fingers. At Glastonbury, you can wee into a urinal, with the aid of a cardboard tube that you place in your undercarriage. You don't think it will work, but it does, and you feel really amazed that it does, as you stand there, in a field, knowing for a glorious moment what it is to pee as conveniently as a man. One day, doctors and midwives will provide peeing tubes. Until then, women everywhere are destined to urinate over themselves.

As I thoroughly washed my hands, I almost lost the

precious contents of the pot down the plughole; it was lidless and balanced precariously on the side of the sink. I screwed the lid on and washed and dried my hands one more time, before emerging to be greeted by a long and disgruntled-looking queue of people. I was very careful to cup the warm sample in both hands, conscious that anyone might think that the thing I was carrying in a urine sample jar was a urine sample.

"Goodness, what happened?!" said Margaret, when I eventually returned. "Did you fall down the toilet? I almost sent out a search party!"

"Sorry," I mumbled, handing her the jar.

"There we go."

Margaret took the pot from me like it was a birthday present.

"You'll lose count of the amount of pots you'll have piddled in by the time I'm done with you!"

I laughed weakly.

"Well," Margaret said, pulling a small sliver of something out of the jar and inspecting the colour on the end, "you are definitely pregnant."

"I thought you might say that."

"First baby?"

"Yes."

"Lovely. A primagravida!"

"A what?"

"Primagravida. It's a fancy Latin word for someone who's having a baby for the first time. Like you."

"Oh, right."

"When was the first day of your last period, love?"

That was easy to remember: a sweltering morning spent

stuck inside the university library, typing up an essay that was already a week overdue, necking ibuprofen and kneading my swollen stomach.

"Now, let's see . . ."

Margaret shuffled the wheel around on a dog-eared cardboard dial, the good old-fashioned way of determining a woman's due date. I didn't have the heart to tell her that I'd used every birth date calculator on the internet, that the date was imprinted indelibly in my memory.

"A spring baby!" she declared. "Perfect!"

It seemed as good a time as any.

"Now then, what do you do for a living?"

"I'm a student. Sorry, I *was* a student. I've gone full-time at work now, so I suppose that makes me a travel agent."

"Oh, lovely! Do you get to go to all kinds of exciting places?"

"Well, I *did*."

"Good." Margaret beamed. "Probably best not to do a lot of flying with a little one on board. So, no work hazards to worry about: standing still for long amounts of time, exposure to radiation, operating heavy machinery?"

"No. Just the terminal misery associated with sending people to places you know you'll never get to see."

"Deary me, cheer up! Now then, missy, do you smoke?"

"No. I've given up." It had been surprisingly easy.

"Good girl."

"There was other stuff though."

"Go on . . ."

"Drinking, before I found out I was pregnant. And I put antibiotic drops in my ears." I had actually laughed when the doctor asked me whether I was pregnant as she prescribed those eardrops.

"Just a formality," she'd said.

"Yeah, of course. Sorry. I'm definitely not pregnant. At least I hope not! Ha!"

"Listen," said Margaret, swotting invisible midges with her hands, "absolutely everybody does things they mustn't do before they find out they are pregnant. The main thing is that you do know now and you're staying as healthy as possible. Right?"

"Right."

"Here's a list of the foods you should avoid." She thrust a sheet of A4 paper in front of me and I skimmed over it.

"Halloumi?!"

"Yes?"

"I ate halloumi. Last Friday." Anna had taken me out for a Greek meal to cheer me up. I thought I was being good by not drinking and it turns out I wasn't even supposed to eat cheese.

"Unpasteurised cheeses can make you very poorly. Looks like you were OK this time, but don't do it again."

There was literally nothing left worth having, apart from perhaps chocolate.

"Your teeth can weaken when you're pregnant," Margaret went on, "so look after them and drink plenty of milk. If you do need to see a dentist, you'll be entitled to free treatments."

Yep. Chocolate was off the menu too. Officially, anyway.

"Good. Now, any history of diabetes, heart disease, asthma?"

"No."

"What about Dad?"

"My dad?"

"No, baby's dad."

I looked at the floor. It was a very light grey with swirls of puce and white. "The only thing I know about his health is that he was supposed to be infertile."

"Right, then!" Margaret clapped her hands together with a loud pop. "We don't need *him*, do we? No, we don't, thank you very much."

Clearly, we did need him. We needed him at the very first hurdle, to fill in a lengthy questionnaire about his medical history.

"How important *is* this bit?"

"We'll manage just fine," said Margaret, ticking and crossing and leaving the 'father' column blank, "and so will you, you know."

"Thanks."

"Honestly. You're not the first and you certainly won't be the last. I see a lot of mums in your position and most of them do very well."

"Really?"

"Yes. Between you and me, I think a lot of them do *better* without having a man to worry about as well as baby."

"Thanks," I said, "that means a lot, coming from you."

"No problem. Any questions?"

"I don't think so. Actually, I was just wondering, are you allowed to have sex? Not that I am going to have any. Probably never again, actually. But I was just wondering. Curiosity, I suppose."

"Oh, absolutely. The only thing too big about any chap who thinks it might make a difference to baby is his head."

"Oh, right. Well, like I said, I won't be doing it. I suppose I never really thought about being pregnant before and it just made me wonder."

"Who says you can't do it? As long as it's safe, jolly well go out and get it while you jolly well still can, that's what I say."

"Right." Great sentiment from Margaret, but I had never felt less like having sex.

"Now I'm afraid I'm going to need to take lots of pots of blood from you, rather like a very nasty vampire."

I offered out my arm and looked away. Needles didn't bother me, but I was vaguely aware of the notion that there was a lot of pain ahead.

"Sharp scratch now, that's a good girl."

As I felt the blood being sucked out of my arm, the frame of my vision went fuzzy. On the opposite wall, a 3D poster of a foetus blackened at the edges like a vignette.

"There we go. All done." Margaret spoke with the same soothing tone of the school nurse on vaccination day.

I looked down and saw a tiny peony blooming through the pale skin of the plaster.

"Are you alright, lovie?"

"Yeah, fine just a bit woozy"

"Don't worry, that's perfectly normal. You'll be right as rain when you've had something to eat. Now, off you go and send all those people off on their lovely holidays. And just remember – you're going to have a super little baby."

In theory, Margaret's high-octane happiness should have pissed me off, but it seemed to have the opposite effect. I practically skipped from the doctor's surgery to the bus stop, trying to imagine what my super baby would be like.

Eight

O N M Y W A Y into the hospital, I passed a pow wow of pregnant women, clad in towelling and slippers despite the torrential rain. A column of smoke rose from their centre and I realised why they were outside. For a second, I judged them, then I wanted to ask if any of them could spare a cig, then I realised that I didn't really want that, and anyway, I was going to miss my appointment.

"You're late," said Mum.

"Sorry," I said, slumping into the plastic chair next to hers. "Bloody students."

"You haven't been for a wee, have you?"

"No, but I really need one."

"Well hold it in. You'll get a much better picture if your bladder's full."

"I know. It said that on the letter. And you've told me at least five times over the phone."

Mum sounded so excited that I wanted to tell her to eff off. I almost did, but I stopped when my two front teeth were resting on my bottom lip. Mum had taken the news that I was pregnant by a mysterious, infertile, vanishing man better than she had ever taken me saying the eff word in her presence.

There were a lot of messages for me on the wall of that waiting room: aquanatal classes every Wednesday at Moss Side Pool, help to give up smoking was available and breast was most definitely best.

"What's the matter?" Mum asked.

"Nothing," I said, crossing and uncrossing my legs, then crossing them again. "I'm just looking at the posters. And I need a wee."

"Well you can't go, not yet."

"I know. You said that."

I needed a wee and I needed a cigarette. I kept thinking about those women, my comrades, standing outside in their sodden slippers.

"Emily Morris?"

There was my name, incongruously echoing off the walls of the Early Pregnancy Unit.

The jelly was cold, just like the sonographer promised. It came out of the bottle with a flatulent sound that might have made me laugh, under different circumstances. The screen was black. I couldn't look. I shut my eyes tight and clenched my jaw until there was a roar in my ears. Mum squeezed my hand.

I wanted there just to be one. Mostly, I wanted it to be healthy, like everyone says. Being healthy was more important than being the only one in there. But ideally I didn't want more than one.

"Em," Mum said, after a few seconds, rubbing my thumb with hers. "Em?"

I closed my eyes tighter.

"Well, there it is, in case you were in any doubt." She squeezed my hand twice, gently. "There's only one of them, if that helps."

I looked.

It danced.

That was not my insides; it was a film, playing out on the big screen. I was expecting a still shrimp, floating in space.

46

This thing had arms and legs and it danced. It was twirling around, showing off its stack of perfect vertebrae and its funny, ghoulish face, splaying out the hands I didn't think it would have yet.

"That's your baby's heartbeat," said the sonographer, pointing to a fuzzy flicker in the middle of the screen.

When I was a little girl, Mum used to say: "I love you so much. I loved you from the moment they showed me your heartbeat on the scan." And she'd pulse the tips of her forefinger and thumb together.

I never knew what she was on about; she said it so often that it became as familiar as the doorbell going or the theme tune to *Coronation Street*. Now I got it.

Afterwards, we bought souvenir photographs. We slotted coins into a vending machine and it spewed them out on thin slivers of paper. They gave us a frame to put them in: shiny cardboard with pastel alphabet blocks spelling out MY FIRST SCAN. The photographs looked the same as the scan photos people showed off at work, but this one was different: it was mine. It all got real in that windowless room.

"I can't believe how mobile it is," I said, breaking the awe-struck silence that had filled Mum's car since we pulled out of the hospital.

"I know. I'd forgotten how much they wriggle."

"You see the pictures and you tell people they're nice, but really it's not very interesting. It's the moving that amazed me the most though. The pictures don't show you that."

"Speaking of moving, when are you coming home?" said Mum.

Silence returned to the Peugeot 106.

"I said, when are you moving in with me, Emily?"

"I'm not," I said, "I mean, thank you so much for offering, but I can't leave Manchester."

Some people miss home when they move away to university. I thought I might when I'd left three years earlier, but within a week, I had no need to worry: Manchester was home and Mum's house was for birthdays, Mothers' Day and Christmas.

"Where will you live?" Mum said, braking at the pelican crossing outside the university. Students dawdled in front of the car, clutching folders and laughing, looking like they were posing for cover of the next prospectus. So soon after the elation of the scan, I was hit by a pang of irreversibility.

"I haven't thought about it yet."

"Well, you need to think about it."

"Mum, I've got nine months."

"Actually, you've got six."

She was right. I'd been thinking of the pregnancy as nine months, almost a year, the birth ages off. But the weeks were passing like pages in a flick-book and I was already nearly a third of the way through. "I'll work something out," I said.

The lights changed, the last student straggler stepped on to the kerb and Mum edged forwards. We sailed past familiar buildings: the Church of the Holy Name, the bridge of the dingy shopping precinct and the sixties Maths Tower that they were tearing down, piece by piece.

"You can't carry on living in that room. What about your housemates? Babies cry a lot, you know."

"Jesus, Mum. I know I don't know much about babies, but I am pretty sure I know that they cry."

"Well, you're going to need help. That's all I'm saying. And I'm offering it to you."

We carried on past my university and I remembered the stacks of redundant books at home that I really should have returned.

"They're helping me at uni," I said. "I might be able to get something through the council or a housing association."

"You might. Those places have waiting lists, you know."

We were nearly there. As we passed the end of my old street, I strained to see the corner of the halls I'd lived in for my first year. That place was a total dump inside, but living there had been the best few months of my life.

"I'm sorry," I said, when Mum pulled up outside the call centre. "Thanks for coming with me. And thanks for offering me somewhere to live."

"Go on," she said, leaning over and kissing me on the cheek. "I'm on double yellows and there's a bus up my backside."

When I got to my desk, I propped the scan photo up next to my computer, because that's what people do.

Nine

E VERY MORNING I got out of bed, walked over to the full-length mirror and pulled up my pyjama top. Every morning, it looked the same. Every morning I made a mental note to scrub the ancient hairspray flecks off the mirror.

If anything, my tummy had reduced in size since I found out I was pregnant. A swift end to drinking, middle-of-the-night pizzas and hungover cravings for anything savoury had done me good. As the weeks passed by, I began to wonder if there would ever be any outward evidence of the agile dancer I'd witnessed on the big screen (and until there was a bump, I wouldn't truly believe it was happening).

Then one morning, when it was extremely inconvenient, it popped up. Just like that, overnight, an undeniable dome. It was 6:30am, I was fourteen weeks in and I needed to get to Liverpool.

Once I'd come to terms with the fact that I was not going to New York to be an intern on an art magazine, I realised I needed to do something else. In order to pass my degree, I had to complete ninety hours of work experience. Ninety hours is a lot when you have to squeeze it in around a full-time job, but I knew it would be easier to arrange before the baby came out. So, I secured myself a placement at a cultural press office in Liverpool, which is ridiculous when I think back, because the last thing I needed on top of everything else was a commute. I like Liverpool, though: half of my family are from there; I adore the accent and the sense of humour and I once had a job typing up the funeral notices in the *Liverpool Echo*, which were often quite poetic. Plus Liverpool has a waterfront and some pretty good art galleries, so it wasn't all that different to New York. Somehow, I condensed all my shifts at the call centre into four long days and spent the other three in Liverpool. It was knackering, and I had no day off, but I was fine with that, because spare time would have quickly been filled up with worrying. Given the fact I was clinging on to the vague hope that I might one day be able to return to university and finish my degree, I kept going. Until the bump was visible. Suddenly, all the feelings of shame I thought I'd dealt with came flooding back. The bump was like a massive dunce hat permanently strapped to the front of me, cast-iron proof of my own foolishness.

I was late for my work placement that morning. After I saw the bump in the mirror, nothing I tried on would hide it. In the end, I went for a wrap dress because the pregnancy magazine recommended them a lot. What I hadn't grasped was that they're recommended not because they make you look less like you're pregnant, but because they're adjustable and comfortable. I realised this as my train sighed into Lime Street Station. As it slowed past the dark, damp walls that flank the track, I caught sight of my reflection in the blackened glass of the train window. The wrap dress was 'very clingy', as Mum would say. There could be absolutely no doubt in anyone's mind that I was with child; I looked about eight months gone.

There was no way I wanted my new, temporary colleagues to know that I was pregnant. It was just really embarrassing. Plus I probably shouldn't have been working seven days a week. If they sent me back to Manchester with no reference, I'd never be able to get my degree.

When I got off the train, I spent a sweaty, panicky few minutes in the maternity section of a high street shop before realising that I was going to be even later than I already was and the last thing I wanted was all eyes on me when I walked in the door.

It didn't occur to me that my colleagues might be too busy to notice, or even care, that I was pregnant. I spent my morning alternating bump covers: a lever arch file, the hot drinks tray and my desk, when I wasn't clinging on to the photocopier for dear life.

Just before lunch, David, my supervisor, called me over. It was time to fill out my progress report for university. I sat down opposite him and folded my arms.

"Right, well nothing to worry about, you've been great so far. That press release you did last week was perfect."

"Thanks."

"Do you think you'll want to work somewhere like this when you finish uni?"

"Maybe," I said, staring over David's shoulder at his computer screensaver. I couldn't imagine where I'd work when I finished uni, if I ever finished.

"We haven't put you off, have we?"

"Oh no, it's not that. It's just that I've decided to take a year out."

"Oh aye." David smiled and shook his head. He'd heard that one before. And so had I. I looked at his screensaver again, and the familiar white kidney bean on a black background made me brave.

"Actually, I'm taking a year out because I am pregnant."

"Oh, right." He nodded slowly, eyebrows raised. "Congratulations."

"Thank you."

David was interested. Apart from my mother, no one I had spoken to about the pregnancy had been that enthusiastic. He knew stuff, like the fact pregnant people are supposed to count in weeks. His wife, it turned out, was ten weeks ahead of me. They had been talking about names and gorging on ice cream and the gender was a surprise.

"Anyway, I'd better let you get some lunch," he said, when we'd been talking babies for at least ten minutes.

Something about the fact he was male and didn't recoil in horror or look uneasy really got to me. I imagined what it must be like to have someone to share everything with, the ice cream and the naming and the scary stuff too.

"Thanks."

"You're alright. Fancy coming to a press call this afternoon? The boat race is setting off from the docks next week."

"Yeah, that'll be good, thanks."

"I'll write on the form for your uni that you're crap and we sacked you."

"OK, ta." I stood up and wheeled my chair back under the desk next to David's.

"Hey."

"Yeah?" I looked back and David nodded at my tummy.

"So you are."

"Yep."

So, is your fella excited then?" David asked me later, as we walked downhill to the docks. Behind the Liver Birds, the sky was angry and grey.

"No."

"You what?"

"I mean no, I haven't got a boyfriend."

"Oh." He didn't know what to say. Seagulls cackled overhead.

"And no, he's not excited. Actually, he's not remotely interested." I followed that up with a tiny, pointless laugh.

"Oh, right. Sorry about that."

David did not want to have that conversation; who would? I felt bad that he had to respond in some way to what I was saying, wondering if I should have just told him that I had a fella and he was excited.

"It's OK. I'm getting used to the idea. Gradually."

"Nice fella, then?"

"A gem."

"Manc?"

"Yeah."

"What team does he support?"

"I don't know . . . City, I think." I hadn't thought of that. People buy their babies tiny football kits. I didn't know how to play football, or how to watch it. I wondered if my child would like it, and which team, if any, he or she would support.

"Oh well, you don't want your baby to be a Manc, anyway."

Actually, I didn't care. I wondered where my baby would be born, what accent it would grow up with, whether it would like Liverpool or Manchester more, or whether, like me, it would love them both.

I was trying to stride from the dock to the deck of a boat when David said it out loud. It was the first time I'd heard anyone say it about me, and it was more difficult to hear than telling people myself. "Be careful, she's pregnant!"

The man on the boat grabbed my arm with both of his

hands and pulled me on board. He made me feel safer than I'd felt in weeks. I didn't see a face beneath his battered cap; only a blur of sinew and stubble and tan.

"Thank you."

"Alright, love."

Be careful she's pregnant.

I flopped down on a seat at the edge of the deck. The man who'd helped me was on the dock, talking to David and somebody else. The seagulls were hysterical. Something metallic was ticking quickly against the mast. I looked up. The sky had swirled from grey to a furious mauve. The ticking got quicker and became a pinging, alarm-like, jostling with the laughs of the gulls. There was a cold gust and the boat bobbed a little, scraping the harbour wall. Around me, the thick, red columns of the Albert Dock were spinning on repeat, like a heliotrope in my head. I saw flashes of a school trip to the Slavery Museum, childhood visits to the dockside, Friday night launches at the Tate Modern. I buried my head between my knees but it kept spinning.

"Are you alright?" David called down.

"Yeah, I'm fine. Just need to get my sea legs. " I seriously wondered whether anyone would notice if I hid below deck until the race began and stowed away to the Caribbean.

3rd May 2004, Manchester to Montego Bay. The date of the flight was etched in my brain and stamped in my passport. I'd spotted a ridiculously cheap last-minute deal on the system at work, and a week later, two of my colleagues and I were there. At night, roaches rattled around on the tiled floor of our hotel room and in the morning, skunk smoke drifted through the broken air conditioning unit. The bolts on our room door were rusty and the gaudy, floral bedding was damp. None of that mattered to me, though: outside, the sand was like talc and the sea unbelievably turquoise. Half way through the week, we ran out of money and flashed our business cards at the luxury, all-inclusive resort just along the beach. As we were shown around rooms with mirrored ceilings and a nightclub with a glass-bottomed Jacuzzi on the roof, it became apparent that we were in a very specialist establishment. I've never shared a restaurant with couples in gimp masks before, or watched people enter a competition to see who can fake the loudest orgasm, and I'm happy to say I never will again.

Swinging hotels aside, Jamaica was the most exciting adventure I had ever been on. As a child, I had never even been abroad on holiday; now I was exploring a tropical island. Whilst my companions were happy to lounge by the pool, I took off on adventures: swimming behind waterfalls, sailing through mangroves, spotting hummingbirds, crocodiles and egrets. I held on tight as my tin-can tour bus zigzagged precariously down hazy mountain roads, the singing of birds and insects a constant backing track. Besotted with the tropical landscape, I decided that when I finished university, I wanted more. I arrived back from Jamaica just in time for Mum's fiftieth birthday, complete with a box of birds of paradise and badly bitten legs.

"Em." When I got home from Liverpool, Mum was waiting for me in the same corner of the train station where she met me after Jamaica, where dirty stalactites drip from the ceiling and stumpy-footed pigeons peck pastry flakes from the floor. "How was work experience?"

"Alright," I said. "I nearly fainted on a stationary boat."

"Oh, love." She was beaming, as though she might be proud of me or something.

"What?"

"It just that last time I saw you standing there, you had that box of fancy flowers and bloody great blotches all over your legs. Now look at you."

She'd noticed the bump.

"Yeah." I hugged her. "Now look at me."

Ten

HAVING JUST ABOUT got over the shock, I was dealt another blow: my job, which I loved and I really needed, was in jeopardy. The company I worked for had been taken over by a bigger firm and was being shifted out of town to cheaper premises in the middle of nowhere. My boss had assured me that I would be one of a select few 'home-workers' who would be given the equipment to sell holidays from home, rather than make the unfeasibly long journey by public transport. With the nights drawing in and my belly getting bigger, I was excited by the prospect of working in my slippers.

Things had changed though: the move was only a few weeks away, and the new head office had withdrawn the home-working offer. My employers had to purchase individual trading licences for each home-worker and doing so for me, when I was about to go on maternity leave, was deemed a futile exercise. In other words, I was a waste of money. The news was delivered by strangers in suits from the Human Resources department, not than the manager I knew, who'd been understanding about my predicament.

"Perhaps you could borrow a car from someone to drive to the new offices?" the suited strangers suggested.

I didn't drive. And who knows people who can just *lend* them cars, anyway? Cars are not like jumpers or books.

In the absence of a car lender (and a driving licence), my only other option was a two-hour commute, involving taxis, trams and buses and a long walk late at night. The pregnancy had started to make me feel knackered, and the thought of a long journey like that (with very limited access to much-needed loos) was daunting. By then, Jane had another job and was working different shifts to me, so getting a lift from her wasn't an option.

And so my friend insomnia returned. I desperately wanted and needed to sleep deeply, but I couldn't. So I began to make stuff, under the light of my desk lamp. When I was on my work placement in Liverpool, I'd stumbled across a bead shop. It reminded me of a hobby I'd had when I was eleven or twelve, making necklaces and earrings and selling them in aid of a hedgehog rescue charity. Mum had dug my old pliers and craft boxes out of the loft and I was straight back into it, channelling my pregnant creative energy not into knitting booties and crocheting blankets, but twisting charms on to chain. I became obsessed with winning cheap lots of old, broken jewellery on eBay, pulling them out of padded envelopes in great, tangled clumps, dismantling them and sorting the parts into the colour-coded compartments of my plastic boxes. It was calm and meditative, a way to curb the ever-present anger and fear. People liked my stuff, too: I photographed it, listed it on eBay and watched the bids come in. At that point, I would have loved to have left work and focussed on my jewellery-making: the office that meant so much to me was almost an empty shell and it was autumn, anyway, so the calls had slowed right down, but I knew that making jewellery wouldn't give me the job security and maternity pay I was going to need.

After the visit from HR, I went straight from the call centre to the Student Advice Centre. As I was still officially a student, I had access to their service, and it had been invaluable. They'd explained all the things to me that I didn't understand: childcare options, accommodation, what support was available. Every time I left that place, it was with hope that there might be a possibility I could one day return to university and finish my degree.

I took the lift up to above the Students' Union and plonked myself down in one of low, brown chairs that had become so familiar. To stave the tears, I avoided eye contact with my advisor. Instead, I looked at my library across the road, just visible through the ribbons of the vertical blind. I wanted to be in there, stressing over an essay.

I was expecting my advisor to help me write a pleading letter to the HR department, begging them to reconsider. Instead, she told me, quite confidently, cheerily, even, that my employer was in breach of the Sex Discrimination Act.

"Why?" It seemed drastic to me. Yes, they were massively letting me down, but the *Sex Discrimination Act*?

"Emily, none of what is happening to you could possibly happen if you were a man."

It was as simple as that.

Eleven

THE WOMAN SITS bolt upright in bed.

Was that what she thought it was?

She thinks it was.

She switches on the bedside lamp. Her husband groans and pulls the duvet around his eyes.

"Darling," she says.

"What?"

"I just felt the baby move."

The husband opens his eyes. "Really?"

He puts his hand on her tummy, groggy but awestruck nonetheless.

They sit still, shushing each other, like they're in a bird hide; as though making the slightest noise, even rustling the duvet, will prevent the baby from moving again.

"Shhh!" says the woman, giggling, "I felt it again. It feels like butterflies in my tummy."

The husband can't feel it yet, but he is still amazed. He tells his wife he loves her, snogs her and perhaps, if neither of them are too tired, they go on to have sex.

That's how I imagined baby's first movements happening to normal couples. I'd read a lot about it on Motherboard (OMG felt LO moving 4 1st time!!!!!!!!!! DP so happy ☺ ☺ ☺ xxxxxxxxxx can't w8 to meet our DS or DD).

This is how it happened for me:

My housemates were having a party. I could hardly get annoyed about the parties; they were young and none of them chose to live with a pregnant woman. I didn't know I was pregnant when I moved in with them, but I was. They were brilliant about it, sympathetic and kind, but they needed their parties, which was understandable.

As well as being pregnant, I was stressed: my Student Advisor had put me in touch with the Equality and Human Rights Commission, who'd helped me draft an email. I'd sent it to my company's Managing Director and he'd replied, almost instantaneously, with a date for a 'hearing'. The events of the preceding months had weakened me and left me embarrassed and apologetic. Part of me wanted to say sorry, call off the meeting, leave and move to my mum's. As I lay awake listening to my housemates having loads of fun, all I could do was worry about the hearing, and the fact I'd spent fifty quid on smart maternity clothing that I would never, ever wear again.

The last thing I needed was a house full of people determined to stay up until dawn, but I didn't have much choice. Last time there had been a party, I went to stay at Anna's, and came home the next day to find my bed slept in, a dented Red Stripe can abandoned on top of my maternity notes. There were no locks on the doors in our house because everyone was friends, and I would have looked completely neurotic had I had one fitted. Still, having already lost control of my own body, I felt then like I had lost control of my only sanctuary, my bedroom, as well. This party was a spontaneous, mid-week affair. There had been no warning, but even if there had, I think I'd have wanted to occupy my bed.

My bedroom was actually a living room, rented out by the landlord to make extra money. This meant that when there were parties, which there frequently were, I was right next door to the action. I was tucked up in bed, but I might as well have been lying in the middle of the next room, amongst the beer-can ashtrays, spent laughing-gas balloons and the filthy shoes of strangers.

I sat up and leant over to my bedside drawers, rummaging around in the old shoebox I kept there, which contained mainly redundant things: condoms, foreign coins, cigarette papers, tampons. At the bottom, squashed and studded with glitter, I found one half of a pair of earplugs. I crushed the foam between my thumb and forefinger, pushed it into one ear and pressed a pillow down hard on the other. Every time I almost drifted off, my hand relaxed, releasing the pressure on the pillow and letting in the bass.

That was how I was lying when I felt my baby move for the first time. It wasn't wind or indigestion or muscle spasms or anything else, it was one hundred per cent the feeling of my baby twirling in my womb. I'd been dreading feeling the baby move, sure it would feel like an alien invasion, but when it happened, I was amazed. I shuffled up on to my elbows, switched on the bedside light and gazed at the flat gap on the other side of the bed. I froze, willing it to do it again.

"Is that you?" I said, as though I might get some kind of response.

It happened again. A ripple, a flip, a feeling in my tummy like the one I used to get every morning when my school bus careered too fast over the little stone bridge.

"Hello!" I clasped my tummy with both hands, grinning.

The beautiful moment was ruined when a wide-eyed boy who I'd never seen in my life burst into my room.

"Is this the bathroom?"

"Jesus. No!"

"Am I in a K hole?"

"No, you are in my bedroom."

"DON'T GO IN THERE A GIRL IS TRYING TO SLEEP!" shouted the boy, clattering out and slamming the door behind him. "Who tries to sleep in the middle of a *party?*"

The baby was enjoying the party, even though I wasn't. I wanted to tell someone, anyone. I even considered going into the living room and announcing it to the revellers, but that might have been a bit weird. So I just chatted to my baby. Maybe that was weird too, but it reminded me why I couldn't cancel the meeting, why I had to save my job.

Twelve

YOU'RE PUBLIC PROPERTY when you're pregnant. As soon as your bump is visible, everybody wants a piece of you. On one of many visits to the midwife, a woman sat next to me in the doctor's waiting room and laid her fingernails, which were curled and ridged like rams' horns, on my belly.

"Well, we all know why you're here, don't we love? God bless you."

People say they'd punch anyone who dared just touch them like that, but it's easier said than done: I have a hard time getting annoyed with people who are just trying to be kind.

More annoying than the touching though, are the questions. Generally, people think it is totally acceptable to interrogate you when you're pregnant. There's a standard set of questions that people ask. This list isn't exhaustive, but the usual ones are:

1. When are you due?
   (March.)
2. Do you know what you're having?
   (A baby.)
3. Have you thought of any names?
   (Yes.)
4. Are you afraid of the birth?
   (Fucking petrified.)
5. Are you excited?

(Very occasionally.)

6. Is your husband excited?

When your baby bump begins to show, you might as well wear one of those badges that shop staff have. You know the ones: "Ask me anything about . . . DIY/skincare/my life." Maybe the quizzing doesn't feel too invasive if you're in a conventional scenario, but when the father's AWOL, it doesn't take long for things to get more than awkward. You have a choice: tell the truth or lie. The truth had made me feel pretty embarrassed when I'd spoken it on my work placement, so the next time I was confronted with the questions, in the hairdresser's chair, I decided to experiment with lies.

It was my birthday and I wanted to go very blonde. It felt like the closest I'd get to celebratory debauchery. I felt like I was being deprived of something wonderful by not being able to go out. Anna said there was nothing stopping us, but I didn't want to be stuck sober in the middle of a packed dance floor, inhaling smoke and getting splashed with drinks that smelled of vomit. My birthday treat to myself would be getting my head smothered in peroxide.

First, I checked whether I was allowed to have my hair bleached on Motherboard. One woman, a hairdresser, told me I didn't need to worry – the only dye that could harm me or my baby was a specific kind of dark one. A couple of others took the time to reply, telling me they had no idea but I should probably check with my midwife. Other members told me that bleaching my hair was fatally dangerous to me and my unborn child, that I wouldn't care about things like hair in a few months, I should probably just get a crop and that I should put my baby before my own selfish vanity. All of it came with an IMHO (in my humble opinion). Motherboard, it emerged, was the place where people who lurk in newspaper comments sections went when they reproduced. Anyway, I checked with Margaret and she did that fly-swotting thing again and said it was fine.

"HI! My name's Zoe and I'll be your stylist today!"

Zoe was REALLY ENTHUSIASTIC.

"Hello."

"What are we doing, then?"

"Blonde, please. Platinum. As white as you can get it without it falling out."

"OK!"

"It's for my birthday," I added, as though that might improve my chances of achieving optimum whiteness.

While Zoe was mixing my colour, I stared at myself, bloated and blotchy, in the mirror. Perhaps making an appointment that involved sitting right in front of my own reflection for several hours hadn't been such a good idea.

"Right, let's get you in a gown!" Zoe said, holding up a black nylon cape.

I saw her eyes flick down quickly to my belly and back again. There's nothing more awkward than thinking someone is pregnant, but not being quite sure, and not knowing whether to congratulate them in case they're not. I definitely was though, and from the smile on Zoe after her second glance, she knew it. Which meant the questions were coming.

"So, how far gone are you?"

She hadn't even finished painting the first highlight. As much as I would have liked to tell her to get lost and let me enjoy my hairdo in peace, she had a sweet smile on her face and my hair in her hands.

"Four months."

(I was actually nineteen weeks, but I'd learnt that only midwives and other pregnant people count in weeks.)

"So, when are you due?"

"March."

"Do you know what you're having?"

"I find out next week."

I felt like a machine, repeating the same answers in monotone. Midwives should dish out Dictaphones to pregnant women so they can fire out the answers at the touch of a button: March. Don't know yet. A bit tired. No. Yes. Terrified. Thanks.

"Ooh, exciting!" Zoe continued. "Have you got a feeling what it is?"

"A boy."

"Is your other half excited?"

"Yes."

"So, are you doing anything special for your birthday?"

"Just a meal."

"Aw, just you and your fella?"

None of your business, I thought. But that's not what I said. "Just me and a couple of friends."

That much was true. I'd booked a big table at a posh restaurant that did a good midweek offer and invited everyone I knew. The guest list was dwindling by the minute, as more of my student friends texted me to say they had no money, or they had too much work to do, or they just didn't want to spend their money on fancy food when they could quite easily get a two-quid Domino's.

"Oh no, can't your partner make it?"

"No."

"That's a shame. Why not?"

Jesus. "He's working."

There was no escape. If I ran out, the chemicals that were stinging my eyes would frazzle my hair and burn my scalp. So I remained seated in the big leather chair, feeling like I was on *Mastermind* (specialist subject: my messy life).

"Oh, you'd think he'd be able to get the night off for your birthday meal, wouldn't you? What does he do?"

I looked down at the celebrity gossip magazine Zoe had placed on my lap: *Yummy Mummies Show off Flat Tummies!*

"He works nights. He's a barman. I mean a fireman. He's a fireman. He really can't get the time off. Under no circumstances. It's very strict."

"Ah, I suppose saving lives comes first."

"Oh yes, no willy nilly time off for him whenever he wants!"

"You must be dead proud."

"I am." I smiled, past the point of no return.

"I'd love to go out with a fireman, me. Is he good-looking?"

"Yes."

I could almost picture him in my head: stacked, gelled hair, not my type.

"Muscular?"

"Yes."

"Ooh. Tanned?"

"Not really. He lives in Manchester."

"What's his name then?"

And out of my mouth came "Mike".

"Mike?"

"Yeah, Mike."

"So, will he be able to make sure he's at the birth? I mean, he could be on duty when your waters break. You know like how the WAGs arrange to have caesareans in case the baby comes in the middle of a match?"

"I don't know, it's a long way off."

I stared at my moony face in the lit mirror, the ruddy puffiness of my cheeks, the sooty semicircles beneath each of my eyes, the halo of flopping foil parcels. I did not look like the girlfriend of a handsome, muscular fireman.

"I'd rather have a caesarean, me."

"Me too."

It was true: giving birth terrified me. I tried to come to terms with it by watching birthing documentaries, usually before bed, giving myself recurring nightmares about irreparably ripping open. A caesarean would give me some semblance of predictability and control over the situation, but Margaret had already told me I wouldn't be allowed one without good medical reason.

"So," Zoe was still going, "will you be doing something special with Mike to make up for him missing your actual birthday?"

"Yes," I shifted my numb buttocks and had a quick think, "he's taking me away. The Peak District. I didn't want to fly, so he booked us a weekend break in a fancy hotel."

I could see that too: honey-coloured brick, sweeping driveway, flocked wallpaper, claw-footed bath.

"Ooh, what a romantic! And that's not too far away, either, is it? The Peak District."

"No. He thinks of everything. It's even got a spa."

What the hell was I on about?

"Ooh, do they do those pamper packages for mums-to-be?"

"Yep. Those are the ones."

When it came, hours later, the hot roar of the hairdryer

was like a sweet serenade.

"What do you think?" Zoe asked, angling a hand mirror at the back of my head.

"Thanks. You made it white."

"Really sexy." Zoe narrowed her eyes. "You're a proper yummy mummy now! Mike won't be able to resist."

I was pretty sure Zoe knew that Mike was a work of terrible fiction, but at least I'd look smarter for my imminent hearing at work.

When Zoe chirpily told me the extortionate cost, I panicked, feeling guilty for spending money on a hairdo when I didn't even know where I was going to be living in a few months. It had hardly been a relaxing experience, but I handed over the cash, with tip, and escaped as quickly as I could.

"Enjoy your romantic weekend, hun!"

"Thanks."

I hailed a black cab outside the salon. More guilt: I should have got the Magic Bus, especially given the fact I could quite possibly soon be unemployed, but the white lies had exhausted me.

"You OK, darling?" The taxi driver's voice boomed through the speakers, jolting me out of my sulk.

"Yes, thank you."

Why did everyone want to speak to me? I couldn't wait to get home and hide in bed forever, or at least until I was rudely awakened by my bladder.

"You are looking very tired."

"Yes, I am." I sighed, flipping open my phone: another cancellation for the meal.

"How long to go now?"

"Five months."

"Five months! This is a long time! You are looking very, very big already," the driver shouted, in surround sound.

"Yes."

"I have a young son and let me tell you, it is the best thing in all of the world when you see that baby for the first time."

"Thank you." I smiled at him in the rear-view mirror.

People kept telling me about that moment, when the baby had just come out and their life felt complete and overwhelmingly purposeful and the pain didn't matter anymore. Apparently, the love and fulfilment made you high. I hoped it was true, but I wasn't convinced.

"Your husband, is he excited?"

Yes. He is very excited and he is Mike the fireman and he is taking me away to—

"Actually, I don't have a husband."

"Sorry. Your boyfriend – is he excited?"

Ever had a deep and meaningful conversation with a taxi driver on the way home from a night out? I have: loads of them. Once, a driver turned off his engine outside my house, ordered me to listen to the dawn chorus and asked me how I could possibly consider not believing in God when such an amazing thing existed. I'm not sure how we got on to the subject of creationism, but I ended up agreeing with him so he would turn off the automatic door locks and I could get out and go to bed. Another time, I had a driver on the verge of tears after he told me about how his wife had had an affair while he was out working nights saving up to take her on a cruise.

There isn't really an excuse for deep taxi discussions when you're sober and pregnant and it's the middle of the afternoon, but I was knackered and I'd run out of fibs.

"I haven't got a boyfriend, either."

"But where did he go? The father of your child?"

"I don't know."

"Is he in Manchester?"

"I don't know. He was my friend. He isn't any more."

"But he is going to be father; doesn't he want to see baby?"

"Apparently not."

"I don't believe." He shook his head. "He will come. When baby is born, he will come and he will want to see."

"Perhaps."

Raindrops wriggled down the taxi window like worms. Outside, the trees were rusting from green to orange. Some of them were starting to look bare already. I knew that by the time they were green again, I would have had a baby.

When he stopped the cab, the driver peeled a passport-sized photograph from the dashboard and passed it to me via the coin tray.

"Here," he said, "Mustafa. My son."

The boy was wearing pale blue. He had his father's gleaming, mahogany eyes and a small, dribbly smile. I wondered whether my baby would look like its father or me or a strange combination of us both.

"He's lovely," I said, really meaning it and not just saying it to be kind.

"Yes, yes he is. Thank you."

I handed the photograph of Mustafa back to the driver, along with a crumpled tenner, and opened the cab door.

"Listen. You will be OK. If this man doesn't want baby, he is not good man. You will be good mother. I can see this."

"Thank you."

I was putting my key in the lock when the taxi horn

beeped, making me jump and spin around. The driver was waving through his wound-down window.

"Smile lady, you are blessed!"

Thirteen

"**H**APPY BIRTHDAY BREAKFAST!"

"Thanks, love."

"Woah, big baby belly!" Rebecca said, clocking my bump with even wider eyes than normal.

I was wearing a monochrome striped top, which only accentuated the mound. Everyone knows horizontal stripes make you look bigger, but those tops were in, and I didn't see why I shouldn't wear mine if I wanted to. Besides, it was one of the few tops I had that was stretchy enough to still fit.

"Yes," I sighed, "big baby belly."

Rebecca hadn't been able to come out for my birthday meal, so I met her for breakfast a couple of days later.

"So, you're having a baby. This is weird."

"Yes," I said, "yes it is."

Rebecca was another of my call-centre friends. She didn't work there anymore though, preferring to do the odd stint of flyering and a bar job. When she was in England, anyway. Since graduating, Rebecca spent a lot of time in the tropics, learning to surf and falling in love. She regularly saved up, vanished, reappeared suddenly, saved up and vanished again.

Rebecca used to send round-robin Hotmails to me and her other friends saying things like: *Hey I am in Bali, long story sorry I didn't say bye before I left it was a bit of a mad rush. Crazy times! Not sure if I am going to have enough cash to stay here. Argh! Sun is shining though and it is fun, big love, Bec x*

When the Boxing Day tsunami hit in 2004, I was convinced Rebecca had been swept away. She had sent one of her updates a couple of days before Christmas, telling everyone she was living happily in a beach hut in Thailand. After the tsunami, she sent nothing, despite numerous emails from me and many others. I spent days and nights worrying frantically, hanging around in the corner shop because they had Sky News and you could read the ticker-tape messages along the bottom from tourists who wanted to let people at home know that they were OK. Just when I was about to try to figure out how to make contact with her father, Rebecca got in touch:

Hi Guys, I am fine! Sorry if you thought something bad had happened. Last minute change of plans! So horrible what happened back there. Not in Thailand any more. With my boyfriend's family in Oz. Flew here on Christmas Eve.

I'd been in awe of Rebecca's free-spiritedness since I'd met her, and secretly hoped that I would one day live a life in which deciding to fly from Thailand to Australia was as trivial a move as getting a cab from Fallowfield to Withington. Deep down, I don't think I'd have ever been carefree enough to pull it off, but with the baby on its way, I knew I'd never find out.

"Have you heard from the man then?"

"No, I don't think I will."

"Yeah, he sounded like really bad news, anyway."

"Yep. Anyway, where are you off to next?"

"Well, if I keep working for another two months, I'll have enough money to be away for Christmas. I could work in a ski resort. I'm thinking: snowboarding or surfing?"

"Probably the surfing? Better weather, anyway."

"Yeah. Not as festive, but better weather. I can go back to Australia, but I am thinking I really would like to see South

America and this guy I met in Thailand last year is in Brazil, so maybe that's an option."

"Yeah, maybe that's an option."

"Yikes, so when you have your baby I might not be around, sorry. But I really want to meet it, you know."

"I know."

I looked at the grease bubbles swirling in my veggie fry-up.

"Babies are cute!"

"Yeah."

"And it won't be a baby forever, anyway. It will grow into a kid. Kids are great! You can have loads of fun with kids!"

"I suppose," I said.

There was no way that Rebecca or anyone else was going to be able to convince me that having a kid could possibly be anywhere near as much fun as flitting between tropical countries, surfing and snowboarding and falling in love.

I devoured my breakfast, but Rebecca said she was full, leaving her toast to go cold.

"What was that you said about work, then?" she said, "on your text message?"

"Oh, God, be glad you got out when you did," I said. "They've been bought out and they're moving to the middle of bloody nowhere. First they said I could work from home, but now they've changed their minds. If things don't go my way, I've got no job."

"I might be able to get you a job at my work," Rebecca said. "You've done bar work before, right?"

"A bit," I said, "but I'm asleep by nine these days. And I can't be around smoke."

"Shit, sorry, of course."

"It's OK, you were only trying to help."

"Hang on, have you given up smoking?"

"Yeah, it was easy, actually."

"Really? Maybe I should get pregnant! Haha!"

Haha.

"What about flyering? You've done that before, you've done it with me!"

I thought back to the hours Rebecca and I had spent under the railway bridge on Oxford Road, cold and numb and needing a wee, handing out flyers to passers-by in exchange for a crap, cash-in-hand wage that never actually materialised. I imagined doing it in my current state and almost laughed.

"I'm not sure that would be the best job for me right now, Bec. Thanks, though, love."

Rebecca was sitting front of me, but she might as well have been in Thailand or Bali or Brazil. It wasn't her fault; we were just on totally different trajectories, and her particular trajectory was way more appealing than mine. To both of us.

"Good luck, miss," she said, when we'd paid the bill and were standing outside in the sharp autumnal air, "be brave."

"I'll try," I said. "Keep in touch. Send pictures of you in whatever exciting place you find yourself in."

"Yeah, of course."

We hugged. Then Rebecca pulled on her bobble hat and hopped on her battered shopper bike and cycled off along misty Wilmslow Road.

Fourteen

ONE OF THE many things Motherboard taught me was that some women love nothing more than to complain about how utterly useless their 'darling partners' are. Did you know that when going to B&Q to select the paint for the nursery, ahead of spending all weekend decorating it, some men *buy the wrong shade?* Did you also know that some men fail to bring chocolate home from the shops when they have been ordered to do so? Or that they *snore?* Or invite their mothers over for the weekend? Disgusting.

Early in high school, before I realised how difficult GCSEs were going to be, I made a conscious decision never to get het up about exams. Cross country running? That had me hyperventilating and telling the PE teachers I suffered from weekly periods. Gymnastics in gym knickers? See above. But academic exams? I wasn't bothered. I'd have a quick flick through the text books, learn the keywords and mosey into school the next morning like there was nothing to worry about.

Everyone else revised, though: they revised loudly at the bus stop and on the bus and in form time and at lunch. They'd recite passages of novels and equations and the features of oxbow lakes while I told them to shut up, all the while secretly wishing I could be a bit more like them.

That was how I felt about the other mothers: while they were throwing themselves into an exciting new world of techniques, terminology and equipment, I was avoiding *The*

Complete Guide to Conceiving, Pregnancy and Giving Birth (a thoughtful birthday present from my mum – "you got the first bit right, love," she said) because I was terrified of what lay inside. A quick flick through on my birthday morning had revealed a lot of DPs with side partings and polo shirts, rubbing beautiful, not-really-pregnant women's backs. Rather than getting myself into a panic by intensely revising and reading up, I was hoping I could turn up on the first day of motherhood and work out what to do.

Of course, Margaret disagreed with that approach, as did my mum. They both thought I should be making friends with other mothers-to-be and comparing notes on stretch marks and breathing exercises. Margaret kept trying to convince me to go to aquanatal classes, but there was no way I was getting in a cozzy in my condition.

"You won't be the only one," Mum kept saying. "There are loads of single parents these days."

"I don't think the pregnant ones are single yet," I said.

In the end, I agreed to go to a class at the hospital that promised to tell me what was going to happen to my body in pregnancy and childbirth; something I really didn't want to find out about, but knew I probably should.

"Come in ladies, we don't bite!"

Two women were standing at the front of the dingy room. On a table in front of them, a doll lay next to a plastic pelvis. I slipped into the back row and chose the most isolated seat I could find, tuning in and out of conversations about numbers of weeks and maternity dresses and weight gain.

Turns out when people refer to their husbands in real life, they don't say DH, or 'darling husband', but 'hubby', which is at least sixty times more annoying. And I know that makes me sound bitter, but I hereby declare that in the highly unlikely event I ever marry, I will never, ever use the word 'hubby'.

Those who weren't married talked about 'partners', which sounded like it should be prefixed by 'howdy' and made me think about the now defunct high-street stationery chain.

"Right, ladies. Are we all ready to get started?"

The midwives introduced themselves as Jackie and Rita. Jackie handed out a roll of sticky labels and told us to take one and pass them on. We were required to write our names on the labels and stick them to our chests because, Jackie told us, just like every person who has ever led any sort of workplace training session, she would forget her own head if it wasn't screwed on.

When we were all labelled, Jackie held on to the plastic pelvis while Rita raised giggles by referring to her as her 'glamorous assistant' and slowly threaded the doll through one side and out of the other.

"Now don't worry, ladies," Rita said, "our bodies are amazing things and this is what they're designed to do."

I crossed my legs, trying to work out if there was a way of leaving without attracting the attention of Rita and Jackie and the other mothers.

"Now," Jackie continued, "you've probably heard some of your friends say that since they had their baby, they've been more prone to . . . *accidents*."

I looked around and saw that I was the only one who wasn't nodding or giggling, so I did both.

What sort of accidents? I thought, tripping on piles of filthy nappies? Slipping on snot?

"O-Kay," said Jackie. "Yep. It's a familiar tale. Now,

incontinence isn't nice for anyone, even if it's only temporary, but thankfully there *are* ways to try to avoid it."

Incontinence.

"That's right," said Rita. "Now. Can anyone tell me what the group of muscles that we have *down below* are called?"

That was easy; I'd learnt it in *More!* magazine when I was way too young to be reading it.

No one else knew though. Either they were a coy bunch or their hubbies had been missing out.

I put my hand up and Jackie nodded at me.

"Yes?" She narrowed her eyes to read my label. "Emily?"

"Pelvic floor muscles."

"*Well done!* Pelvic. Floor. Muscles. And it's exercising our pelvic floor muscles that can help stop us from any surprise little wees when we laugh."

I didn't know how anyone could possibly ever laugh again after going through what Rita and Jackie had just described.

Jackie encouraged us to practise. We had to pretend we were stopping a wee mid-flow. No one would be able to tell what we were up to, we were promised; we could do it when we were watching the soaps, cooking the tea, even standing in the supermarket queue!

Next came perineums and olive oil, which had me crossing my legs even tighter.

"Just get your hubby to give you a nice massage down there and it could reduce your risk of tearing," said Jackie.

"*Extra virgin* works best," said Rita. "Only joking, ladies!"

"Now, you all know you shouldn't be fetching and carrying in your pregnancy, don't you? That's really important. So make sure your partner does any heavy lifting for you. And that goes for after the birth; there's nothing worse than seeing a woman who's just birthed carrying her baby in a heavy car seat. You'll need to ask your partner to help you get your baby in and out of the car, especially for the first few days."

I looked around the room, my eyes darting from woman to woman, desperately trying to find my kindred spirit, the one woman who was also here under duress and going it alone, the one who didn't have a partner or a car, but all of them were nodding.

"Now, birthing balls!"

Jackie produced a silver gym ball and sat astride it, her legs wide open.

"Birthing balls are *brilliant* for an active labour, which can really help to speed baby along, because we *can't wait* to meet our babies, right?"

More nods, accompanied by murmurs of excitement.

This was not exciting; it was horrible. Why couldn't any of these women see how terrible the whole thing was?

"I've got my birthing ball already," said a voice from a couple of rows in front.

"*Brilliant!* That's what we like to hear!"

"I was bouncing on it in front of the telly the other night and my hubby came home and laughed at me. I said, 'I'd like to see you on one of these, you cheeky bugger!'"

"Ooh, I'd have given him a slap!"

Suddenly, everyone was guffawing and comparing the uselessness of their hubbies. And I was tearing off my name sticker and walking out into the rain.

Fifteen

BEFORE THE HEARING, I went to the toilet. Three times. I didn't know how long it would last and I didn't want to need a wee in the middle of it. Also, in a weird way, I felt sentimentally connected to those dingy, beige toilets, the place where it all began (or the place where I found out what was happening, anyway).

My baby was a boy. I'd had a hunch he would be, but there was a fifty percent chance of me being right about that. Still, I wanted to confirm my suspicions. And to stop calling him *it*.

"Stop blubbing, will you?" I said to Mum, as we waited for my twenty-week scan to start.

She was sitting in a chair at the head of the bed, kneading a tatty tissue.

I couldn't see the baby in its entirety this time, only parts of it, gliding across the screen like fish in a murky tank.

"Is it alright?" I asked, my voice tinged with worry.

"If you'd just bear with me. . ."

The sonographer sounded impatient. I shut up, embarrassed, realising that I sounded like a neurotic mother already.

"Everything seems to be progressing normally," the sonographer said, eventually.

My shoulders dropped and I sighed and thanked her.

"Do you want to find out the sex?"

"Yes, please."

"Alright, then, Mum. I can tell you that you are looking at

. . . are you sure you want to know?"

"Yes."

Yes, goddamnit.

"OK. You are looking at your little boy."

My little boy.

"Now who's blubbing?" said the sonographer.

It was me.

Knowing the gender changed everything. Instead of a nameless, parasitic thing, I had a son: Tom. There were pictures in my head, pale and vague as distant memories, but very definitely there, of the two of us hanging out together, walking to school, playing in the park. Tom would be my companion, my ally, my friend.

I looked in the mirror. My hair was still icy white and my make-up looked good. Thankfully the mirror was too high for me to be able to see the polyester boot-cut maternity trousers, the only ones I'd been able to find, and the cheap "smart" shoes I'd bought especially for the occasion. I clutched the washbasin taps tight, until my knuckles blanched. I was ready to take on HR, inequality, the world.

The fact that the meeting was called a 'hearing' made it sound terrifying. I had been told I'd be allowed a colleague in there with me, and a brilliant woman called Farah had agreed to join me. Farah and I had bonded a year earlier on an educational trip to a cruise ship, recreating the 'King of the World!' moment from *Titanic* on the breezy front deck. In the early days of my pregnancy, she regularly sat down with me on the steps at the front of the office, talking through my options, calming me down. She was also a law student, and the best possible person to accompany me to the hearing.

"You'll be fine," she said, winking at me as we sat down.

The hearing, when it finally happened, seemed informal. There was me, Farah, my boss and a woman from HR. It wasn't even in a separate room; we were in a cluster of bucket chairs in the corner of the call centre.

"So we're here to hear the grievance you submitted," said the HR woman, clearing her throat and shuffling papers. "Can you just go through what was in your letter, please?"

"Yes. I was denied home-working because I am pregnant and I really, really need it. Because I am pregnant, and the new offices are far away, and I don't drive. I am good at my job – you only have to see my sales figures to see that. I've been told it's not worth the company investing in a licence for me because I'll be going on maternity leave in a few months, but I've also been advised that that's in breach of the Sex Discrimination Act, because it wouldn't happen to a man."

I glanced at Farah and she nodded at me, beaming.

"We all know that January's one of the travel industry's busiest months. I'll be able to work later from home and help at that hectic time of year. Plus if I do work from home, I'll be able to keep going right up until when the baby's born. Well, obviously not *right* up to it . . ."

A smattering of laughter, a good sign.

"Emily," said the HR woman, uncrossing her legs, "first of all I'd like to apologise that you felt the need to put in a grievance. As you know, our staff are very important to us. I'd also like to apologise for what seems to have been a mix-up."

"A mix-up?"

"As you know, we are only able to offer the home-working package to a select number of employees, based on their performance. That's where the misunderstanding occurred. When we analysed your figures for the month of May, one of our busiest sales periods, they were quite low. What we didn't realise, and therefore didn't take into account, was the fact that a) you were away in Cyprus for one week of that month and that b) because of your studies, you were only working part-time during in that period. When the amount of time you were actually at your desk is taken into account, your conversion rates are actually very impressive."

I looked at Farah, who was suppressing a grin.

"Impressive enough for me to be a home-worker?"

"Absolutely, Emily. We'd very much like to reinstate our offer. You're definitely on the home-working list."

In five minutes, the dreaded hearing was over and Farah and I were hugging in the toilets.

Misunderstanding, or no misunderstanding, Tom and I had got what we needed. January would be busy enough for me to make plenty of commission, which I'd put away for when I was on Statutory Maternity Pay.

Now all I had to do was find a place to live: a home for me and my son.

Sixteen

I SPENT MOST of my pregnancy looking at the ground. The pavement became my landscape: discarded kebabs spewing slices of slimy tomatoes, pats of blackened chewing gum, fluffy cigarette ends, dog shit, pigeon carcasses, flattened rodents, crisp packets faded by the sun, oil rainbows in puddles, vomit spatters tattooed on to concrete long after the rain had washed the worst away.

With the money I was saving by not going out (and before baby paraphernalia became a considerable actuality), I invested in an iPod, chunky and pink, with a green LCD screen, the freshest technology. Whenever I left the house, I shoved my hands in my pockets and my earphones in my ears and listened to the music I'd danced to on all my favourite nights out. One of my favourite albums at the time was *Hot Fuss* by The Killers. The final track on that album soothed me, temporarily, every time I heard it. It was called 'Everything Will Be Alright' and as it flowed dreamily into my ears, I felt, fleetingly, like Brandon Flowers really was reassuring me that things were going to work out OK. Until the next song started and I realised that a beautiful Mormon from Las Vegas knew nothing of my situation and was in no position to let me know my fate. The iPod was always on shuffle, so I never knew what was coming next. I liked it that way, living track-by-track, in three-minute chunks. I didn't think beyond the next song, which meant I didn't have to think beyond the next week, which was useful when my time left was counted in sets of seven days.

The weeks were flipping by quickly, my belly swelling and time running out. I knew I had to find somewhere to live, and I was beginning to realise it might not be in Manchester. Even if I found a place and got help towards the rent through Housing Benefit, I didn't know how I'd afford to pay the bills.

The fast passage of time was never more apparent than on my daily trudge along the long, tree-lined road that led from my house to the bus stop. The feverish, sap-sticky summer where it had all begun was long gone, replaced by an autumn that hurried up and happened sooner than I'd expected. Before long, I was stepping over spiky conker cases, the contents nestled inside like perfectly polished wood. Soon after that, the leaves fell, papery at first, until the first deluge of autumn rain turned them into a slippery, smelly sludge.

On Bonfire Night, I caught the train to my mother's to escape another house party. I'd spent most of the afternoon hiding in the avocado bathtub, watching my jellyfish tummy poke, bluish, through the water's filmy surface. My housemates thundered up and down the stairs, cleaning ahead of the in-evitable destruction, shouting to each other about what was needed from the shop. I camped out for as long as I could, topping up the hot water with my big toe every time it went lukewarm. Sylvia Plath was right about the bath: it really does make you feel better, but you can't stay in it forever. By the time I had hauled myself out and dried my shrivelled skin, it was dark, the party was imminent and I wished I'd left the house earlier.

That evening, the noisy walk to the bus stop had me riddled with anxiety. The pregnancy, the desertion, the problem with my job: all of it had turned me into a nervous wreck. I was constantly wound up and worried, which was probably no good for the baby, which made me worry more. What was happening to my body was so all-encompassing that it never crossed my confused mind to address my mental health. There were plenty of visits to medical professionals, but all of them concerned the physical. As I walked to the bus stop, I was convinced that the fireworks peppering the sky were going to land on me and set me and my baby alight. Each time one screeched overhead, I ducked, and whenever one exploded, I jumped, certain that the baby could hear the bangs too. I'd got over my fear of fireworks when I was about five, but now it was back. At one point, when a spent rocket nosedived a few feet in front of me, I considered turning back and enduring the party. I kept going to the bus stop though, and the train station beyond that until, eventually, I reached the cosy safety of my mum's front room.

Mum had been bidding on boxes of second-hand baby clothes on eBay. After tea, she brought them into the living room, delicately unfolding and refolding every tiny vest and sleepsuit. It was the happiest I'd seen her look in years. I wanted to be as excited as she was, but there was too much to worry about. The birth was like a bloody wall blocking my way, and I couldn't see past it. All I knew was that beyond it lay at least eighteen years of absolute commitment to a role I really wasn't sure I was capable of. Mum wanted to talk about Tom, but exhausted from the stress of my journey, I couldn't think about him. I thanked her for the clothes and left her sorting them into size-ordered piles.

"Move in here, Em," she said, as I trudged upstairs to bed.

The next evening, when I returned home from a slow shift

at the call centre, the pavements were littered with the remains of the night before: tubes like giant Sherbet Fountains; sharp, wooden sticks and fragments of charred cardboard. As the week wore on, the fireworks were joined by red paper poppies, petals trodden into the tarmac around the gates of the nearby primary school.

Soon after that, the first frosts arrived. I'd forgotten about the beauty of frosted concrete, probably because it had been years since I'd actually been up and out early enough to see it. The ground actually glittered, the last few fallen leaves were sparkling and the gutter on next door's house dripped with jagged icicles. It was beautiful, but it made my daily walk to the bus stop a treacherous mission. I've never been the most graceful person, and with the extra weight I was carrying and the bulbous shape of me, balancing on glassy pavements was a challenge. There's added pressure to stay upright when you're carrying a baby, too. With the days seeming to get dark quickly after they'd become light, it was a real effort to not just stay in bed.

On my days off, I did. One bleak and blustery afternoon, after I'd spent all day in bed making bracelets, I needed to go to the post office to send off some packages of jewellery. I wrapped up warm, my gloved hands fumbling with the slippery carrier bag full of padded envelopes. The pavements impossible, I kept reaching out for something to hold on to, but there was nothing apart from the odd twig protruding from a garden hedge, which inevitably snapped. My waddling shuffle was getting me nowhere. The post office was a ten-minute walk away, but it felt like it was going to take a lot longer that day. Once again, I toyed with the idea of turning back towards home, but I knew I had to keep going. There was a couple walking a few steps in front of me, anyway, so I didn't feel completely alone.

When I had almost made it to the main road, where the pavements would be gritted and I knew I'd feel a lot safer, I stepped on to a deep, frozen puddle, hidden under a pile of leaves. There was a sharp crack as the the ice broke under my bulk. To take control of the situation, I sat down, triangular shards jostling at my ankles, icy water seeping into the seat of my jeans. I looked up, wondering how the hell I would haul myself out. The man in the couple looked over his shoulder, definitely saw me, turned around again, caressed his girlfriend's bum, and continued on his wintry stroll.

I was on my own, sitting in a freezing puddle, too heavy to get myself out. The puddle was a metaphor. I laughed – what else could I do? Then I made sure no one was looking, got on all fours and used a wall to drag myself up. I pulled my coat down over my numb, soaking buttocks and carried on my quest to the post office. My journey couldn't get any worse, I reasoned, popping in my earphones and looking at the ground. Only I couldn't see the ground. When I looked down, all I could see was my belly, poking out of the front of my too-small coat.

So I stopped looking at the ground and started looking forwards, because it was my only option. When I got home, I ran a bath, called my mum and asked her if I could move in with her after all.

She said yes, obviously.

Seventeen

A WEEK LATER, I cleared my desk and went to the significant toilets one last time. The call centre was deserted; most people had already made the move to the new premises or were on their annual leave. Cardboard cut-outs of cruise ships keeled over on the carpets, piles of holiday brochures had toppled and splayed into colourful fans, and posies of wires spewed out of circular holes in the desktops. As I strode past the debris, I had a little cry, remembering the naïve twenty-year-old I'd been when I first started working there. Anna laughed at me because I was late on my first day, saying she thought I'd never last. Neither of us could have predicted I'd be leaving, three years later, to have a baby.

At home, I was nowhere near packed. Some of my stuff, mainly university books and essays, had remained in the banana boxes I'd brought them in; there'd been no point in fully unpacking once I realised that I wouldn't be living there long-term. Most of my clothes didn't fit me anymore and had been stuffed into bin bags, infused with the damp smell that constantly hung in the room. The carpet was strewn with shards of cracked CD cases, twisted-up bus tickets and stray beads from my jewellery-making.

One thing I hadn't managed to dispose of was the confidential waste: piles of letters that I'd been too scared to open but knew I couldn't just put out for recycling in case someone wanted to commit identity fraud (although they wouldn't have got far as me with my credit rating). I knew what the credit card statements said: that I'd maxed out and was paying off the minimum amount per month and would probably be doing so until I was seventy-eight. The bank statements would be a similar story: month after month of going over my overdraft limit, then charges for the privilege, which made things worse. It was all there: the evidence of the overseas trips with work, hungover shopping trips, student nights out. There was no point in going through it all, or carting the burden to Mum's. I put everything in the 101 *Dalmatians* tin wastepaper bin that had been in the room when I moved in. The bin and I had become well acquainted during the summer's many spewing episodes, so it felt like a part of the story too. I took everything into the garden, stood on the crunchy, frosty grass, and set fire to it all. The flames caught fast and I watched as they turned green and the Dalmatians melted away.

In the background, sirens wailed, the constant soundtrack to the city. I thought back to my first winter in Manchester, the promise and excitement of it all, the absolute freedom that had turned into the absolute opposite.

When all the bills had turned to grey scales and dust, I scattered the ashes at the bottom of the garden.

Eighteen

"IF WE HAVE to make two journeys, we have to make two journeys," Jane said, calmly, when she arrived to collect me.

She actually laughed when she saw the abomination that was my bedroom. If ever anyone laughs affectionately at your failures, they are a true friend and a keeper.

It took three journeys in the end, me squished into the front of Jane's Citroen with a load of bin bags of clothes, ricocheting up and down the M6, listening to fuzzy football commentary and Jane talking to me about Manchester United as though I knew something about them. Mum had broken her ankle and couldn't help me move, which was probably a good thing, given the fact we'd almost killed each other the last time.

When the third journey was over, Mum was waiting with tea and Mr Kipling cakes. We sat around in the living room together, Mum and Jane telling me over and over again that I was in the right place now, that everything was going to be fine. I wanted to believe them, but I was homesick already.

When Jane set off back to Manchester, I made my way up the familiar stairs to my room. With the help of her friends, Mum had managed to shift things around a bit in readiness for my arrival - and the baby's. People from her church and other friends had rallied round to provide me with a cot and a thing called a changing unit that you apparently needed to put the baby on top of while you changed its nappy. Mum had replaced my bed with a smaller, three-quarter-sized one, "to make more space for the cot". It hadn't been assembled yet, but there was a neat space waiting for it, parallel to my bed, just behind the door. Uncle Paul had been in and gone over the 'fizzy orange' paint I'd chosen at sixteen with white, because he thought it would be better for me and the baby to be in "calmer surroundings" (and he was probably right).

It touched me that all these people, some of whom I hardly knew, had been so generous. I knew that most of them would be wondering who or where the father of the baby was, but that none of them probably dared to ask. Most of all, it meant the world to me that Mum still hadn't bollocked me for getting pregnant, and that she was happy to take me in. I knew that her lack of judgement and generosity made me extremely lucky for a woman in my shoes.

But that doesn't mean I was happy.

Apart from the cosmetic changes, my room was exactly as I'd left it, three-and-a-bit years earlier, a trail of clothing and expletives in my wake. Beneath the orange and white paint, there was still woodchip. The tubular water lamp I'd got for my seventeenth birthday, a 1999 antique, stood next to my bed; as well as plastic fish, it now had fronds of hairy algae floating in it. On the shelf behind my headboard, dust and dead moths lay next to framed photographs of horses, resin animal figures and a naked, purple-haired Troll. And the flat-pack, wonky wardrobe was full of clothes I hadn't been able to bear to part with in case they one day fitted me again (and now never would): weird, asymmetric tops; iridescent, bengaline dresses, and a pair of flared jeans with love-heart pockets on the bum.

The thing I remembered most about the jeans was that I'd been wearing them the day I went for a psychic reading with Maureen when I was eighteen.

People came from miles around to hear what Maureen had to say. Lucky for me, she was based above the hippy shop just down the road. I was on a waiting list for months, then one day she called me to tell me she could offer me a cancellation the following Saturday morning. I was hungover from the night before, but I sprang out of bed as soon as I heard my alarm. It was a special day: the day I got to find out all about my future.

Maureen didn't look like how I thought a psychic would. There was no floaty blouse, no cat-flick eyeliner, no crystal ball on the table. She was wearing a baggy jumper, Deirdre Barlow glasses and a scrunchie in her mustard-coloured hair. The man in the shop had nodded at a narrow doorway, festooned in beads.

"Through there, love, up the stairs."

When I approached the room, Maureen's head was in her hands, her elbows were on the tie-dye tablecloth and she was staring out of the dust-caked window at the main road. A rash of black mould crept up the pale blue wall behind her. She'd been burning patchouli, and the room smelt of cat piss.

I stood in the doorway, clearing my throat so she'd know I was there. Some people would say she should have known that already. She swung round and squared up like she was ready for a fight.

"Come on then, don't dilly dally. I've someone else in at ten."

Maureen sounded like she was going to wax my bikini line, or yank out a tooth.

I sat down at the table.

"Right. You listen to me, love. I do the talking. If I ask you a question, you answer, but otherwise you keep quiet. Do. You. Understand?"

I nodded, terrified.

Maureen had an old-school tabletop tape recorder, like the ones they used in police interviews. Her chipped nail was poised on the big red button. It squeaked as she pressed it down and she leaned in towards the mic.

"This is a reading for Emily. The date is July 21st 2001. My name is Maureen, world-famous clairvoyant and psychic medium. For bookings, please call zero nine zero one three double six treble six."

Why was she putting an advert on there? Who was going to listen to this shit apart from me? If she was world-famous, what was she doing there, in a damp, single-glazed room above a joss-stick shop in the back of beyond? She was a charlatan and I was being ripped off. But I still wanted to know what she had to say about my future.

I watched as Maureen dealt out cards with pictures of towers, cups and skeletons.

"Don't panic, a skeleton doesn't always mean death," she said.

"That's good."

"Right . . ."

And she was off, speaking too fast for me to be able to register or consider anything she said, throwing in a load of generic phrases that could be applied to just about anyone: hot-headed, soul-searcher, big thinker, worrywart, little madam, daydreamer.

I sat agog, waiting for her to say something that made

sense. Maureen didn't look at me, she didn't stop for breath. She just kept flipping the cards over fast and arranging them in some kind of formation. Then she stopped and looked up.

"You're here to see me about a man, aren't you?"

I wanted to say something clever like, "Actually, you're wrong. I'm a lesbian," but the fact was I was there to see her about a man and a tiny part of me was still hoping she'd tell me what I wanted to hear.

Maureen spoke to me like I was stupid (which, of course I was - I had just handed her thirty quid, after all.)

"He's bloody useless."

That was pretty accurate, actually.

"When was the last time you saw him?"

"I don't know."

"You can't lie to me, love. When?"

Why was she asking me if she already knew?

"I can't remember. Maybe a couple of weeks ago."

"Hmm. I think it was more recently than that."

It was the night before, but there was no way I was going to admit to that.

"He's bad bloody news. Stay away."

"Right."

"You won't listen to me. You'll carry on going to bed with him. You'll go to bed with him tonight, in fact."

"Thanks."

It was nice to be told these things in advance.

"Pregnancies," she announced with no warning. "You'll have six."

"SIX?!"

"Are you listening to me? Not six babies. Six pregnancies.

That's including miscarriages, abortions and twins. Or triplets."

"Oh."

"Your first one will be a little boy. Bloody useless father. He'll go AWOL. The two of you will end up living with your mother."

I laughed, awkwardly, adamant that I would never let a thing like that happen.

"It'll happen, in your early twenties."

Maureen was shit. I wanted my thirty quid back. Not least because that meant I'd be able to afford to go out that night and fulfil at least one of her predictions.

"Don't you smirk at me, missy. If I say you'll have a baby, you'll have a baby." She looked at me over the top of her glasses. "Mark my words."

I ran home feeling robbed, the most expensive cassette tape I've ever bought stuffed into one of the love-heart pockets.

Later, Mum and I huddled over the ghetto blaster in my room and laughed.

"Bloody hell, you've only got a couple of years left," Mum said.

"Yeah well, you should make the most of the peace and quiet, according to Maureen, the bloody baby and I are moving in with you!"

The tape was still there somewhere, in my room, wedged behind a chest of drawers with the rest of the cassettes that had clattered off their plastic rack years ago. I could probably find it if I reached down the back, but my bump would get in the way. Instead, I climbed into bed, shivering and wrapping the duvet tight around me. I'd forgotten how cold the room was. I needed to sleep because I was starting a new job in the morning: the home-working scheme had been delayed by 'technical issues' so my boss had found me a job at a high-street travel agency near Mum's. Going out to work somewhere new was the last thing I felt like doing at six months pregnant, but I didn't really have a choice.

I couldn't sleep. Tom was kicking and wriggling and it was too quiet. Mum's house was at the bottom of a cul-de-sac in the far end of a town that was the last stop on the line from Manchester. It was deafeningly silent. There was nothing to fall asleep to. No mice scratching in the skirting boards, no sirens, no bass. All I got was the occasional eerie screech from a pheasant in the fields beyond the back garden. At dawn, when it was time to get up, they were silenced by the distant pop of a shotgun.

Nineteen

I T WAS A fresh start. Literally. I put my hands in my pockets and shuffled out of the close, breath tumbling out of my mouth like cigarette smoke, trying to forget the fantasy I'd had about selling holidays in my slippers.

I felt like an idiot waddling into that travel agency on the first day. Everyone else who worked there was dressed like an air hostess, all neckerchiefs, red lipstick and pencil skirts. I had to wear a men's XXL polo shirt bearing the company logo over the bootcut trousers I'd bought for my hearing. As soon as I saw the others, I wanted to reverse out of the door, but I remembered why I was there: I needed the money and, if I stayed in bed at that stage, there was a danger I'd end up marooned.

"It'll be busy in January," said Helen, a girl who it emerged I'd met on a night out six years earlier, "but not many people want to book holidays at the moment."

"No," sighed Alice, the manager. "They'll come in out of the cold, put their Christmas shopping down for a bit, have a seat and look at the brochures, then be on their way."

In other words, there was no point me being there.

My belly wouldn't fit under my desk. On my first morning, I sorted out my pen pot three times and completely studded my rubber with staples. The brochure racks needed restocking, but I wasn't allowed to do that because it was deemed too dangerous a task for pregnancy.

"It smells nice in here," I said, breaking a deathly, mid-morning silence.

"What are you on about?" asked Helen.

"It's all the brochures," I said. "It smells like a bookshop."

"You won't like the smell in here on Saturday, love," said Fiona, the girl on the foreign exchange counter, whose voice was constantly muffled by bulletproof glass.

"Why not?"

"Oh yeah," said Helen. "People piss through the letterbox at the weekend."

"Oh."

"Watch yourself when you come in on a Saturday; you don't want to be slipping on frozen piss in your condition."

I spent my lunch break wandering around Southport, twice having to duck into shops to avoid people from my past. Seaside towns in winter are like the dregs of parties on a Sunday afternoon: bleak, deserted, horribly depressing. An icy wind was gusting in from the Irish Sea, sending litter skipping noisily along the pavements. Pastel ice-cream signs, faded by the long-gone sun, swung and squeaked and made me shiver. Fanfares, beeps and the clatter of coins spilled out of amusement arcades and sticks of rainbow rock, sugar dummies and cock lollies dangled in front of kiosks. The warm smell of frying food lured me into a dingy takeaway and, before I knew it, I was shuffling along the front by the Marine Lake, stabbing greasy chips with a plastic fork and shovelling them into my mouth. I'd long given up caring about the getting-fat thing: food was my main source of comfort.

I hunkered down in a chilly Victorian shelter, watching gulls riding the miniature waves in the muddy-coloured lake. The sea was miles away: across the coast road, over a wall, beyond a strip of imported sand and kilometres of sinking mud. I liked the idea of living near the sea, but Southport is famous for being the seaside town that the sea rarely visits.

After my lunch break, my first real customer arrived: a woman pushing a buggy that contained a shrieking child. The mother smiled thinly. She looked as though all the energy had been siphoned right out of her and injected into the baby, who was now almost standing up, rigid in the buggy and about to tip it over.

"I need a holiday."

It felt like I was a doctor and she was my patient, begging me for drugs that would make her better.

"OK, where to?"

I was shouting over the little girl.

"Sorry," she said, "she's teething. It's her back ones, I think."

I nodded, as though I knew exactly what she was on about.

"Maybe you'd like to put her in the ball pool. She is old enough to go in the ball pool, isn't she?"

The small, inflatable pool in the corner of the shop was designed to keep bored little darlings entertained while their parents pored over package holidays.

The baby scowled at me, her ruddy cheeks encrusted with snot, a smattering of hairs splaying out from her crown in a tiny top-knot. I hadn't been in such close proximity to a small child for as long as I could remember; I didn't know how to look at her, what to say to her, how to act around her. It was awkward, and I was never awkward when I met new people.

"Would you like to go in the ball pool?" I said.

Nothing, save for the evils.

Eventually, having persuaded her child to sit in the ball pool without screaming, the woman returned to my desk.

"Right," she said, "Spain. We don't want to fly too far with her, you see. And no night flights."

I'd heard parents say that so many times when I worked at the call centre and wondered what difference another hour or two or an evening journey could possibly make. Suddenly, confronted with the full force of a toddler, I totally understood.

"We need kids' facilities too. Obviously."

I flicked through the options, finding identikit tower block after identikit tower block, all with the same crowded swimming pools and the same buffet restaurants, all with some poor sod dancing whilst dressed as a giant teddy bear in the 30-degree heat. It really didn't matter which one she chose, or where it was, they were all the same.

"I'll have to talk to my hubby," she said. "He wants to go to bloody Mexico, to a fancy hotel with a Jacuzzi in the room. Can you imagine that with her? Men don't have a clue. You and your fella make the most of it, before the baby comes along, I mean."

Right on cue, the baby resumed her screaming, a string of spit drooping between her tragic mouth and the plastic ball in her hand. The woman raised her head gracefully, tilting her nose northeast.

"Oh, Isobel, you haven't, have you?"

She darted over to the ball pool, grabbed the child and sniffed her.

"Oh God, yeah, she has."

She looked at me for reassurance I didn't think I could give.

"It's alright, you know, she's got tights on. It'll stay in the tights. There won't be any poo on the balls."

"It's OK," I said, holding my breath, "these things happen."

"You've no changing room in here, have you?"

"No, sorry."

"You'd have thought they'd have given you a baby changing room when they gave you the ball pool."

"Yeah. Sorry."

"It's a proper stinker, this. Teething poo," she said, wincing.

"Oh dear. I'm afraid I can't let you in the back for security reasons."

Even if there weren't any security reasons, there was no way the teething poo, whatever that was, was going to stay in the shop a minute longer.

"Never mind," she said, strapping the child, who was now roaring, back into the buggy, "I'll take her to McDonald's or something. I'll come back about the holiday though, promise!

I went into the back and brought out a can of air freshener, holding my finger on the button continually as I walked to the front of the shop and back again.

"This glass might be bullet-proof, but it isn't smell-proof," said Katie.

"I don't think I like the smell of this shop anymore," I said.

Twenty

"HO HO HO, merry Christmas!"

My last shift before Christmas took forever; travel agencies are probably the least busy shops during the festive season and the hours dragged. When I walked into the house, knackered and wanting a drink I couldn't have, I was smacked in the face by a stuffed Father Christmas dangling on a string.

Christmas at Mum's house has always been intense. Every January she stockpiles cut-price decorations to add to her already excessive collection the following December. If it lights up or plays a tune, she wants it; if it does both, she'll take two. Still, Mum's house is virtually minimalist compared to some of the others in her neighbourhood, where residents compete to create the most impressive festive display.

"I'll just take you to this one at Number 3," Mum would say, pulling up in front of a giant plastic snow globe, next to a slowly-grazing mechanical deer. "But wait! You haven't seen Number 253. It's only a couple of doors down. They've got a Santa stuck up their chimney! And a singing snowman on top of their porch."

Mum doesn't go for the full grotto effect, but she does throw taste out of the windows (all of which are draped in fairy lights, set to strobe mode). You can smell the cinnamon and ginger pot pourri when you're walking up the driveway. In September.

The fat Santa, which was bungee-jumping from the upstairs banisters into the downstairs hall, was the newest addition.

"Ho ho ho!" he said again, as I shrugged off my coat and brushed past him. "Merry Christmas!"

"Oh, fuck off!"

"Emily!"

Mum's tone told me that she had visitors. Visitors who weren't supposed to hear me tell Father Christmas to fuck off.

I sloped upstairs to my room, climbed into bed fully clothed, and fell deeply asleep, waking later to the sound of Mum and her friends in the hall.

"Ooh, you haven't even seen Emily yet, have you?" Mum was saying.

I cowered under my duvet. Mum's friends were kind, polite Christians. One of them was my primary school teacher. I couldn't handle the thought of them seeing me knocked up.

"Emily! My friends are leaving now, come and say goodbye."

"Not to worry," someone said. "I expect she's getting tired now."

"Yes, what a shame," Mum was shouting. "She must be *sleeping*."

When I'd heard the car engines start and watched oblongs of light flick along the walls as they reversed down the driveway, I went downstairs. Mum was gathering glasses and plates of dented mince-pie cases.

"Who was here?" I said, picking up a broken breadstick.

"My friends. It was rude of you not to come down and say hello."

"I was asleep."

"No you weren't. I could see the light under your door."

"I'm tired. I fell asleep with it on."

"You should have come to say hello when you got in," she said. "They all heard you. Swearing at Santa."

"I didn't want them to see me like this."

"Don't be silly, they all know you're pregnant."

"Don't they wonder where the father is?"

"People don't ask, Emily."

"They don't ask you, but they go home and talk about me. They say: 'Ooh, Emily's living at home with her mum and she's pregnant and there's no sign of a man.' I'd rather they did ask, if I'm honest."

"People aren't interested in that, Emily. They're just excited about the baby."

"Oh, come on."

Mum didn't say anything. She carried on picking up the plastic trays smeared with dip, the glass dishes of crisp crumbs and the shrivelled sticks of celery. No one ever wants the celery.

"Perhaps they think it's the Immaculate Conception," I said.

Mum glared at me and carried the stuff out of the room.

"I just wish people would talk about it!" I shouted after her. "I'd rather that than the wondering. I know what they'll think of me. And I know what Nan will think of me if she comes at Christmas."

I hadn't been to visit Nan since that day in the summer. The guilt was getting to me, but not enough to make me want to go there and risk her clocking the bump.

"Emily," Mum shouted from the kitchen, "your poor nan hasn't got a clue what's going on."

I picked up a hardly-touched box of red wine, wishing I could drink it.

"She has moments, though," I said, following Mum into the kitchen, "moments of clarity. You told me that."

Mum was loading the dishwasher and humming 'Silent Night'.

"I'm going to bed," I said.

As I checked the front door was locked, I ducked to dodge the dangling Santa.

"Ho ho ho!"

"Oh, Jesus Christ."

"Don't say that." Mum followed me in the hallway. "What do you think of my new Father Christmas?"

"Not much."

"Will the baby like it?" I asked. "Next Christmas, will he be old enough to be into the Santa?"

"Let's see," Mum counted out on her fingers, "he'll be eight months old by then. I expect he'll pull it and chew on it and giggle at it, yes."

"God, I can't imagine."

Uncle Paul brought Nan from the nursing home to us on Christmas Day. I held a cushion in front of me the whole time she was there, a fact that amused Mum, Hannah and Paul.

"You can put the cushion down now," they said, as we sat down for Christmas dinner.

I wasn't willing to risk it.

"Ugh! This tastes like poison," Nan said, screwing up her face after a sip of the alcohol-free wine Mum had bought for her and me.

"You're right, Nan, it really does."

In the evening, after Paul had returned Nan to the home

and driven back to Mum's again, we all gathered round to play the *Countdown* game I'd bought Mum for Christmas. But I was still the butt of everybody's jokes.

"Aren't you missing something?"

"Yeah, where's your cushion, Emily?"

My family didn't mean to piss me off, but they did: Christmas without parties had cemented my feelings of being lost and alone and the last thing I needed was to be laughed at. I stomped upstairs to my room, where I sobbed and filled pages of my notebook with scrawls about how scared I was. For the previous three years, when I'd returned home for Christmas, I'd been itching to get back to Manchester by Boxing Day. It wasn't that Mum did anything wrong; Christmas in her house was cosy, relaxing, delicious, but when I left home at nineteen, I left home. There was only so much time I could spend there without missing the life I loved in Manchester. This year was different, though: I wouldn't be on the first train home when services resumed on the 27th December, because this was home now.

My baby was due in March, and I knew that was going to come around quickly after Christmas. Downstairs, everyone was laughing, and the board game was playing the signature tick-tock countdown from the TV show.

Diddum, diddum diddle de dum. Dong!

Tom began to wriggle, as he often did when I lay still. It was more than just a flutter these days; he was a big baby and my whole belly would shift when he moved. I felt bad, knowing he would have heard me crying, wondering if sadness could travel down the umbilical cord. He was the reason I was sad, but he hadn't done anything wrong.

"Hello, you," I sniffed, "I love you."

And I did.

That morning, Mum had received a happy Christmas phone call from Violet, an old lady we hadn't seen for years. When we were children, we used to go on holiday to the block of flats where she lived by the seaside in Eastbourne. We spent hot summers playing with her granddaughter, fishing in the rock pools and putting on plays in Violet's apartment. Mum passed the phone to me after she'd told Violet I was pregnant. Apparently, she wanted to speak to me. I recoiled, feeling the same sense of shame I felt around my nan, but Mum widened her eyes at me and I knew I'd have to do it.

"Hello?"

"Congratulations," Violet said. "You will never be alone again."

I liked that. I would never be alone again. And Christmas would never be as boring (or as cheap) again.

Twenty-one

NEW YEAR'S EVE. The biggest party of the year. A night when everyone, everywhere is drunk. Even my mother. A night when I should have been in Sydney but I was on the Wirral, the only sober one at the family party. I'd wanted to stay at home and mope, but Mum was having none of it. She bundled me into the car with a spare duvet and drove me over to my Auntie Joy's house.

"It's great," she said. "You get a gorgeous view of the fireworks from the end of her road."

"I should be in Sydney right now," I said, as we sped through the Mersey Tunnel.

"They've already had their fireworks," Mum said. "I saw them on the telly earlier. They didn't look very good, love."

While everyone gathered in Auntie Joy's kitchen, drinking and laughing, I made myself at home in the front room, cradling a tin of Quality Street. Within an hour, I was sifting through empty wrappers, trying to find an actual chocolate.

What was I doing this time last year? That question had been stuck in my head on repeat for the previous few months. I'd spent the last New Year's Eve working behind the bar at a warehouse party, pouring eight-quid shots of champagne into plastic party glasses. At midnight, I watched everyone around me fall into each other and slur. The most significant thing about the new year, as far as I saw it then, was that I'd be going into my final year at university in the September.

"Come on Em, let's go down the front!" Mum shouted at five to midnight.

Mum lost her Scouse accent decades ago, but when she's tipsy or in Merseyside, it magically returns; when she's tipsy *and* in Merseyside, she's Cilla Black.

"I think I'll just stay here," I said, sliding the near-empty chocolate tin behind my back.

"Don't be silly, you can't be on your own at midnight, come on." She grabbed my hand and tried to drag me out of the armchair. "Bloody hell, you're a dead weight."

It would have been easier to roll down the frosty hill to the river than walk with my mother as support.

"Hold on tight, queen," she said. "If you fall over, you'll end up in the drink and take me with you!"

The fireworks over Liverpool started as soon as we set foot on the blustery promenade. I walked to the edge and clung on to the cold railings, feeling the icy mist from the estuary sting my face. In the distance, ship foghorns bellowed, signalling the start of 2006.

Behind, a crowd of people wished each other happy new year and burst into 'Auld Lang Syne'.

Mum and my auntie and everyone from her house had joined a huge circle of strangers, crossing arms and singing. Everyone is supposed to be happy at the stroke of midnight at New Year. If you're frightened, though, or sad, or lonely, or depressed, there's no moment on the calendar that could possible make you feel worse. I knew that my friends were all out there, somewhere in Manchester, being typical 22-year-olds. I knew that the father of my child was out there, somewhere, and I wondered if, in that moment of emotional magnification, he had still managed to block out thoughts of his baby to-be.

I could hear Mum shouting: "Where's Emily? Oh heck, she's near the water. Emily!"

I sloped back over to where Mum was standing and linked arms with her and the stranger next to her.

For Auld langs syne, my dear, for auld langs syne, blah blah blah blah blah blah blah, for auld langs syne.

(How many people actually know all the words to that song?)

"Happy New Year," Auntie Joy said, leaning in to kiss me but not getting close because of the bump. "This'll be an interesting one for you, eh love?"

Interesting. It would definitely be that.

Twenty-two

"**C**AN I NOT just buy this stuff online?"

Mum had driven me to the baby superstore: a corrugated metal behemoth in the middle of a windswept car park. The trip was an attempt to cheer me up. I'd been on course for a caesarean because my baby was upside down (or the right way up, depending on which way you look at it), but against the odds, he'd gone and done an about turn. Most mothers don't want a caesarean and are upset when they find out their baby is in the breech position; I had completely confused my midwife by beaming when she'd carefully delivered the news. Finally! I'd got out of giving birth. The Motherboard women couldn't understand my joy; some were going through the complicated and painful procedure of attempting to have their babies turned around in their womb to avoid the caesarean. I was thrilled, until I went to the consultant for a checkup and was congratulated and told that my baby was now facing the right way and was on course for a natural delivery. The consultant initially thought I was crying with happiness, then realised that wasn't the case.

"Don't be daft," Mum replied, slamming the car door and grabbing my hand. "Where would the fun be in that?"

As far as Mum was concerned, this was an excursion.

Inside, there were a lot of pale pink things and pale blue things and a lot of couples.

Thanks to the generosity of Mum's friends and her eBay

habit, most of the essentials were covered: my cot was sorted, as was the pram, as were the clothes. I wasn't sure what was actually left to buy, but Mum was more of an expert on this sort of thing than I was, or imagined I ever could be.

"This shouldn't take too long, right?" I said, looking up at the high walls stacked to the top with stuff.

"You'll have to get some Mexican hats," Mum said, handing me a thing that didn't look anything like a sombrero.

"Nipple shields," I said, reading out the wording on the packet. "Jesus. It sounds like I'm going into battle."

"Well, you might be. It took you nine weeks to get the hang of breastfeeding."

"*Nine weeks?* Didn't I starve?"

"No, you'll be glad to hear you didn't. I had a breast pump. Which reminds me, you should probably get one of those."

I could only imagine how they worked and what they did.

There were an awful lot of pads on offer: maternity pads, breast pads, changing pads, cooling pads, warming pads, disposable pads, washable pads. All needed to soften the blow of it all, I presumed.

Mum tossed another packet into the trolley with a joyful flourish: disposable briefs.

"*Disposable briefs?*"

"Real ones would just get ruined," she said.

As Mum educated me in the pastel-plastered aisles, all I could do was wonder how people who didn't have a mother to help them were supposed to cope? How could a darling partner/hubby/boyfriend/girlfriend possibly know all this? I learnt more in that trip to the shop than I'd learnt from reading the books and Motherboard.

"Best get some scratch mitts."

"Scratch mitts?"

The first thing that sprung to mind was those loofah gloves for exfoliating in the shower, but I was pretty sure you weren't supposed to exfoliate babies.

"Yep. They stop them from scratching their own faces when their little hands are flailing about all over the place."

Mum was holding up a packet of tiny mittens, which I would have thought were for keeping babies' hands warm.

"Oh, right."

I thought about the news the consultant had given me that day.

"Hang on, do they have sharp fingernails, then?"

"They can be long when they first come out, yes. You're not supposed to clip them for a while."

"So do they scratch you on the way out?"

"Emily, their head and shoulders come through. The last thing you're worrying about are tiny fingernails."

I looked at Mum and seethed. She was absolutely delighted about it all, the prospect of her box-fresh grandchild, but she wasn't the one who was going to have to give birth to it.

"Hopefully you won't need dummies, but best to get a couple, just in case," she said, throwing them into the trolley. "Bottles. We'll cross that bridge if we come to it."

"How are people supposed to know what they actually *need*?" I asked as Mum wrestled a baby bath into the trolley.

"They ask other parents, I suppose."

I felt bad for the seething; I'd be completely stuck without my mother, willing not just to give me and the baby a roof over our heads, but to throw herself completely into the confusing technicalities of it all. I was just going to have to get used to the gloating.

"Thanks, Mum."

"What for? You're paying for all this."

"I know, but thanks for telling me what I need. And everything else."

"You're alright."

I wasn't though.

Beep went the checkout as the first item scanned. *Beep*. It quickened *Beep*. *Beep*. *Beep*. The total on the till went up and up and up.

The lady at the counter asked me the questions I'd learnt to answer off by heart. Christ, it must get boring when you work in a baby shop. I flushed as I handed over my debit card.

"Enjoy!" she said, handing me my receipt.

"I'll try," I said.

Twenty-three

I SAW MORE crap films in my pregnancy than I have ever seen in my entire life put together (including the whiny cartoon musicals I endured during the first few years of motherhood). Cheesy rom-coms, terrible chick flicks, predictable thrillers. If it was shit and it was on general release during those nine months, I saw it.

Where else was I going to meet my friends? Bars and clubs were off limits and sitting in the dark watching a film for a couple of hours meant not having to speak about The Baby. It suited everyone concerned. My closest friends at that point were Alex, who lived on the other side of the world, and Anna, who totally had my back but was busy with work and being in a relationship. Most of my student friends kept in touch, but none of them really knew what to say about the whole baby situation. It was weird enough for me and it was happening inside my body, so I couldn't expect anyone else to get their head around it.

So we'd meet in the foyer of the multiplex for formalities and an awkward hug. The best thing about it was the popcorn, which I'd buy by the overpriced bucket load and pretty much polish off before the trailers had finished. Afterwards, my friends would tell me they had to get the bus home as they had a load of work to do, though I strongly suspected they were off out for drinks or the kind of school-night party that only happens when you're a student. When I got home to my student digs, I would sit on my bed and exhale, unfastening my stiflingly tight bra. Yellow shells of popcorn would rain down from my cleavage on to the carpet, where they remained until the mouse came and noisily cleaned them up in the middle of the night.

When I moved to Mum's there was a film on that I actually wanted to see: *March of the Penguins*. I'd seen the trailer on a previous cinema outing: endless lines of identikit, human-like Emperor Penguins, trudging through blizzards to reach the freezing sea where they had to dive in to catch their food. The cinematography looked stunning and the penguins looked cute, so I couldn't wait to go.

Mum said she'd pick me up after work. It had been a long day because Tom kept getting wedged under my rib cage and it hurt. The only relief was to stand up and lean backwards, limbo-like, but it was January: people finally actually wanted to book holidays and I was sitting at my desk for most of the day, with very few opportunities to stretch. One couple booked flights to Australia to visit family.

"Lucky you," I said as I took down the details. "I was supposed to be going to Australia, before this happened." I pointed at the bump, which by now was unfeasibly huge.

The woman, a retired midwife, told me with a mild, wise confidence that I was going to be a brilliant mum. "Hey," she said, as I confirmed the spring dates she wanted to book, "your little one might arrive while we're there!"

I smiled, but the proximity made me panic.

It was probably the busiest day I ever had in the shop, and when it was officially over, I was still filling in paperwork as the manager vacuumed around my desk, worrying that Mum would be waiting for me in the side street outside.

She was and we bickered as we crossed the hail-lashed car park to the seafront cinema.

"Sorry, you're too late," said the woman in the box office, stony-faced.

"Surely it's still the trailers. Can you not just let us in?" I pleaded.

"You're just too late. Would you like to watch another film?"

"No. I only wanted to watch *March of the Penguins*."

I broke down. I turned away from the woman and stared at the Pick n Mix stands and I sobbed.

"Sorry," said the woman.

"It's alright," said Mum, steering me towards the exit, "we can come back tomorrow."

I wasn't crying because we missed the film; I was crying at the realisation that watching a documentary about penguins with my mother on a Wednesday night was going to be the most exciting thing that had happened to me in months. The more I thought about it, the more I cried. I couldn't explain it to Mum; she thought I was just crying because of the bloody penguins.

"Goodness me," she said, "it's like when we went to that holiday park in Wales when you were ten. Inconsolable you were, because the kiddies in the next caravan went home a few days before us."

I remembered it: the overhead sounds of seagulls' feet and non-stop rain, fuzzy footage of the Barcelona Olympics on the tiny TV, me sulking on the bottom bunk, reading *Smash Hits*.

All I could muster through unstoppable tears and bubbles of snot was, "It's not the penguins, it's not the penguins."

"I'll tell you what it is, love: it's your hormones."

We managed to catch the penguins the following night and I wished we hadn't. They get together forever and the males look after the eggs; even the fact of the male penguins' dedicated and responsible parenting had me blubbing. That was before I watched one female return from her fishing mission miles and frozen miles away, only to find she was too late and her adorable, fluffy chick was dead on the ice in front of her mate's feet. She wailed, I wailed, it was bloody awful.

But I didn't stop there: my final trip to the cinema before the birth of Tom was just as disastrous.

"It's your last weekend of freedom," Mum said, like she was planning a hen party. "Why don't we go to the cinema?"

"It won't be my last weekend though, will it?"

First babies are usually late. I knew this from Motherboard where people bemoaned the agonising wait for the agonising birth to begin, while I would have been happy to put it off for forever. People sent each other sprinklings of 'baby dust' (rows of asterisks) and posted recommendations for things to do to persuade the baby to dislodge.

According to Motherboard, the most common ways to induce labour were:

Eating curry

Drinking RLT (raspberry leaf tea)

Eating pineapple

HYF ('How's your father?') (Sex) (Who even calls it that?)

It baffled me how anyone could do HYF when they were that pregnant. I spent some time thinking about the logistics of it all and whether it would be even remotely comfortable or good. I was certain that, taking into account the statistics for first babies, my track record with timekeeping and the complete lack of all possibility of sex, my baby would be late. There would be weeks spent pacing the house, scoffing curry and pineapple, knocking back raspberry leaf tea and not having sex, all of which was fine by me.

"He's due on Wednesday," Mum said.

"Yes, but that doesn't mean he'll come on Wednesday."

"Well, let's just go and watch a film, anyway," Mum said. "Come on, love - it's Saturday night!"

"Since when were you so wild for Saturday nights?"

Mum wouldn't even look at the film times, she just bundled me into the car and drove me to the cinema. I think she just wanted to get me out of the house: I had been marooned on the sofa in my pyjamas since I'd gone on maternity leave two weeks earlier.

The film was terrible. Pierce Brosnan was parading around in underpants and cowboy boots and I couldn't even see it properly because there was a shadow that kept floating in front of him.

"Keep still!" Mum hissed.

I realised I was swaying from side-to-side in an attempt to see round the persistent blob.

"There's a big black blob in front of Pierce Brosnan."

"No, there isn't."

But there was. I blinked and it shifted, then floated in from the corner again. It was making me dizzy. In fact, all of me felt fuzzy. My left hand in particular seemed to be numb, so I quickly splayed out my fingers then curled them into a fist (a move that I would later know well as the main action to accompany 'Twinkle Twinkle Little Star').

"What are you doing?"

"Pins and needles," I whispered. "Actually, I'm just going to go to the loo."

The black blob floated out of the auditorium and into the corridor, bouncing past the popcorn stalls and along the psychedelic carpet. In the toilets, I was confronted with a choice of empty stalls, which never happens when the film's just finished and you're bursting. Each cubicle was named after a female film star. I plumped for Drew Barrymore; her bog had to be alright. It wasn't though: the door was out of sync with the frame, so I had to lift it to lock it, but as I tried, I realised that my left hand had no feeling in it whatsoever. I sat down quickly on the loo, stretching one leg out in front of me to block the door in case someone tried to come in. Looking down, I discovered something that the midwives, Motherboard and books had warned be about: The Show. The Show is not a show, nor anywhere near as entertaining as any kind of show should be. The film with Pierce Brosnan in his undies and a Stetson was more entertaining than The Show. If you don't know what The Show is, don't look it up; all you need to know is that it's gross and it means the baby is imminent.

"Em, are you OK?" Mum's voice echoed in the empty room.

"I think I've got The Show," I said, wondering if I might have to give birth on the floor of Drew Barrymore.

"Bloody *hell!*"

"I haven't even packed a bag," I said, as Mum ragged the Peugeot 106 along the dual carriageway towards the hospital.

The Motherboarders, who were due at the same time as me, had packed their hospital bags (and posted a full inventory) about three months earlier. Not even the trip to the giant baby shop had made me want to do mine; if anything, it had put me off.

"I don't want him to come tonight," I sniffed, as a midwife strapped a blood pressure monitor to my arm.

"Why not? He's all cooked," said the midwife, who had introduced herself as Beth.

"I want a caesarean."

"No, you don't."

"I *do*. I really do."

"A caesarean is a major abdominal operation. You don't want to be recovering from that as well as looking after a newborn baby, believe me."

I'd heard it all before and no one was going to change my mind.

"Am I safe to go to the canteen for a brew or is the baby going to shoot out while I'm gone?" asked Mum.

"I think you're safe," said Beth, smiling.

"What's up with you, then?" Beth said, when it was just the two of us. "I get the feeling you're not too excited about all this."

"I'm not," I sighed. "No point in pretending I am."

It didn't help that the room I was lying in was called a Delivery Suite, nor that I could hear blood-curdling screams from down the corridors, nor that I had gone to the toilet to find a nightie hanging on the back of the door that was covered in every bodily fluid imaginable.

"I'm here about the weird thing in front of my eye, anyway, primarily."

"I know," said Beth, "but we had to admit you to this ward because you're full-term. How *is* your eye, by the way?"

"It's a bit better," I said. "Still a bit blurry, though. Am I in labour?"

"No, it was probably a migraine brought on by hormones, but you're definitely not far off. We need to keep an eye on you. I'm going to do an ECG, to monitor your heart."

Beth nodded at the monitor that was attached to the great strap around my belly.

"You're having some pretty mighty Braxton Hicks there."

I knew about Braxton Hicks (BH) from Motherboard. They're practice contractions that don't actually hurt. I didn't know where the name was from, but every time I heard the phrase, 90's soul hit, 'Unbreak My Heart' by Toni Braxton went off in my head.

"So, when will the baby be here?"

"I can't tell you that."

"I just want to be ready. I'm not ready. I don't think I ever will be."

"Was it a surprise?"

"Yeah." I half-laughed. "Or a massive fucking shock. Whatever you want to call it."

"Are you going to breastfeed?"

"I hope so."

"Good," Beth said, sticking an electrode to my chest. "You've got great nipples for breastfeeding."

"Thanks. That's the nicest thing anyone's said to me in a while."

"Baby's dad not around?"

"Nope. Not seen him since the day I told him."

"Well, he's going to miss out."

"That's what everyone says, but I'm not so sure. I just feel like a complete idiot most of the time, to be honest with you."

"You're not an idiot. I can tell. What do you do?"

"I was at uni, studying History of Art. I want to go back eventually, but I'm not sure how probable that is."

"You will go back. So, what kind of art do you study?"

"Ancient stuff, modern stuff, a bit of photography. People

think it's just looking at paintings, but it's so much more than that. We do gender studies, politics, anthropology – you can tell a lot about a time and a place from its art. And art's not just in galleries, either, have you seen the Iron Men on Crosby beach?"

Beth nodded and smiled.

"I want to write my dissertation about them, about how people think they're a waste of public money, but you go down there and see people looking at them, taking pictures of them, touching them. . ."

I hadn't thought about university, or talked about it, for so long. Everything had been about the baby and the pregnancy and my job and the move. I'd forgotten what it felt like to feel positive and passionate about something.

"You love what you do, don't you?"

"Yeah. I really do. And I really miss it. I hope I can go back to it."

"Oh, you will."

"You reckon so?"

"I know so."

"Thanks. I'd forgotten how it made me feel."

"Listen. Your baby is one lucky little boy."

"What?"

"Just look at his mum: clever, funny, beautiful."

"Beautiful?!"

"Yep, beautiful."

"When you were talking about art then, you came alive. Your eyes lit up. All that energy and love you put into your subject you will put into being a mother. You have got no idea how much fun you're about to have."

I wanted to hug Beth. All I'd seen was a wall of pain and

blood and she'd made me see that beyond it there would be adventures.

"Thank you."

"I'm not going to lie to you," Beth said, "it is going to hurt, and there will be sleepless nights and filthy nappies, but you are getting a *son*. It's time you started getting excited, missy. You're going to be someone's mum."

They sent Mum home and I couldn't sleep. Feeling a heady mix of fear and excitement, I couldn't stop thinking about what Beth had said. I lay on my left side, in the foetal position, the only way I was comfortable. Between the slats of the blind next to my bed, I saw snow coming down. I pulled myself up and walked over to the window, watching thick flurries rush down beneath the orange lamps of the car park.

"Don't come yet," I said, in my head, "you're supposed to come in spring."

It *was* March, but when Margaret the midwife in Manchester had clapped her hands together and announced a spring baby, I'd imagined blue skies and daffodils, not blizzards.

I was discharged in the morning; the doctors were sure I'd had a focal migraine and there was little else they could do for me. The first thing I did when I woke was ask for Beth, but she'd finished her shift and I felt abandoned. When Mum came for me an hour later, she was traumatised.

"I hate driving in the snow," she said to me, doctors, midwives, anyone who'd listen. "I'd have camped out in the canteen for the night if I'd known it was going to snow."

"Sorry, Mum."

"It's not your fault," she said. "Just don't go into labour while the roads are still slippery."

"I'll try not to."

"It would have been nice if Tom had come last night," Mum said on the way home, not taking her eyes off the road for a second.

"Why, so you wouldn't have had to drive in the snow?"

"Partly that," she said, "and partly because I think you were ready. That Beth really put you at ease."

"Yeah, she was alright."

I looked out of the car window at the stark, white fields, the skeletal trees with their capillary branches, the sharp sting of the thorns on the gnarly, black hedgerows. Cold air smelling of cabbages and sprouts blasted into the car through the vents on the dashboard.

"The snow never sticks when you want it to, does it?" I said.

"What do you mean?"

"When you're a kid and you want the snow to stick so you can get a day off school and build snowmen, it never does."

I'll never forget my first proper snow day; I won a certificate for writing about it. My exercise book was bound in sugar paper and smelt like fish and chips:

I woke up and I was astonished: the world was caked in white. My gloves got wet and my fingers went numb but I didn't mind. Before I went to bed, I tucked Lupin (my Tiny Tears doll) up warm and looked out of the window at the snowman and it felt magical. He was wearing my purple hat.

Mum still had that exercise book somewhere. And I had a picture in my mind of the oversized, HB-pencil handwriting and the colourful illustration beneath it. It struck me, suddenly, that beyond all this, there might be another magical snow day.

Twenty-four

I STAGGERED TOWARDS my target: the leg holes of a pair of Floral Full Briefs, gathered sadly on the carpet near my feet. The paper ones I'd bought were far too small and the first pair I'd tried on had torn. I was almost there, but before I could fully pull the full briefs up, I lurched forward, grabbing the landing banister, pushing my bum against the small piece of wall between Mum's bedroom and my sister's, and emitting a sound I wasn't aware I could make. The moonlight cast a silver streak across the slates of next-door's roof and made me think of a sharp blade, cutting into my stomach and my back and the tops of my streaky thighs.

I affectionately nickname my period pains Dubstep Womb because the grinding cramps feel like a particularly filthy bass line is dropping in my uterus. This was a whole new level of pain though, a whole different genre. This was Death Metal Womb.

"Ooh, she's off again," said Mum, who was on the phone to Hannah, giving her a running commentary that was far too jovial for my liking.

My waters had broken that morning. It was nowhere near as dramatic or Niagara-like as it ever looked on the telly.

"Mum," I said, shocking myself with the calm, matter-of-factness in my voice, "my waters have gone."

Mum called work and told them she needed to take the first day of the 'paternity' leave she'd been granted and, after

I had persuaded the midwife on the phone that I was absolutely positive that I hadn't just weed myself, we headed to the hospital. Only to be sent away again to wait for things to 'properly' start. We stopped off at the supermarket on the way home and I bought a few final essentials: batteries for my camera, the knickers ("just get some that you won't mind chucking in the bin after the first time you've worn them," was Mum's ominous advice) and nachos and guacamole: my final meal.

Later that night, in my freezing cold bedroom, when I was supposed to be "getting some rest", the pains began in earnest. The hospital had advised paracetamol, which doesn't even touch the average slightly sore head. I began every contraction telling myself I could handle it, but the pain came in ever-increasing waves and when it reached its peak, it was all I could do to grab on to the cold metal of my headboard and roar.

In preparation for giving birth, I had watched a lot of TV programmes on the subject and read a lot of books. Midwives had been keen on my going to antenatal classes, but the thought of sharing a room with a load of panting women with adoring partners massaging their lower backs was too much. I didn't think there'd be any other situation that could make me feel more alone; not even sitting at home, eating chocolate and watching graphic footage of babies popping out.

I hadn't made a "birth plan" either. It seemed ridiculous to me to plan for one of the most wildly unpredictable things that would ever happen to my body. Surely a birth plan would only set you up for disappointment? The midwife gave me an A4 sheet to fill in and I returned it, tatty and crumpled, with "a caesarean please, if not all the drugs" scrawled across it. Meanwhile, over on Motherboard, enthusiastic mums were sharing their essay-length birth plans, which included things like ambient playlists, naked partners and, bafflingly, no pain relief.

There was no earth mother idyll for me; I was under no delusions. I knew that giving birth was going to fucking hurt and that, statistically, given the fact this was my first baby and my body had never done it before, the chances were it was going to take ages: not just hours but potentially days. The pain lived up to my expectations, too. Later, I learned that Tom was 'back to back', his spine against mine, which is apparently many times more painful than when the baby is in the correct position, with its back to your front. At the time though, with no point of reference, I was sure that the agony I was experiencing was totally normal and that my pain threshold was pathetically low. I didn't have a scrap of positivity or bravery in me: this was the culmination of it all, the thing I had been dreading most, and it was every bit as dreadful as I'd imagined.

With paracetamol my only option and the hospital continuing to fob me off until my contractions were closer together, I began to draw desperately on the fragments of hippy advice I'd picked up from the TV, books and Motherboard.

Visualise yourself in a relaxing place.

I thought back to the temple that Stu and I had visited in India a year earlier. Tucked deep within the jungle, it was the only ancient Hindu temple to survive the area's Catholic invasion. Surrounded by trees alive with chattering monkeys and hissing cicadas, it was one of the most beautiful places I had ever seen. When the next contraction began, I closed my eyes and breathed as deeply as I could, pretending I was in that tropical forest clearing, thousands of miles away. But as the pain reached its crescendo, the dreamy picture in my head turned to dark images of the heavy, grey basalt of the temple walls crushing my insides. All the worst memories of that wonderful trip flooded my mind: the searing heat of the pre-Monsoon days, the poisonous snake I almost stepped on in the forest, the powerful waves of the Arabian sea knocking me over and snatching away my bikini, a crow pecking the throat of a dead rat on a Mumbai street. I cried out, not just in pain but in anger. I was angry that my body could hurt this much, angry that I couldn't handle it, angry that I'd believed for a second that visualising holiday snaps might make me feel better. And angry, really, really angry, that the man who'd made me pregnant was probably in the pub at that moment, having a perfectly normal evening.

"Can you try to keep the noise down, love?"

Mum burst into my room and switched the light on. I looked up and saw her standing in the doorway, looking more terrified than I felt.

"Nothing, nothing, nothing."

What I was trying to say was "nothing makes it better."

"I know it hurts, love, but I'm worried you might wake the neighbours."

"I don't give a shit about the fucking neighbours!" I spat.

"Emily, please don't swear."

"I'm sorry, Mum, it's just that it's really fucking awful."

"I know." She sat down next to me on the bed. "I counted eight minutes between your last two contractions though, love; the hospital have said you're not to go in until they're five minutes apart."

"I'm scared." I was weeping. "The next one is coming in a few minutes and I'm scared of it."

"Let's try the bath," Mum said.

"How's that going to help?"

"I don't know, but the water does, somehow. Just try it."

"But I don't want to get naked in front of you."

I was wailing like a child who's just fallen and grazed her knee.

"Right, put on one of those big pairs of knickers you bought earlier," Mum said, rolling her eyes.

"What about my top half? The only bras that fit me are the breastfeeding ones and they're in my bag."

Mum sighed, marched into her bedroom and came back holding one of her own bras in voluminous, plum-coloured satin.

"Go on, shove that on."

I sat on the toilet while Mum filled the bath, swirling her arm around gently, the iridescent foam clinging to her forearm in crackling, honeycomb clusters. It was a long time since she had run a bath for me, but I still remembered the soothing slowness of her stirring the bubbles, the comforting scent of baby bath.

Another one came. I gripped the temperamental towel rail and crouched, an ungraceful ballet dancer at the (very wonky) barre.

"Watch that towel rail," said Mum, "don't go pulling it off the wall."

Immediately, I did, exposing squinting red rawl plugs in the glossy blue tiles.

"Oh, heck," said Mum.

"Sorry."

"Oh, don't worry about that. It's only a towel rail. We've got more important things to think about than a towel rail."

I smiled, grateful for her soothing tone; the same one she'd used when I was little and sick; the tone that reassured me that, no matter what was going on, it would all be alright in the end.

As I lowered myself into the warm water, both sides of my bloated body slid against the bath, making elephant trumpet sounds. It was weeks since I'd even tried to fit in the bath; the shower just seemed easier. At thirty-two weeks, my fundal height (the size of my bump) was measuring abnormally huge and I was tested for gestational diabetes. I was sure the results would come back positive, but no, I was just absolutely massive. I'd felt disgusting, but in that moment, in my mother's bathroom, dreading the next bout of agony, my size and weight were the last things on my mind. The underwear suckered slimily to my skin. It felt like childhood lifesaving lessons, when we had to jump in the pool wearing baggy T-shirts and shorts. I stared at the wooden slats of the ceiling, listening to the familiar whirr and tap-tap of the bathroom fan, looking at quivering cobwebs and the dusty dolphin wind chimes, a souvenir I'd bought Mum from some holiday or another.

Now Mum was perched on the lid of the toilet, timing it all on her watch.

"Good girl," she said.

If I hadn't been in agony, I'd have laughed at the irony of that statement.

When the contractions hit, I shunted up and down the bath like a piston, sloshing water over the side. Mum had been right (and so was Sylvia Plath, again): the water did help soothe the pain.

Mum's pet hate was my ability to turn the bathroom floor

into a paddling pool whenever I came to stay. Once, when I was seventeen and still living at home, things got so bad that an actual toadstool sprouted on the ceiling beneath the bathroom, right above the front door. That night, lukewarm water cascaded on to the laminate floor like a waterfall in the monsoon. Mum said nothing, she just discretely mopped up the mess with her foot on a faded beach towel I'd had since the lifesaving swimming lessons, my name still sewn on the hem.

When the islands of solace between the pains got smaller, Mum said solemnly that we'd have to go. She knelt at the edge of the bath, arms stretched out like Christ the Redeemer, and wrapped me in two bath sheets because one wouldn't have fitted all the way round.

There were three more contractions before Mum managed to get me out of the house and with each one I begged her to let me get back in the bath, but really, I knew she was right: I knew we had to get to the hospital.

"Eat this," Mum said, as she climbed into the driver's seat. "It's going to be a long night and you need the energy."

"This" was a sandwich: vegetarian ham on diet bread that was so called because it was made of at least seventy percent air.

"Thank you," I said, inspecting it. I didn't feel remotely hungry. "Can we go now?"

"Alright, alright. Have you seen how frozen these windows are? I need to warm Poppy up first."

Poppy had been my car, an incentive to pass my driving test when I was eighteen and had more money than sense. It hadn't worked: twice I'd screamed "get out of my car!" to an expressionless examiner in a distractingly noisy cagoule, clutching the steering wheel and banging my head on the horn as he tried to tell me where I'd gone wrong. I'd eventually succumbed to the idea that I'd never be a driver and sold Poppy to my mother.

I couldn't even drive a car and I was about to have a baby. That thought hit me at the same time as my next contraction. I stood up in the foot well and grabbed the handle near my head.

"Alright, love, try to be calm. Just think: when you come home again, you'll have your baby with you. Now, eat that butty."

It was the driest thing I'd ever tasted, but I devoured it because my mother had made it for me and I loved her for making me a butty when I was about to have a baby.

However many hours later, I was on all fours on a birthing ball on the floor of a delivery room, wearing nothing but a ruched-up nightie Mum had bought me in the supermarket sale that said something about being a princess on the front and involved diamante. When I'd changed into it, the midwives had cooed over its loveliness, a sweet but annoying attempt at distraction.

"I don't know," Mum was saying, from the comfort of a PVC-covered throne in the corner, "all that palaver with the undies in the bath and now look at you."

I ignored her, biting down hard on the Entenox tube, hearing the delicious tick and tasting the dry sweetness as it flowed in through the valve and disconnected my brain from the pain that I was still aware of but no longer particularly bothered about. The agony ebbed and I resisted the urge to carry on chugging, having already received a stern telling-off from a midwife for not giving the gas and air a rest between contractions.

"The court!" Mum tutted, crossing and uncrossing her legs. "What are you on about?"

"The court! These magazines always include a photograph of the court, as though that adds weight to the story."

I'd grown up around Mum's crappy magazines: museums of misery, rolled-up and dimpled by bathwater or the sea. She usually bought them when she was off work or on holiday, but I wasn't sure why. You could win £25 for sending in a top tip, like making napkin rings out of the innards of a loo roll, or dinting an apple pie case to form an ashtray. Apart from that, it was all crosswords and tragedy.

Mum brandished the magazine in front of me. I saw a headline about a love rat and a cheat, and glimpsed a thumb-nail-sized photograph of a sixties brutalist building behind a roundabout.

"The bloody court," she was still laughing to herself. "I am so glad they included that photo of the court."

"Mum!" I roared. "I am in agony and I am having a baby and you're just sitting in the corner reading *Take a Break*."

"I thought you didn't want me to make a fuss."

"I've changed my mind. Make a massive fucking fuss."

"Stop swearing, please." Mum stood up, flung the magazine on the chair and rushed over to me and the ball. "What do you want me to do?" she said.

"Hold my hand please, Mum."

And she did. She held my hand when the midwife put me in the bath and I repeatedly observed, high on gas and air, that the ceiling fan made precisely the same noise as the one in the bathroom of my student halls. She held a plastic cup of cool water to my lips every time I gasped "water" between contractions, like I was lost in the desert. Mum held my hand when it felt like I was a kite and our arms were the string and had she let go the pain would have launched me through the ceiling tiles, out of the top of the hospital and into the cold March sky. When I squeezed her hand so tight that I felt something crunch, she didn't say anything but looked at the midwife and winced. Mum held my hand when I argued with the midwife that I was definitely not being silly for shouting out "if you gave me a loaded gun now, I would just shoot myself in the head." Mum held my hand when an anaesthetist on a power trip refused to give me an epidural, then again when her decision was overruled and I had to pretend not to be in pain and remain absolutely still while she begrudgingly stuck a needle in my spine. Mum held my hand when, many hours later, it transpired that my son's head would not fit through my pelvis and would never emerge the conventional way. She held my hand as a doctor stared into my vagina and announced that I needed an emergency caesarean section. She held my hand while someone roughly shaved my pubic hair off with a disposable razor. She only let go of me when she had to go and get into her theatre greens and it was time for them to wheel me down.

"See you in the theatre," she said, sniffling.

"See you down there," I smiled, weakly.

We were very nearly there.

Twenty-five

THIS IS THE still.

Finally, I get to rest. As they slice me open, I savour the calm.

Thirty-five weeks of anger and fear became thirty-six hours of agony and panic and it all transmuted to this heavy hush.

Silence, save for clinical beeps and the chink of surgical steel. I shut my eyes tight so as not to catch a glimpse of my guts in the gleaming light fittings above.

For eight months, I've wanted to run away. Now, I'm glued to a table by the numbness in my legs. I couldn't move, even if it wasn't physically impossible. I've had enough, I am knackered. This is what is happening now.

Apparently, I am about to experience the greatest moment of my life.

"It might feel like someone is doing the washing-up in your insides," the doctor warned me.

And that's precisely what it feels like.

I close my eyes and wait.

The cry, when it comes, is much croakier than I imagined and far less offensive. The midwife holds him up to me and he is bigger than I expected, purple and wizened. He's organic and waxy and fleshy. He's of me but his eyes are not. How did they grow in the dark? They don't make eye contact, not when they're this small; I've read that in one of my books. But he is looking right at me. He knows me, he knows everything. I know him, I always have.

"Hello, Mummy," coos the midwife.

"Hello."

What I really want to say to him is: "I'm sorry you got me, love."

I'm shaking.

"Memory full?!" Mum's fumbling with my camera. She's wearing ill-fitting theatre greens and she looks ridiculous. "Memory full! Nine bloody months you've had to prepare for this moment and now it says memory bloody full!"

I can hear his raspy cry as the midwife lays him on the scales. "Eight pounds, four ounces!" she exclaims.

"That's what I said, isn't it?" Mum's still playing with the camera. "When we were in the delivery suite before and we were taking guesses, I said he'd be eight pound four."

"He's bigger than I thought," I say.

"Memory full!"

The memory card's full of photographs of dresses that no longer fit me, hanging limply from the back of my bedroom door in Manchester, ready for eBay.

"Press the button with a picture of a bin."

Mum jabs the camera as she schleps across the room in her funny shoe covers.

"Memory bloody full! Nine months you've had to prepare for this."

Nine months to prepare. Nine months and thirty-six hours. Nine months, thirty-six hours and one moment of peace.

The chaos is over now, but it's been replaced with a new chaos of a different kind. They're starting to stitch me back together.

"Here," Mum says, holding up the camera, "his first ever picture."

He's being held aloft, red and crude and brand new, his bottom lip jutting out, shiny as a tomato. With his tiny, purplish fingers, he looks exactly like he's making a hand signal. His thumb and forefinger are touching, making a circle, and his other three fingers, caked in vernix, are splayed out wide. It's the sign that divers use when they're underwater, the one that means OK.

Twenty-six

THE SKY OUTSIDE was azure. In the hospital car park, birds were calling in the dawn from the silhouettes of the bare trees. It was my favourite time of day. The time of day when the street sweepers breeze in and magic away chip wrappers and broken bottles and the remains of the night. It's when shutters rattle down over kebab shop-fronts and up over newsagents, when streetlights cast an orange glow on navy tarmac and foxes slide silently between overflowing bins. It's when parties recede, when you find yourself under a sleeping bag on a stranger's sofa, or in a taxi you can't afford, or tying a scarf over your weary eyes, squashing in earplugs and sliding between cool sheets for a sleep that'll end when it ends.

Or it's when you find yourself in a hospital bed, wide awake, brawling with nature.

I didn't know anything about looking after babies, but I knew that breastfeeding was natural, healthy, free, the thing I was going to do. As a relatively young mother, I was statistically less likely to do it. Throughout pregnancy, I was asked by almost every health professional I encountered whether I was going to do it and I could tell that a few were surprised when I told them I was. Society's male-focused over-sexualisation of the breast makes some people find the thought of a suckling baby weird and/or disgusting, which is really sad. I was by no means fanatical about all this; it was long before the arrival on the scene of 'lactivists': people who seem to think it's their job to tell other mothers how to feed their own children (they probably were around, actually; I just hadn't encountered them, which is a good job). Breastfeeding just seemed to me to make the most sense: baby milk was designed for babies, so I would give mine to my baby. How anyone could be cool with consuming the milk of a goat or a sheep or a cow but recoil at the idea of humans drinking human milk was beyond me. But aside from the politics and the health benefits of it all, why on earth would I want to do anything that involved unnecessary housework? Bottles had to be kept not just clean but sterile, and washing-up had always been (and continues to be) my downfall. There was no decision-making process involved: I was going to breastfeed, I just knew. As such, I didn't really do much research into the process of breastfeeding (or BF, as the Motherboarders called it, which just looks like 'boyfriend').

"It can be quite hard, you know, Emily," Mum had tried to warn me. "You can take a baby to a boob, but you can't make it drink."

I was going to be fine though; how hard could it really be? Plus, I was never, ever going to forget what Beth the midwife had said: I had great nipples for breastfeeding.

Newborn babies have the natural urge to suckle the moment they come out. In an ideal world, they are immediately placed on their mother's chest, naked and squirming, and the first feed begins. The skin-to-skin contact helps the baby's instinct to suck and a rush of oxytocin, aka 'the cuddle hormone' starts the flow of the milk, or, in the first few days, colostrum: a tiny trickle of nutrient-rich, golden liquid that's packed with antibodies.

Tom and I didn't get the skin-to-skin contact. Mum asked

for it, on my behalf, in the hurry between the doctor telling me I had to have a caesarean and it happening, but it was forgotten in the chaos of the theatre. It's hard to hold a baby when you're lying flat on your back, temporarily paralysed from the waist down, a small sheet of cloth the only thing stopping you from glancing your own open guts. In a caesarean scenario, it's usually the baby's father, or in our case, the grandmother, who is tasked with holding the baby close to the mother while something like a vacuum cleaner is used on her insides and her organs are carefully rearranged with layers of muscle and skin deftly stitched back together.

Tom must have been an hour old by the time I was mended and we were in the recovery room. A midwife untied the hospital gown at the back of my neck and helped me pull it down at the front, revealing my swollen breasts, striped with veins and stretch marks. She hiked up the back of the bed with the foot pump so that the top of my body was at right angles with my legs, and told me to lift Tom to my breast, not bring the breast to him. I was ready, ready for nature to do its thing, ready to feel officially like a mother.

But nothing happened. Tom ignored my breast. He ignored the other one. It didn't work.

I tried again when they'd wheeled me back on to the ward, but he still wouldn't do it. Sometime in the middle of the night a midwife appeared and asked me what formula I'd like. I didn't know, because I wasn't going to give my baby formula.

"Emily," she said, "your baby hasn't eaten anything since he was born. He's hungry and he's thirsty. Won't you give him a bottle, just for tonight?"

She had a point. Surely he should have had something by

now?

"Will it jeopardise my breastfeeding?" I asked, knackered and confused.

"No. It just means you and Tom can get some rest. You can try feeding him yourself when you're feeling stronger."

It sounded like a good deal to me. I'd been awake and in labour for thirty-six hours; the idea of tackling the feeding again after a good sleep seemed like the best plan for Tom and for me. Before I knew it, Tom was glugging back a bottle of formula and the two of us were drifting off into a well-needed sleep.

But it still didn't work in the morning.

I had my catheter removed, ate some toast, tested out my legs again with a foal-like wobble down the corridor to the shower. Even after all of that, my baby did not want my milk. I'd failed at the first hurdle of motherhood, the bit that was supposed to come naturally. It didn't bode well for the rest of the experience; a worry that was cemented the first time I tried – and messily failed – to change a nappy. It didn't occur to me that my baby might kick, despite the fact he'd been kicking me on the inside for months. So when I realised, after undoing the dirty nappy, that I'd forgotten to get the cotton wool, I hobbled off to get it. When I came back, seconds later, Tom had kicked shit all over himself and the bed. I was forced to bath him, which was a traumatic experience for us both, while a nurse stripped and remade my bed, tutting "deary me".

Eventually, I got Tom to 'latch on', which would have been progress had he not pulled away immediately, howling. The bottle I'd given him on the first night meant Tom expected to get an instant hit of plentiful milk the second he started suckling, rather than having to work for a few droplets of colostrum. With the help of several midwives, I managed to get him to ingest what must have amounted to just a couple of drops. I found that the most effective method was also the most convoluted: the midwife milked me, holding a cold teaspoon beneath my nipple to catch the drips. She would then carefully syringe the precious drops out of the pool on the spoon and deposit them into Tom's mouth. Once I got the hang of it, I was able to do it myself. Even the inevitable stains of the stuff left in the bottom of the syringe felt like a terrible waste, but a few millilitres had to be better than nothing at all. This tiny sprinkle of goodness might have had health benefits, but it wasn't going to satisfy him and he kept on screaming. Worried about the other women on the ward and their babies, all of whom were bottle-fed and sleeping, I kept caving and agreeing to a bottle, which exacerbated the problem.

Around the third or fourth day after giving birth, your 'proper' milk arrives. This is when things really start to kick-off, and, thanks to the timing and a flush of hormones, lots of women are struck by the full hit of what just happened. The days leading up to this event dragged. I was looking forward to it because I was hoping that I could stop using cutlery and other tools to feed my newborn baby and just do it the way I was supposed to.

When I woke on the Saturday after Tom was born, 1 understood what it must feel like to come round after breast augmentation. There were two solid, throbbing rocks on my chest and the urge to empty them was similar to the sensation of being desperate for the loo. I lifted Tom to them, just as I'd been taught, relaxed my shoulders, exhaled, ready for the relief.

Nothing.

All Tom wanted was the bottle. He would latch on for a few seconds and it would feel like a bulldog clip was on the end of my nipple and the midwives would tell me the stinging meant he must be on wrong. So I'd take him off, changing position: him on a cushion, him lying down with me leaning awkwardly and painfully over him, him lying on his side, facing me. An incredible midwife spent hours of her shift at my side, encouraging me to relax, to try scores of different tricks. Despite all her sterling efforts, nothing would work. At best, Tom would suckle for a few moments, until there was a break in supply, which meant he had to work a bit harder, at which point he pulled away, screaming with frustration, seemingly craving the instant and easy supply that the bottle had given him.

I was tired of being hooked up to the brutal breast pump when I was supposed to be resting, watching it drag my nipple unfeasibly far down a clear plastic tube, all for a few thin threads of milk that culminated in a pathetic, bluish pool that was nowhere near enough to feed my baby. The less frequently babies feed, the less milk mothers produce, and I was terrified of running out. When Tom came near me, the stuff literally leaked all over his cheeks, but he didn't want it. When he was asleep and I tried to harvest it for him to drink later, there was hardly anything. Only his cry and the feeling of his skin next to me would trigger enough oxytocin to get things going; cold, hard plastic and the whooshing of the pump just weren't enough.

That Saturday, the midwife who'd helped me came to see me before the end of her shift.

"You're getting there," she said.

I thanked her and told her I was determined to crack it by

myself that night. I would not give up and ask for a bottle, I would spend the whole night, if that's what it took, persuading my baby to feed.

"Emily! Get up, get up now and feed your baby."

The midwife sounded like she was shouting at a passed-out drunk (she kind of was).

I opened my eyes, gradually tuning into the situation. Tom was lying parallel to me in the transparent cot next to my bed, crying so hard it looked as though he could explode. The last thing I remembered was him falling asleep, exhausted, after another breastfeeding battle, and me placing him down gently in his cot. Morphine had knocked me out so hard that I'd slept through the unbearable din of my own child screaming right next to me.

"Sorry," I said, "I didn't hear him."

"Well the rest of the ward did. It's not fair on the other mums in here, or the babies."

This midwife, who I'd never come across before, clearly dealt in tough love.

"Sorry." I pulled myself up as quickly as I could, my caesarean wound smarting through the fug of the drugs.

"Here," she passed him to me, "you'd better feed him."

"I can't do it," I whispered.

By this point, my disbelief in myself wasn't helping things – instead of just scooping Tom up and getting on with it, the very thought of trying to feed him filled me with tenseness and dread, neither of which are conducive to breastfeeding.

"Course you can."

"I can't though. I've tried everything and it won't work."

"Well, you'll be home alone in a few days and you'll have

to feed him then. Either feed him yourself or buzz for a bottle."

And she was gone, with a flick of the jazzy, Aztec curtain that separated us from the rest of the ward. And the rest of the world.

I looked over my shoulder at the small, rectangular window next to my bed. The sky outside was royal blue now. I knew that light so well. It had always felt like a secret: the time when night bleeds into day and you are awake to see it when most of the world is asleep. It was the gloaming, and the gloaming that turns Saturday into Sunday is the greatest of them all.

I thought of my housemates back in Manchester, probably still awake, dancing round the living room. They'd sent me a text message earlier telling me how happy they were, that they'd be toasting me and Tom that night. I imagined the tops of lager cans knocking together, the slurred cheers and off-kilter hugs. And I thought of Tom's father, out there somewhere, possibly also still awake, wondering whether he'd got the text message I'd sent him the morning after the birth:

I know you don't want anything to do with him, but I had to tell you he exists. He weighs 8lb4oz and he is perfect and beautiful.

He'd probably changed his phone number, I reasoned with myself. I hadn't, though. I'd kept my email address the same, too, just in case. Despite all the vitriol, I hoped that when the baby was tangible, he'd be at the very least intrigued. Tom had been born on the exact day he was officially due, something that happens with only a tiny percentage of babies. Whatever the date, his father must have known that he was due that month, so he must surely have been wondering.

"Oh God, just make him shush will you, love?" moaned the mother in the next bed.

She was bottle-feeding her baby; I had overheard the midwives advising her to keep her boobs away from the water in the shower, to avoid stimulation and speed up the drying-up process.

"Sorry," I murmured, by way of an apology.

The gloaming was a familiar friend, but not like this. It was a time to be sitting on a flip-down seat in a black cab as it rumbled to the next party, to be putting the world to rights with someone you'd only just met, to be walking to the park, amazed at the volume of the birdsong.

Feeling like the shittest mother in the whole world, I slid my feet into my slippers and shuffled down the corridor to the midwives' station.

"Just give me a bottle," I said, each word separated by a sob. "Please, just give me a bottle."

The teat of the bottle was magic, muting Tom's cries the moment it reached his mouth. Silence – just like putting earplugs in. I lay back, listening to the soothing sound of satisfied gulps. When he was done and winded, I laid him in his cot, tied one of his sleepsuits around my eyes, and settled in for a sleep that would end whenever my baby woke.

Twenty-seven

MUM'S DECISION TO make me wait in the hospital chapel may or may not have been an attempt to set me up with God.

"I'll just bring the car closer to the entrance," she said. "You wait in here with Tom."

She plonked his car seat down next to me on the pew, and quickly disappeared. Tom immediately began to scream.

"Sssh," I tried.

There was no one else in the chapel, but I got the feeling we were supposed to be quiet in there.

Tom was very unhappy; his cheeks were shiny and raw. I could see his uvula quivering at the back of his throat, like a screaming cartoon baby. I was pretty sure I could see lumps where his teeth would be, too: little brick walls waiting under his gums. I tried to imagine him with teeth and with more than his thin crop of dark hair, and a father.

"It's alright," I said, offering my forefinger.

He clutched on with his tiny corned-beef fingers, his miniscule fingernails blanching from mauve to yellowy white.

"It's alright."

It wasn't alright, really. We were going home and I had no idea what I was doing.

They couldn't wait to leave, the other mums. Not only were they sick of listening to my hungry baby scream all night, they had hubbies and other halves and even other children to go home to.

Each morning, the consultant would come on his rounds, and each morning, women would tell each other how much they hoped it would be their turn to go. Each morning, I crossed my fingers and desperately hoped that I would be allowed to stay.

Life was good in Bay 5 of the Postnatal Ward. I got all my meals in bed, even if the only vegetarian options available were jacket potatoes that looked like they'd been cast in bronze. (Also, tuna pasta bake, because somehow some people will never understand that tuna is meat.)

There was a little button next to my bed with a picture of a nurse on it. I am almost certain it's the same button you get on an aeroplane for when you need a drink: small, square, a woman with isosceles triangles for legs. Anyway, whenever you pressed that button, they came running, pretty quickly, because thankfully, they did not have isosceles triangles for legs. And they might not have been able to bring me a mini bottle of wine or a gin with a little tin of tonic and a plastic glass, but the midwives did bring shots of oral morphine in tiny paper cups.

Most of the midwives wanted to help me feed my baby. The wonderful mix of healthcare assistants and midwives did everything, from teaching me to change nappies, to helping me with the painful and distressing task that was going to the toilet. One of them, a night-shift worker, just sat on the end of my bed in the soft gloom and listened. She listened as I told her I didn't know where my baby's father was and it didn't look as though he was ever going to reappear. She listened as I laughed, tearfully, at the surprising faces my baby could make: tiny 'o' shapes with his mouth and adorable yawns. She listened as I told her the whole story, from the very beginning, and how I didn't know how it would end.

The day after my failed breastfeeding all-nighter, things went a bit wrong.

"I feel like I'm falling down a lift shaft," I said, to the midwife, clutching Tom tightly, genuinely feeling as though my bed was plunging down several storeys at high speed, taking me and my baby with it.

Next thing, I was having a psychiatric assessment and being asked whether I felt like harming my baby or myself.

"No," I said. "I just keep feeling like I'm falling from a great height." I didn't want to harm my baby; I just wanted the plummeting to stop.

A few weeks later, Mum, who was visiting me when it happened, told me that she was taken off into a side room and quizzed on the likelihood of me hurting Tom. I knew why they had to ask, and I am glad they did, but really, I just wanted to stop falling.

Thankfully, the psychiatrist believed that I didn't pose a threat to my son. I was told I was suffering from exhaustion and prescribed temazepam, whilst Tom's cot was wheeled off to the midwives' station for the night. In the morning, I woke from a gloriously fuzzy sleep to find my baby at the foot of the bed, No. 5 scrawled on a green paper towel that had been taped to the side of his cot, his nappy dirty and ready to be changed. Normal service resumed. It would have been terrifying, were it not for the fact that I was surrounded by professionals. Being on the postnatal ward made me feel safe and capable of scraping by.

Bay 5 had become home. But after a week of pampering,

opiates and crap food, I knew my time was up. "You can go home today," said the consultant, with a firm nod and a smile, leaving me cowering behind the jazzy Aztec curtain.

When Mum arrived an hour later, Tom was asleep and I was pretending to do the same, scrunched up under the starchy sheets.

"Get up," Mum said sternly, rolling me like she used to when I was fifteen and I didn't want to go to school.

I groaned, like I did when I was fifteen and didn't want to go to school.

"I thought you'd be ready to go when I got here."

"You didn't think that."

After a disastrous photo shoot involving a livid baby and some 'anti-fatigue' foundation that made me look like I'd face-planted a barrel of glitter, it was time to leave the ward. Mum gathered up the flowers and the cards and the cuddly toys and I thanked the midwives, who told me I had a gorgeous baby and I was going to be a brilliant mum.

Then Mum went to get the car and left us in the chapel, with Tom screaming for his next feed and me still not actually knowing how to do it.

"Ssh," I said, again, willing my mother to hurry up.

Tom's cry was all right, actually – to me, anyway. I'd based all my experience of crying babies on the ones I'd heard in shops and on public transport: high-pitched and horrible. Tom came out sounding all gravelly, though; something to do with not having been through the birth canal and clearing out his chest in the process. I think that was one of the first things I said: "Hasn't he got a deep voice?" I was expecting a car alarm and instead I got Tom Waits.

I wished he'd pipe down in the chapel though. I was

worried someone might come in wanting to pray. And my nipples were tingling because of the sound. That's a weird thing: it's like an itch that has to be scratched. On the rare occasions that Tom actually managed to latch on, I felt a kind of relief that I'd only ever experienced in a service-station toilet when I'd been needing it since a few junctions back. I had to put rustling pads that looked like hotel bathroom coasters inside my bra in the hope that they would absorb all the leaking milk. One thing I hadn't realised until my breast-pumping was that nipples have loads of holes, like a watering can or a shower head.

"It's alright," I said, yet again, letting Tom squeeze my forefinger tight, like I'd done with Mum's hand a week earlier.

I just wanted her to hurry up. What was I supposed to do if someone came in? Would I apologise or just leave? I could barely lift the car seat by myself, and the midwives had told me not to try.

I looked at the white lilies on the altar and the hand-knitted kneelers and I thought about all the reasons a person might find themselves in a hospital chapel. I looked at Tom, screaming and needy but beautiful and alive, and I closed my eyes and blocked out the crying for a second and said thank you.

My phone rang. I didn't think I was supposed to answer it in the chapel.

"Hello?" I hissed.

"I'm outside," said Mum, chirpily, as if she was just picking me up from the pub.

"Can you come and help me lift the car seat, please?"

It took us ages to figure out how to safely strap the thing into the car, and I couldn't bend down because of the caesarean scar, so I was pretty useless. Eventually, though, when we'd wrestled the helium 'It's a Boy!' balloons that were tied to it into the car, we were on the road, Mum driving terrifyingly slowly. It couldn't have been the movement of the car that sent Tom to sleep, but perhaps the rumble of the old engine did.

Outside was greyer than I'd imagined. Instead of the bright, spring day I'd envisaged for my baby's homecoming, we were greeted by snow; not pretty snow, but the ugly dregs of a wintry storm that shouldn't really have happened at that time of year anyway. Stubborn crusts of grubby slush clung to hedgerows and roundabouts, and the sun failed miserably at poking its way through a neat circle, a bullet hole in the milky sky.

When we got home, Mum took Tom into the house and set the car seat down on the rug in front of the sofa. He looked out of place, like the Christmas tree when it first goes up. I tried frantically to remember how to change his nappy, bath him safely and, most frightening of all, how to feed him. He read my mind, like an animal sensing fear, and suddenly he was shaking his head from side to side, grumbling and pulling a disgusted face. Next came the now-familiar hacking noises, which quickly morphed into a full-crescendo cry, just as Mum came into the room, laden with flowers and gift bags.

"Pass him to me please, Mum?"

The sting of my stitches meant I couldn't even bend down to pick him up.

Mum handed Tom to me and I didn't worry about how I'd cope again because I didn't have time.

Twenty-eight

THE GUILT BEGINS in the delivery room, or the operating theatre, (or the car park, or the bathroom, or wherever the baby is born). It wracks you from the very start. The doctors ask if you'd like your baby to have a vitamin K injection, which helps prevent spontaneous bleeding in the first few weeks of its life. Of *course* you want it to have that injection (or I did, anyway). So, within minutes of arriving into the world and wondering what the bright lights and sounds and space were all about, Tom was stabbed in his tiny heel with a needle. I couldn't explain this to him or comfort him; all I could do was listen as his already bewildered cry grew several octaves higher.

If you are the only parent, you get double helpings of the guilt – lucky you. In my case, I was guilty for the fact my child did not have a father, and that the hope I realised I'd been clinging to for eight months that he might magically materialise when Tom was born had not come to fruition. I was also guilty because I couldn't feed my baby, that even the natural mechanics of it wouldn't work. It's not just single mothers or those who can't master breastfeeding who are affected by the guilt; from talking to other parents, I know that the guilt gets to most of them. They feel guilty that their baby seems to suffer from perpetual insomnia, guilty that they were unable to deliver it the natural way, guilty for the very fact it exists in this world. I want to say that the guilt dissipates, or at least eases off a bit as babies get older, but it doesn't. With walking and talking come inevitable questions about the world, the answers to which are often bleak; with nursery and school the realisation that not everybody you encounter smiles at you and adores you and, if you work, there will always be the constant battle between your job and your child, which will manifest itself in dilemmas like being unable to attend the school play. Again, for single parents, the guilt is galvanised by the lack of any kind of understudy to join the audience in your place.

Anyway, long before school plays come the very early days at home, when you're in pain and you really need a rest but you find yourself busier than you've ever been. In the immediate aftermath of coming home from hospital, Mum's house was busy with visitors. On the first night back, Uncle Paul, Auntie Joy and Hannah came round to see Tom. ("Oh my God, is that it?" Hannah gasped, when she first caught sight of Tom. "It's tiny!" Then she picked him up and didn't want to put him down – and she's been a devoted auntie ever since.) Mum ordered a Greek takeaway (because the restaurant was my favourite), and the living room was full of foil trays and croaky crying and love and it felt a bit like a weird version of Christmas.

The next morning, I woke up, cold and soaking wet. I'd lost another breastfeeding battle late the night before and had succumbed to the bottle. I didn't know what time it was, but it was daylight. Tom was in the Moses basket next to my bed, but I couldn't hear a sound from him. I had clearly been in such a deep sleep that I had managed to wet the bed. Hiding under my duvet, I stretched out my hand and found my phone on my bedside table. I grabbed it and dialled the landline, which I immediately heard ringing in Mum's room next door.

"Hello?" she said, her voice echoing through the wall and down the receiver.

"Hi, it's me."

"Oh. Why are you ringing me?"

"Please will you come into my room and look at the baby because he hasn't woken up crying and I have been in such a deep sleep that I think I have wet the bed and I am too scared to look because I don't know if he is OK."

Mum hung up and rushed into the room. I heard the quiet creak of wicker. "Hello, treasure," she said.

Slowly, I peered out from under my duvet. Mum was holding Tom aloft. "Is he alright?"

"He's asleep, or he was - he's coming round now."

"But why didn't he wake before now?"

"Did he have a bottle?"

"Yeah."

"Formula?"

"Yes. I haven't been making enough milk, despite all the pumping," I sighed. "There wasn't much else I could do."

"It takes longer to digest than your milk," Mum said. "That's why he slept for so long. It's OK."

"But I've wet the bed. That's not OK."

I eased myself out from under the sodden sheets and put my feet on the carpet. The long sleep meant I'd missed my latest dose of painkillers, too. Slowly, painfully, I stood up, the cool morning air mixing with my sopping nightie to bring me out in goose pimples.

"You can't help it, love," Mum said. "With everything you've been through, it's no wonder you went off into a deep sleep."

"I need a shower," I said, desperate to peel off the slime of my nightie, but knowing Tom needed me first.

"You haven't wet the bed," Mum said, jiggling Tom, who had by now begun to realise that he was hungry and had a wet nappy and had started to cry.

"I have."

"That's milk," Mum said. "I can smell it."

She was right. While my baby had been taking ages to digest his manufactured milk, I'd been producing litres of the natural stuff, most of which had now seeped into the mattress on my relatively new bed.

A few days later, it was Mothers' Day. I was feeling especially appreciative of my mum at the time, so I had asked one of her friends to drive me to the garden centre, where I bought her a potted olive tree (which is still going strong, and, thanks to Mum's sentimentality, still has the gift-wrap ribbon curling around its thin trunk, albeit faded). It hadn't occurred to me that I had just become a recipient of Mothers' Day cards and gifts, probably because I was so caught up in the fact of new motherhood. On the Sunday morning, after I had presented Mum with her card and the tree and after copious tears on her part, she handed me an envelope. It was addressed to 'Mummy', in the calligraphic writing my mother reserves for special occasions. I opened it carefully and found inside a cream card with a teddy bear on the front. 'To Mummy from Your Little Boy' was the message that welled me up. Inside, calligraphy kisses and a message: 'I love you very much'. The midwives had called me Mummy plenty of times, but something about seeing it written down thwacked me in the solar plexus. I was no longer just Emily, but Mummy, which was outrageous.

The second thing to choke me up on Mothers' Day was the arrival of the community midwife, who I knew was a mother herself. I hadn't been expecting her, but she insisted on dropping in to help me with feeding time. As it happened, I didn't need her help, because for the first time ever, Tom simply latched on with the minimum of fuss and stayed there.

"It must be because it's today," I said.

"I'll leave you now," the midwife whispered, sneaking out of the room. "Happy Mothers' Day".

She'd barely reversed her car out of the drive when it all ended in tears and I was cradling crying Tom in one hand and dunking a hot bottle in a jug of cold water in an urgent effort to cool it down. Still, it was the longest actual feed I'd ever managed, which was a Mothers' Day present in itself.

That afternoon, while Tom was taking a nap, I painted one of his tiny soles blue. Feet are the very best part of a baby. They're miniature and beautiful and cute and nothing like the hairy, bony, monstrosities they're guaranteed to one day become. I studied the network of lines on the bottom of Tom's: he had what looked like a big capital A on his right and a capital X on the left. On his heel (I can't remember which one) there was a minute purple dot, the remains of the vitamin K shot. Along the tops of his feet, the tips of his toes were lined up like strings of beads. To my left, I had a pile of plain, square cards. Tom continued to sleep as I got a production line going, stamping his foot on to a card, topping up the paint, stamping another one. Every card was to thank a friend who'd helped me along the way, and every time I stamped, I thought of what they'd done for me. There was one for Margaret the midwife, for being the first person to make me think having a baby might not signal the end of the world, one for Jane, for everything, one for Anna, too. All the while, Tom slept, his breath slow and soft, his arms up at the sides of his head like a cactus in a Western.

That evening, Mum and I decided to go to bed early. I should have been able to sleep, knackered as I was, but Tom was hacking and spluttering in his Moses basket. Since he'd been born, his chest had rattled; like his gruff voice, it was a result of not having been through the birth canal. Now, the rattling was audible and accompanied by snuffles. The snuffling turned to grunting and the grunting became an angry, snotty cry. I got up and picked him up and felt something on one side of his chest, a lump like a tiny egg. I tore open the poppers on his sleepsuit and yanked down his vest and saw through his thin skin that he had a matching egg on the other side.

"Mum!" I said, running into her room. "There's something wrong with the baby. He can't breathe and there are lumps on his chest."

"It's alright," she said, snapping on the bedside lamp, "let's have a look."

I lay him next to her and showed her what I'd seen.

"I think they're like little boobs," she said.

"Boobs?!"

"Yes, from the hormones in your milk."

Why had no one warned me about the fact that my very small, male baby, might grow a pair of tiny, temporary breasts?

"He's very snuffly, though," said Mum. "I think he's got a cold."

"A cold? Already? He's a week old."

What followed was a lengthy call to NHS Direct, a number I knew off by heart for the first few years of Tom's life.

"Do you have an aspirator?" the nurse on the helpline asked.

"A what, sorry?"

"A nose aspirator. Sometimes they're called mucus extractors. You can get ones you squeeze or ones you suck."

"Suck?"

Mum had not told me about snot suckers when we'd been shopping for baby stuff. (Later, I consulted Motherboard about these contraptions and discovered posts from women who'd actually sucked the snot out of their babies' noses straight into their own mouths and I sat at my computer and balked.)

Given the fact that Tom couldn't blow his nose and I hadn't invested in a snot sucker, we had to bundle him up in the middle of the night and take him to the on-call medical centre.

"Ooh, look at him," said the receptionist, standing over his car seat with her hands on her hips. "They don't stay like that for long."

Good, I thought; he was yet again roaring and red. I'd tried to give him a bottle, but he needed to breathe through his mouth, so that hadn't really worked out.

The doctor confirmed that Mum had been right about the boob thing, which was a relief (and fascinatingly weird). He also prescribed antibiotics, which came with a heavy dose of guilt for me; if I'd managed to feed Tom in hospital, the colostrum would have given him all the antibodies he needed, and he wouldn't be having antibiotics syringed into his mouth at less than two weeks old.

For my first ever Mothers' Day I got the gift of guilt.

Twenty-nine

"THE MOMENT THEY place that baby in your arms . . ." (Insert one of the following):

your life will feel complete

it will all be worth it

you will forget the pain

you'll be overwhelmed by a dizzying sense of purpose and love, like nothing you have ever felt before.

I'd heard them all. Midwives, Motherboarders, Mum, Mum's friends, all of them promising me this incredible rush of love.

"The day I had my baby was the best day of my life," say loads of people who have had babies.

Really? You were knackered, in agony and likely leaking from practically every orifice. Was that really the best day of your life? *Honestly?*

If you are pregnant, I want to warn you that the day you give birth might not be the best day of your life. Obviously becoming a parent is a milestone, and a wonderful one at that, but the actual day you give birth might not be so great. Perhaps it will be, if you're lucky enough to have a chilled-out water birth with no complications whatsoever, but chances are it won't. And you mustn't feel guilty if it's not. There will be other best days, like the first time you finally teach YOUR CHILD to ride their bike without stabilisers, or the first time they draw a surreal picture and tell you it's you, or the time they win a certificate at school. The best is on its way, so don't get yourself worked up about that. Don't be afraid to admit it if the day you give birth is not the best day of your life, or even if it's your worst; it's not your fault and it's certainly not your baby's. Also, don't feel guilty if you don't get the fabled rush of love the first time you hold your slimy, screaming, squirming baby. It will come, in time; sometimes love's a grower. Thankfully, my cynicism stopped me from believing the promises of instant euphoria, otherwise I would have been sorely disappointed.

Shortly after Tom was born, I began to shake, uncontrollably, my teeth chattering together, my hands quivering. The doctors said it was probably a mix of adrenaline and the epidural wearing off. I was in shock. Not just the physical shock of having been cut open while I was awake, but the emotional shock of realising I had just brought a human being into the world who was entirely dependent on me.

When the midwife tucked Tom into the crook of my arm in the recovery room, he was hot and soft and a perfect fit. I knew that he was mine, that he was beautiful and that I must always look after him, so I did. I got swept away on the tidal wave of bodily fluids and I didn't wash ashore for another few weeks, when I was bleeding less, my stitches stopped stinging and I was getting decent chunks of sleep.

The all-consuming, high-as-a-kite, gooey love I'd been promised came at its own leisurely pace. It took its time, showing itself in small glimpses as, between mopping things up, I marvelled repeatedly at Tom's eyes, his little fingers, the tiny squeaks he made.

When Tom was twenty-one days old, spring finally arrived. Sun flooded the living room, lighting up channels of dust like swarms of busy insects. It was warm, so I carefully peeled away Tom's clothes to try skin-to-skin feeding. I was still struggling with breastfeeding: having been to breastfeeding support groups, had daily visits from the midwife and spoken to lactation consultants over the phone, I just couldn't persuade Tom to do it. I'd settled for a mix of bottle and breast, which, I told myself, had to be better than the bottle alone.

Quietly, calmly, I scooped my baby up and held him close to me. His skin was unbelievably soft, like that long, downy grass that grows in meadows in the summer. The moment should have been perfect, but it ended in screams and me surrendering to the bottle, again.

Afterwards, I risked lying Tom on Mum's cream sofa, chancing it that he wouldn't wee or poo. I watched as his limbs moved wildly and involuntarily; his hands clawing thin air and his toes curling as he kicked. It must be strange to suddenly have all that space when you've been hunched up for so long. His eyes didn't move from a certain point above, possibly the reflection of light on a picture frame. I was just as transfixed on him. He reminded me of a chameleon, grasping at branches with clever toes, swivelling its spherical eyes. I could watch them for hours, those awesome products of nature, and I realised that while he didn't have the ability to change colour, my baby was just as awesome, just as magnificent. How babies are made is the most simple of biological facts, but only now that I had the time to stare at mine, right in front of me, free from the madness of his initial arrival, did I begin to realise just how amazing it truly was. Just after I began filming the beautiful moment on my phone, Tom cocked one of his legs in the air like a dog against a lamppost and let out an adult-sized fart.

Before I put him safely back in a nappy, I lay Tom on his front on a cushion and took photographs of him. They're still some of my favourite photos. The skin on his legs is baggy, like oversized tights that he has yet to grow into. And even though he is far too young to really smile, he has a happy, serene look on his face. I had one of those photographs enlarged and made into a chopping board for Mum. Of course, she never chops anything on it, but every time I see it leaning against the tiles in her kitchen, I remember the day spring finally arrived, bringing with it the tardy rush of love.

Thirty

THERE WAS LOVE for my baby, intense and awe-inspiring, but I still felt stranded in Southport, in Mum's house, in bed. It didn't take me long to work out that life with a newborn baby and life as a student have several parallels. Sleepless nights aren't a big deal if you were nocturnal in a former life. Babies famously need feeding in the night, which really isn't a problem if you don't have to be anywhere in the morning, don't have other children to worry about and are used to being kept awake by the boy next door constantly playing the same Jimi Hendrix riff on his electric guitar. Or the boy in the next room belching, farting and having sex. Tom typically needed a feed at 7:00pm and another at 1am, so what was the point in going to sleep between the two? I read more in those first few weeks than I had in my entire pregnancy, the background noise of Tom's breathing so much more soothing than the worry about his arrival could ever have been.

A few days after I came home from hospital, Mum gave me a precious nugget of motherly advice that I will always be thankful to her for: it was OK to put my baby down. I needed the toilet, and going to the toilet was an ordeal, thanks to the stitches in my lower belly and the iron tablets I'd been prescribed for anaemia. Tom was crying, and I was under the impression I wasn't allowed to leave him for a second while that was happening. Exhausted and desperate for the crying to end, I remembered a baby carrier I'd seen in a cardboard box of hand-me-downs, a donation from one of Mum's kind friends. I rifled through the box until I found the carrier, fumbled with the complicated fastenings, and went to the toilet with my screaming baby strapped to me.

Mum was at work, but she called me on her lunch break to see how I was getting on.

"He just won't stop crying," I shouted over the din. "Nothing I try works."

"Have you fed him?"

"Yes."

"Changed his nappy?"

"Yes."

"He's tired. Just put him in his basket."

"But he's crying."

"He's probably crying because he's tired. Put him in the Moses basket, close your bedroom door and get into my bed."

"But I can't just leave him while he is crying."

"Yes, you can. Call me back in ten minutes. If he's still crying, we'll review the situation, but I bet he'll be asleep."

I trusted Mum, and I was willing to try anything. So I did as she said, crawling into her bed, inhaling the scent of her talcum powder, scrunching myself up and trying to block out the crying, which called to a primal part of me. On the alarm clock next to her bed, the glowing colon between the hours and minutes flashed every second. As I counted the flashes, Tom's cry slowed down to a low, lazy moan. Within three minutes, it had stopped. I tiptoed into my room, worried about what I'd find, but from my bedroom doorway I could hear that wondrous sound of my baby breathing. Carefully, I straightened the blanket out over his tiny form; he sighed deeply and went on sleeping. I crawled into bed, lying in line with him and fell quickly to sleep.

Realising it was OK to put my baby down was life-changing. A lot of the time, I could put him in his vibrating rocker ("The Electric Chair" - my mother's name for it) and just get on with stuff while he lay there gurgling to himself or nodding off. I had baths, ate toast, phoned Alex in Australia. My favourite thing to do while Tom was sleeping was to sleep myself. Sleep felt as though it healed me from the exhaustion, the caesarean, the stress I'd been under since the summer before. So, I based myself in bed. As long as I had water, painkillers, food, books, the breast pump and my baby within reasonable reach, I discovered there was absolutely no reason not to be under my duvet, apart from the odd trip across the landing to the loo. My dressing table became a makeshift kitchen; I ordered a miniature fridge from the internet and used it to store the few millilitres of breast milk I managed to pump, whilst an old travel kettle was all I needed to make bottles when Tom inevitably gave up breastfeeding (he'd got better at latching on, but it was only ever ten minutes before there was a break in the flow and I'd have to reach for a bottle). It really wasn't any different to stationing myself in my room for an essay-writing marathon. Despite the fact I should have been loading up on nutrition to pass on to my son, there were few proper meals, but my diet of biscuits, ready meals and toast, when I remembered to eat them, was nothing new.

I lived in my pyjamas, but, I reasoned, I was recovering from a big operation, so that was completely fine. The main thing was that Tom was fed and clean and I was ready to fall asleep, rapidly and deeply, whenever he did. At weekends,

Mum often took Tom out to show him off to her friends, or to see Nan in the nursing home. I was still terrified of Nan's reaction, but Mum said that despite her bafflement at who he belonged to, Nan loved Tom, and he made her crack a rare smile.

While Mum and Tom were out, I probably should have been having a bath or at least getting out of bed, but I just saw it as another opportunity to sleep. It didn't occur to me that I might be depressed, or that what I was doing might be unhealthy. I felt like I'd discovered a secret that new mothers the world over had been missing: I could live in bed! My former self would have loved it. My version of new motherhood really wasn't anywhere near as bad as I'd imagined. All that worrying for nothing, I thought. Tom drank milk, I ate digestive biscuits; Tom looked cute, I took photographs of him on my phone; he slept, I slept too.

It all worked perfectly, until the day I got caught.

I heard Mum's key in the lock a few minutes before she reached my room, but it didn't wake me because it was all a part of the vivid dream I was having at the time.

"Emily, what are you doing?"

I patted my bedside table. Packets of painkillers clattered to the floor and an empty milk bottle toppled into the open drawer below. My hand landed on my book, which was doing the splits on top of the breast pump, but it was too late: Mum was already looming in the doorway.

"I was just reading," I slurred. "Must've nodded off."

Finally, after months of being lovely, Mum bollocked me. She bollocked me for not eating properly, for ruining Tom's routine, for not socialising him.

"*Socialising* him? He's a newborn baby!"

"Exactly," she said. "It's one of the most important stages of a child's development."

Mum worked with nursery children; when it came to child development, she knew her stuff.

"I think you're depressed."

"I'm not," I said, thinking she had a point but still determined to ward off the black dog at all costs. "I'm really not."

Next came the meltdown, the scarlet, stinging face, tears and snot and snot and tears. Tom slept through me talking about how it would be kinder to have him adopted, how he should have a mother who was up for getting out of bed and a father who was up for being a dad.

"He deserves a proper family."

"You *are* a proper family," Mum said.

When Mum had calmed me down, I promised to take Tom to the park the following day. And I did, about an hour before she was due back from work. It took that long to get to a point when neither Tom nor I needed food, cuddles, or some sort of cleansing. And also to pack; I'd stuffed the changing bag full of enough stuff to last us both six months in South East Asia.

If getting ready to leave the house was a nightmare, actually leaving was even worse. My pram was a big, gingham thing from the mid-nineties, a hand-me-down for which I was extremely grateful. My Motherboard comrades had spoken of spending hundreds, even thousands on their prams, many confessing to be so-called pramaholics. As status symbols, prams, it emerged, were up there with swanky cars, designer wedding dresses and bespoke kitchens. I hadn't been able to see the appeal of fancy prams, but I realised, as I wrestled the thing out of Mum's porch, dislodging the glass wall-lamp from its bracket in the process, there had been considerable advances in pushchair design since the mid-nineties.

I didn't need to push the pram down the hill to the park; gravity took care of that. I gripped the handle of the thing like it was the safety bar on a roller coaster, pressing in with my fingernails, cutting indelible crescents into the soft foam. What if I tripped and let go and the pram careered into the path of an incoming car? What if, assuming I made it to the park, I slipped on a banana skin or swan shit and Tom ended up in the boating lake, which had been closed for years because of blue green algae? I imagined the headline in the local paper: SINGLE MUM IN TOXIC POND PRAM PLUNGE. More worrying than any of that, though: what if Tom got hungry and I had to go through the saga of trying to feed him in public?

I made it down the hill without letting go, and managed to push the pram around the boating lake without it ending up in the stagnant water. The park was filled with memories that felt way more recent than they were. On Sunday afternoons in summer, Uncle Paul and Nan used to regularly take Hannah and me there. Our local park had been a recreational field with a rusty climbing frame and piles of white dog shit, so coming to this one had been a real treat. At least Mum had moved close to it now: I had a feeling, as I wheeled the pram along the winding paths, inhaling the scent of wet pine, that the park was about to become one of my closest friends. I saw the bandstand where we used to sit on striped deckchairs eating ice cream, listening to the slow sounds of the brass band, Hannah and I shooting each other with those joke ice-cream cones that eject foam balls on strings. There was an ice-cream stall that also sold tat (as well as real ice creams), and I remembered neon bouncy balls with different facial expressions, the fresh plastic of them smelling somehow good. I saw the slimy stepping stones across the pond where you could usually spot a matted rat, the colourful obstacles of the crazy golf course, and the cave-like tunnels where we'd played hide and seek. On those dreamy Sundays, the park had always been so busy and bright, but now, it was almost deserted. I pushed the pram awkwardly into the park café and ordered coffee and beans on toast.

Despite the greyness outside, the café was filled with light. It was made almost entirely of glass, a giant Victorian conservatory. When Hannah and I were children, the ceiling had been festooned with a menagerie of inflatable animals, and I remembered specifically an argument over a popped parrot. The hard plastic tables and chairs were screwed to the floor, and slipping into the slim gap between them was a challenge. Just as I'd managed to get comfortable, Tom began to stir; the movement of the pram being pushed usually soothed him to sleep, but as soon as it stopped, he was awake. I wanted to scoop him up, pull down my top and discretely feed him there and then, but I didn't dare. Just weeks earlier, a woman had been thrown out of a local restaurant for breastfeeding her baby. I'd been gawping at the comments on local news sites ever since.

"These women just need to plan better," wrote one ignorant fool whose username strongly suggested he was male and who'd clearly never heard the expression 'feed on demand'. "Why can't they just feed their babies before they leave the house?"

The thing is, I couldn't just discretely feed my baby; I had to get him to latch on first, which would inevitably involve hysterical screaming on his part and my swollen, dripping boob flopping out in the middle of the café. I'm all for breast-feeding in public, but not the special brand of breastfeeding/sparring that was mine and Tom's. Instead of attempting to make it work, I dug out the bottle I'd made at home from the changing bag. I made a fist and tipped the bottle towards it, like Mum had taught me. A thin spray arced from the teat and landed in warm drops at the base of my thumb.

"Here," I said, plugging the grumbles with the teat of the bottle.

As I waited for Tom to drain his bottle and tried to eat without dropping baked beans on his face, I was aware of the eyes of the lady at the next table on me. I decided she was judging me for not breastfeeding, as that was the thing that I was judging myself for that day. As it turned out, she was judging me for the thing I'd been judging myself for for months. When her gaze felt physical, I turned to look at her and our eyes made contact.

"Are you married?" she said.

"Pardon?"

"Are you married?"

She looked down towards my left hand, which was holding the bottle. I followed her gaze.

"No." I took a sip of my coffee, which was scalding hot and burnt the tip of my tongue.

"Unmarried mothers."

I wanted to say "unmarried mothers what?" but I didn't. I just stared at Tom, who had almost polished off his milk.

"They're everywhere, these days."

I wanted to defend myself and all the other single mothers in the world, but I was still weakened by everything I'd been through, still hadn't stopped berating myself for my naivety. Also, how did she know that I was single? I mean, I could be unmarried but have a perfectly good partner out at work, waiting to hug us both when he got home.

"It's not fair on the poor kids," she was mumbling away to herself/me. I couldn't hear everything she said, but I picked up ugly chunks: ". . . no father figure. Off the rails. Selfish. Irresponsible . . ."

When Tom finished his bottle, I tipped him into a sitting position and he let out his wind in one huge, glorious belch.

"Good boy," I said, bundling him back into the pram.

". . . Never would have happened. Unmarried. My day. No man. Swanning around. Brazen. Poor child."

I got up as quickly as the stupid fixed furniture would let me, leaving most of the beans and coffee to go cold and the woman to her rant, grabbing a triangle of blackened toast to take with me. As I pushed the pram back out into the park, she was still shaking her head and tutting. Yes, I know I should have confronted her, or stubbornly stayed put and eaten my beans on toast, but all she had done had cemented my shame. I could deal with my own judgement, that was fine because it was all mine, but the judgement of others was too much.

Despite the fact we're in the 21st century now, the vilification of single mothers is a thing, especially in the right-wing press. The rise of the online article and the opportunity for anonymous comments beneath it is a breeding ground for toxic hatred. Single mothers are scroungers, fraudsters, criminals. If a woman who commits a crime also happens to be a single mum, that fact will usually snake its way into the headline. Women have a choice (in the UK, at least), and if they do have their baby, they're thankfully no longer forced to part with it before being locked up in an asylum, but single parents, who by the very nature of the beast are most likely to be mothers, are still demonised. Contraception fails, humans make human errors, people lie, people die, relationships break down, shit happens. Single mothers have probably already been through a fair amount of misery before they're confronted with the people who want to make them feel like society's fucked and they're to blame. Single mothers are blamed for spikes in youth crime rates, for failures at school, for children's poor health. It is always the single mothers, who are making the very best they can of a less-than-ideal situation, who are cited in these articles, never the absent fathers, invisible while the mother struggles and gets by.

That woman was the embodiment of many thousands of others who wouldn't dare say what she had to me beyond their own living rooms, or without the anonimity that the online comments section allows them. I don't know what made her so vocal: downright rudeness, anger or sadness at her own past experiences, maybe mental illness. Whatever it was, it helped me, later, when I was feeling stronger. It reminded me that people still think that way, and that I had to keep cracking on and proving them wrong.

Outside, chastised and shaken, I wheeled Tom into the aviary, where I'd spent many an awestruck afternoon as a child. There were gleaming golden pheasants, screeching peacocks and an enclosure filled with rabbits and guinea pigs.

"So, this is where the animals live," I told Tom.

His eyes were open, but he couldn't have seen anything from beneath the hood of his pram, so I lifted him out.

"Look," I said, shoving him in front of the pens, "that's a chicken, that's a turkey, that's a budgie."

Tom wasn't remotely interested, so I tucked him back into his pram, but I knew that in time he'd love animals and the noises they made. I couldn't wait to have an excuse to visit aquariums and farms and zoos, to show my son the creatures I loved, to be absolutely fascinated all over again.

PLEASE DO NOT THROW YOUR UNWANTED PETS OVER THE FENCE said the ancient, flaky sign on the rabbit and guinea-pig pen. I clung to the wire mesh and pressed my forehead against it, feeling hexagonal patterns pressing into my skin. Inside, a mouldy carrot lay half-nibbled on the concrete flags, but the animals were nowhere to be seen.

Tom sighed and dropped quickly off to sleep, all milky drunk. His little fingers waved at me over the top of the blanket I'd laid over him, hoping it would keep him at precisely the right temperature. The midwife had taught me to check, slotting two fingers between the poppers at the top of his sleep-suit, touching the soft skin of his sternum. I did it every time he was asleep, feeling a wash of relief at the rise and fall of his chest, as well as his temperature.

It was a bleak weekday, and no one was around. I glanced back over in the direction of the café, seeing the distorted silhouette of the woman though the wobble of old glass. Suddenly, I felt very lonely. Walks in the park with new babies were meant for couples, I thought. Mum was at work, my friends were in Manchester and Tom's father was God-knows-where. That fact was ever present, like the stubborn mustard stains on white babygrows, the ones I'd given up trying to wash out. It only got to me when I was on my own, but when it did, it really did. It was why I'd applied for child maintenance. Not because I was a greedy, selfish scrounger, or because I thought I'd get any money (if my memory served me correctly, he still owed me twenty quid), but because it was the only way I had of reaching him. Also, he'd told me, in one of his vitriolic emails, to take that route. He'd questioned whether the baby was his, which was a fair point, given the fact we were never officially 'together', but the authorities would take care of that. When the Child Support Agency contacts a non-resident parent, they can deny paternity and a DNA test happens. It's a horrible business, but I hoped that when the CSA got in touch, he would demand the test, see that the baby was definitely his and that things would shift. Despite the fury in the emails he'd sent, and his cowardliness, I couldn't forget the friend I'd had before any of this had happened. Throughout my pregnancy, I'd clung to the pale possibility of an epiphany and an apology after the birth; I didn't think he really would completely ignore his child's existence. I didn't want to be with Tom's father, but I wanted him to be in his son's life. My hope in opening a CSA case was that when he saw his son's name on an official letter, he might at least want to see him. The money wouldn't matter then; my baby would have a dad.

Until then, it was just a case of waiting: of hiding in bed and walks to the park, of hanging out in the smelly aviary. The male peacock was shrieking, the tall feathers in its fanned-out tail quivering and thrumming together. In the next enclosure, a slow, rhythmic knocking turned out to be the sound of a couple of tortoises getting it on. Then somebody wolf-whistled. I definitely was not in the mood for casual sexual harassment, so I buried my head under the pram hood, pretending to deal with a baby-related issue. The whistles happened again, though, and again. My curiosity got the better of me.

"Hello." The voice sounded like a poor quality recording of a Scouser. "Hello."

There had been a hint of scouse about the lady in the café, but it was the posh variety, with long O sounds and sharper Ks. This wasn't her; it sounded too kind.

"Hello?" I asked.

I began to wring the pram handle, wondering if it could be someone from my past: a colleague, an old friend, someone I really didn't feel like talking to about how I'd ended up back there, pushing a pram around that park.

"Hello."

The voice was definitely real. At least I thought it was. I remembered the lift-shaft incident. If exhaustion could make me feel like I was falling down a lift shaft, perhaps I'd become capable of hearing things that weren't really there. Or maybe I'd become so lonely that I'd invented a companion, like a child with an imaginary friend.

"Hi, who is it?"

"Hello, love."

The voice was comforting and I could tell now that it was coming from my left, where there was nothing but an aviary. And the person talking to me was not a person but a parrot.

"Hi," I said, moving closer to its enclosure, beyond delighted. "What else can you say?"

It eyed me suspiciously, rolling its thick, rubbery tongue in its lethal-looking beak. I put my fingers through the gaps in the cage and pulled them out again when it started to climb towards me, its claws gripping the bars like Tom on my index finger.

"Hello."

"Hello."

"Hello."

"Hello."

"Humpty Dumpty sat on the wall," it said, nodding its head.

"Humpty Dumpty had a great fall," I said, quietly, trying to remember the rest of the words, realising that nursery rhymes would soon be familiar to me again.

Just then, the first, fat dollop of a heavy downpour hit the back of my neck. I grappled with the fastenings on the pram's plastic cover and pulled up the hood of my jacket.

"I've got to go now," I said. "Nice to meet you."

The parrot said nothing, but it did wolf-whistle as I walked away.

Thirty-one

"**I**'LL BABYSIT, IF you like. You and Anna could go out."

Mum's words were magic. Tom was a month old, Anna was coming to visit and I was going to be able to leave the house at night time, something I had genuinely believed would never be possible again.

"You look gorgeous," said Anna.

She was standing at the bottom of the stairs waiting for me, like people do for brides.

"I don't," I said, "but thanks."

I had just spent half an hour trying to stuff the grotesque flap of stripy skin left from my caesarean into a new pair of skinny jeans. The first time I'd seen it was in the hospital, the day after I gave birth. A nurse held on to me as I walked, with jelly legs, down the corridor to the bathroom. I could see her silhouette behind the thin pink curtain as I turned the tap on, a small movement that unexpectedly hurt my tummy.

"I'm here if you need me, honey," the nurse said, gently. "Just try not to get any soap on your stitches."

I was afraid to look down because I was worried I'd see the wound. I've never been very squeamish, but seeing where my own flesh had just been sewn together might be too much. Then the sponge slid out of my hands and landed in the shower tray with the swirling soap suds and blood. Bending down to pick it up would have been impossible, but my instinct was to look down. I needn't have worried about seeing the scar, because it was hidden under acres of wobbly, wrinkled skin.

I gasped, grasping the tap to steady myself.

"Do you want to get out now, love?" asked the nurse.

I did.

The books had warned me about an 'apron' left behind by the surgery, but I didn't know what they were on about.

Now I did. The only difference between an apron and that thing was that you could take an apron off and iron out the creases.

"Well, you look better than you did last time I saw you," said Anna.

"Oh yeah," I said, "the nipple and the spoon. How could I forget?"

Anna had timed her visit to me in hospital perfectly with the moment the midwife was milking me on to a teaspoon. She did an incredible job of maintaining eye contact and keeping a straight face. She also gave me a bag filled with the best presents: a roaring toy lion for Tom, and for me, books, magazines, a peace lily, which felt symbolic (until I killed it when Tom was four), and the Arctic Monkeys album.

"Is this alright?" I asked in the taxi, having tentatively kissed Tom goodbye. "Going out, I mean, and drinking."

I'd made the mistake of going on Motherboard and asking for information about 'pumping and dumping' ahead of the night out. My polite enquiry into how long one should refrain from breastfeeding after consuming alcohol declared open season on me and my morals.

WTF? IMHO *you should not be going for a night out when your child is so young.*

My DP would not be happy if I said I wanted to go out while my LO was so young, especially without him. What does your DP say?

Your LO comes first. Is it fair to deprive him of his food so that you can get drunk? Unbelievable. No wonder this country is going to hell in a basket.

"Course it's alright," said Anna, squeezing my hand. "It's not like we're going on a massive bender. No one has ever needed a night out more than you do now."

We headed in to Southport, to the only bar I suspected might play decent music. When I stepped past the bouncer and through the doorway of the bar formerly known as The Dungeon, I felt as elated as I used to when I pulled off the same trick at sixteen.

Thankfully, they'd got rid of the cobwebs, stocks and dismembered waxwork bodies that used to adorn the place. It still smelt of the same mixture of damp and booze, though, and I could still taste the one pound tequila slammers. Someone had thoughtfully turned the place into Southport's first and only indie bar, complete with seventies wallpaper and egg chairs. It would have been good were it not for the tinniness of the sound system and the fact that everybody else in there was about twelve.

Two drinks later, I didn't care about the sound quality, or the age of the other patrons. Anna had requested The Strokes and I was bouncing around and hugging her tight.

"I can't believe I had a BABY," I shouted into her ear.

"I know, I'm DEAD PROUD OF YOU, LOVE."

"Hang on, I need a sit down."

Turns out dancing hurts when you're wearing two-sizes-too-small skinny jeans that fasten right on a not-quite healed caesarean scar. Anna and I claimed a couple of egg chairs with our coats and did one song off and one song on, until they played 'Atomic' and 'Paint it Black' back-to-back and I had no choice but to keep dancing to them both and ended up in the loos, undoing my flies to relieve the pressure.

"Em, what are you doing?" Five minutes later, Anna's voice echoed off the cold cubicles. "You left me for dead out there. I had to fend off a fifteen-year-old boy."

"Sorry. I needed a wee. And to check my breast pads."

"Are they alright then, your breast pads?"

"Yes, they're fine, thanks; rustling a lot. And itching a bit, but otherwise good."

"And how about you?"

"Yeah, I'm good, thanks."

"Are you sure? You don't fancy *going home* or anything like that?"

"You're joking, aren't you?! This is our BIG NIGHT OUT! We've been waiting for this for NINE MONTHS."

"OK, Em."

I took out my camera phone, sifting through the photographs I'd taken in recent days: Tom drinking his bottle, Tom in his baby gym, Tom in the bath, Tom propped up on my pillow, looking like a Buddha.

Being drunk dulls your physical senses but heightens your emotions, and the combination of the alcohol and being in a place I'd known in another life had cranked up my disbelief at what had just happened.

"He'll be due his night feed soon," I said.

"Do you want to go and see him? I honestly don't mind. No offence, but it's not as if we're having the best night ever in here."

"No, we'll stay," I said. "We've got to!"

"Alright, then, whatever you want."

We got to the bottom of the stairs and they started playing The Kaiser Chiefs.

"Actually, is it alright if we just go home and see Tom?"

"Yes," said Anna, "let's do one."

I was well rehearsed into sneaking back into Mum's house in the dead of night, but I hadn't done it since my late teens. Slowly, quietly, I opened the porch, remembering the peculiar creek of the uPVC frame. I carefully unlocked the front door, stopping the keyrings on the bunch from knocking against the brass lock. At the bottom of the stairs, Anna and I shrugged off our coats and draped them over the banister, whispering about glasses of water.

"Em?"

The silence had been in vain; Mum's voice came muffled from her room upstairs.

"Hi, Mum."

"Hi," she called back. "Feeding time!"

Mum was propped up with pillows on her bed, and Tom was bundled in her arms, making the happy gasps he did when he was fed. When he was done and winded, we passed him around, studying in utter wonderment his eclectic facial expressions, his disproportionately long eyelashes, his miniature ears.

"So, how was your night?" Mum asked.

"It was good, yeah."

"Worth the wait?"

"Yeah, thanks so much for babysitting, Mum, it meant loads to go out again."

But Anna and I both knew that the best part of the night

was that bit, right then, sitting on Mum's bed, sipping water and taking turns to hold the small, warm heft of my new baby boy.

Thirty-two

THE VERY FIRST expression on Tom's face was anger; a deep, cross scowl.

How dare you bring me on to this planet?

Sorry, I wanted to say back to him, completely at his mercy.

For the first few weeks of having a baby, all anyone gets are dirty looks.

When Tom was tiny, I listened to the Arctic Monkeys album that Anna had brought me in the hospital a lot. 'Mardy Bum' by the Arctic Monkeys became his lullaby, the song I'd sing to him in the kitchen after a lost breastfeeding battle, while I waited for the kettle to boil and then sat the hot bottle in a jug of cold water, willing it to hurry up and cool down. It was a song about a girlfriend in a mood, but it suited my newborn baby. No matter what I did for him, all he did was frown at me or eye me suspiciously, even when I changed his nappy.

Changing nappies: the one thing I had been dreading more than actually giving birth. For months, the image I'd had in my head of my future had involved me, nappies and shit.

"We'll change his nappy for you, until you can get out of bed, don't you worry about that," said the nurse, the day after I had given birth.

I was thrilled: I got to miss the first one, which famously looks like tar. The epidural had totally been worth it, I thought; no one tells you that you could get away with not having to change nappies when you're considering your pain relief options.

The following day, though, I was given my first and only nappy-changing lesson, after which I was on my own.

After my first disastrous attempt, I learnt to grab the baby by the ankles like a dead game bird and elevate the lower half of him high above the changing mat. As the weeks wore on, I became deft at the magic trick of swiping away the mess, bundling it into a nappy sack, tying it into a knot and chucking it in the bin. I quickly became an expert, completing the whole routine with the flourish of the midwife who'd taught me. I learnt to change nappies everywhere, a process that got easier when my caesarean wound had fully healed. But my strongest memories are at the changing mat in my bedroom, underneath the small window, overlooking the sleepiness of Mum's street, in daylight, or at night, by the light of the street lamp at the end of our drive.

New baby shit doesn't smell horrible, by the way; it's somehow sweet and inoffensive and combines perfectly with the scent of baby wipes and powder. And I wasn't being biased either – I still get nostalgic when I smell the stuff now.

When Tom was about six weeks old, after I'd finished changing his nappy and he was lying in front of me on the changing mat in all his podgy glory, he screwed up the entire right side of his face, breathing hard, as though he was really exerting himself, and smiled.

The smile had been brewing for a few days, but nothing could prepare me for how good I would feel when it finally happened. It confirmed a number of things: a) Tom was a real human being, b) he appeared to like me, c) he was happy. No more guessing or dirty looks: my child was pleased, I must have been doing things right.

And so it came to be that some of my happiest memories of Tom's babyhood were at the changing mat, once I'd swiftly cleared away the mess. It was where I watched him grow and change, where he lay on his front and lifted his head for the first time, where I squished his irresistible legs when they got so magnificently fat that it looked like he had elastic bands around his thighs. It was where I blew raspberries on his stomach and sung to him and stroked his soft, dimpled flesh. It was where, a few weeks after the smile, I got the chuckle: a raucous belly laugh that shook his entire body and had me making all kinds of ridiculous faces in a desperate attempt to make him do it again.

Nappy changing, it emerged, was an absolute joy.

Thirty-three

"WOULDN'T IT BE lovely if your mummy made friends with some other mummies? Then you could make some little friends of your own!"

Tom grinned inanely and made an adorable noise.

The Health Visitor was talking to me through the baby again. She did it every time she visited, which was frequently, and the only time I bothered to get properly dressed, wash and blow-dry my hair, put on a bit of make-up.

"Doesn't your mummy look lovely today? You've got a lovely mummy, haven't you? You're a very lucky boy."

The lift-shaft incident, a history of depression and my less-than-ideal circumstances meant that I was being closely watched. I received regular visits from the Health Visitor, during which she fed me copious compliments on my sketchy mothering (via Tom), and told me to fill in the Edinburgh Scale.

The Edinburgh Scale is a questionnaire designed to identify signs of postnatal depression. There are ten statements and you have to answer each one by ticking a box that indicates to what degree the statement applies to you. The higher your overall score, the more depressive symptoms you have. I completely understood why I had to fill it in, and was grateful for the care Tom and I were receiving, but the questions were hard to honestly and accurately answer from inside the maelstrom of new motherhood.

Things have been getting on top of me
Dirty nappies
Wet nappies
Clean nappies
Crying
Small, filthy clothes
Sterilising
Bottles
Formula
Guilt
Crying
Antibiotics
Clean, wet clothes
Breast pads
Guilt
Lochia (postnatal bleeding)
Constipation
Sanitary pads
Crying
Teats
Baths
Guilt
Stitches
Crying
The strange case of the missing father
Crying
The strange case of the missing mains lead for the breast
pump
Crying
The breast pump
A lack of breast milk

Guilt

Crying

Yes.

I have been so unhappy that I have been crying

See above. (The baby wasn't the only one crying).

I look forward to things with enjoyment

Yes, but only the next stretch of sleep because I can't really see beyond that.

I felt like I was being tested and that everything was a trick question. Depression was an old acquaintance of mine, a cruel beast that I was aware of, lurking just around the corner in its vicious, postnatal form. As the weeks after birth unfolded, Tom became smiley and I got into motherhood, it seemed less of a threat, but it was very much still there. I was determined to give it the slip, but also aware that, at times, it was catching up with me and wrestling me, albeit temporarily, to the ground.

Most crucially of all, the Edinburgh Scale asks whether you've considered harming yourself. Thankfully, that was easy to answer because I hadn't. Had I been asked the same questions in the immediate aftermath of finding out I was pregnant, I would have hovered my pen nib over the boxes and wondered which one to tick. Pregnancy had been traumatic, and I had built up motherhood to be a horrific thing in my mind. As it happened, it was alright, and I really liked my baby. Also, as each day and night passed, I was amazed to discover that I wasn't totally fucking up. Did I suffer from antenatal depression? Almost certainly. Do I wish I sought help back then? Absolutely. But it was too late by the time Tom was on the outside, so I had to just keep muddling through, grateful for the knowledge that if the depression did catch up with me, there were plenty of people around ready to help me ward it off.

One of the things the Health Visitor was most concerned about was my reluctance to leave the house. My first experience of doing so hadn't been exactly positive. Although I knew the woman in the café's comments were bigoted, they came back to haunt me occasionally.

One Sunday afternoon, when the evenings were still cool and dingy, Mum wrapped me and Tom up and drove us to the pier. We ate fish and chips and watched the multicoloured sunset and pushed the pram along the wooden boards and life outside felt okay, but I knew that when Mum went back to work the following day, I'd be scared to get out of bed again.

"Your mummy needs to meet some other mummies, doesn't she?"

I didn't know how to tell the Health Visitor that I did not want to meet any other bloody mummies. My entire life was spent with a baby; the last thing I wanted to do was go and sit in a room with a load more babies, and their parents, who I guessed lived on a totally different planet to me, and talk about babies. All I wanted was to get on the train to Manchester and go to the pub and talk about politics or music or anything that wasn't being a mummy, with anyone who wasn't a mummy.

"It'll be good for you and your mummy to go and get some nice fresh air, won't it?"

"I do take him out. I take him to the park. Mum and I took him to the pier."

"That's very good, isn't it? But your mummy could make some lovely friends."

"I don't want to do it!" I said, sounding and feeling like I did when I was twelve and on my period and wearing a massive, rustling sanitary pad and my PE teacher was trying to make me do PE in gym knickers with nothing over the top. "I just do not want to go to the mummy groups."

I was fighting tears. Despite my moments of uncertainty, my biggest fear was somehow having Tom taken off me. I had to hold it together in front of the Health Visitor.

"Just try it," she said, finally addressing me and not the baby. "You have to at least try."

She got through to me then. Living at home was my lot, and I had to accept it. Wishing I was in a student bar nearly forty miles away was a pointless struggle with myself, and I'd had enough of those. Maybe there would be another single mother at the group, another woman who didn't call herself a 'yummy mummy', another person who was as clueless and petrified as I was. Maybe there'd be someone who was all three.

"Will you try it, Emily?"

The Health Visitor proffered a flyer in front of me like it was something medicinal.

Thursday Morning Mum's n Tots
Meet Other Mum's. Ask the health visitor.
Coffee and biscuits. Toys n juice.
10am in the Parish Hall.

I immediately recoiled at the font and the apostrophes, before reminding myself that I was supposed to be opening my mind about all this. My kindred spirit could be waiting for me and I would never know unless I braved the church hall.

So I went to Thursday Morning Mum's n Tots.

I was late, but the other mums would understand, I told myself, as I huffed and puffed along the main road, stopping every few paces to hitch up my maternity jeans. It was the first hot day of the year; the one when cars blast out crap music and everyone puts on shorts and goes to a beer garden then freezes as soon as the sun goes down. I hadn't realised this until I'd made it out of the house, when I had to promptly go back inside again to smother Tom in sun cream and put a floppy bucket hat on his head that made him look like a miniature Stone Roses fan. As I adjusted the unwieldy parasol on the pram, he noisily filled his nappy and we had to go back inside again. If anyone knew what it was like to get caught out by a full nappy on the way out of the door, it would be the other mothers, I thought. Despite all my misgivings about baby talk, I was looking forward to spending time with people who at least understood.

The last time I'd been in this particular church hall must have been fifteen years earlier, for an aerobics class. One sniff of the mix of must and disinfectant and I was doing star jumps to Salt-N-Pepa's 'Push It'. Except I wasn't: I was trying to manoeuvre my great hulk of a pram (which probably hailed from the same era as Salt-N-Pepa) into a mother-and-baby meeting. And the other mothers were sitting in a circle, eyeing me like I'd just swung into the wrong saloon.

Once I had got through the door, I realised that there were actually only two other mothers, as well as a uniformed Health Visitor, who was not the one I knew and hated/loved. On the other side of the hall, a tribe of older children in matching England football kits were swiping at each other with plastic swords.

"Are you here for the baby group?" asked the Health Visitor.

"Yes."

I thought that would have been obvious; maybe I didn't look like I was supposed to be a mother, even when I was pushing a pram.

"It's just that we usually start at half past ten."

She grimaced, looking at the clock at the front of the hall; the one I used to will to go faster when aerobics class got too much.

"I know. Sorry. Dirty nappy. Just as we were about to leave, too! You know what it's like."

I looked at the other mothers, both of whom were bobbing babies on their knees. Neither of them smiled.

"We'll let you off, just this once," said the Health Visitor, laughing nervously. "I'm June, by the way."

"Hi."

"Go on then," said one of the other mothers, "aren't you going to introduce yourself?"

"Yeah. Sorry. Right."

I scooped Tom out of the pram and perched on one of the tiny, Sunday School chairs, worrying fleetingly that it might collapse.

"This is Tom," I said, "and I'm Emily."

"And how old is Tom?" asked the Health Visitor.

"Seven weeks."

I wondered how long I would have to keep counting everything in weeks.

"Bloody hell, what are you feeding him?!" shrieked one of the other mothers.

"He's a right bruiser, isn't he?"

"Fi!" the other woman said, trying to stifle giggles.

"Oops, there I go again! I'm always saying what I think, me. I'm Fiona, by the way and this is Ruby Roo."

In case anyone was in any doubt that Ruby Roo was a female, Fiona had lovingly strapped a pink, fabric gerbera to her downy head. The gerbera was almost twice the size of the head.

"Hello, Fiona," I said, "hello Ruby Roo."

"Actually, it's just Ruby to you. Only me and your daddy call you Ruby Roo, don't we, darling?"

"Oh. Right."

"Anyway, I'm Karen," said the other mother, beaming, "and this is Cameron, my grumpy little man."

"Hi. Karen, Cameron."

"The other four are mine too," Karen continued, nodding towards the swordfight that was still happening at the other side of the room, "and before you ask, no: hubby isn't getting the snip. I'm not stopping until I get my little princess!"

"OK."

"Emily," June said, clapping her hands together, "before you arrived, we were having a little chat about sun safety. How do you keep Tom safe in the sun?"

"Well, we've not really had much sun until today, have we?" I omitted the fact that I had hardly left the house since giving birth.

"No, but the sun here can be just as strong and powerful as the sun in hot places," June said.

"Yeah," said Fi, "more dangerous too, when the clouds are covering it."

Everyone nodded.

"Yes, I know that. Well, I suppose from now on I will keep

him out of the sun. And if we have to go out in it, I will keep him covered up, especially his head, and use baby sun block on the bits that are exposed."

"Ooh, Emily," June was shaking her head, "you shouldn't really be using sun block on Tom while he's so tiny, even the baby stuff."

"Right, OK."

"Has he got it on today, Emily?"

I thought of lying, but I glanced down and saw that Tom's chubby legs looked like they'd been daubed in white emulsion.

"Yes. I won't do it again though."

Promise, Mum.

"Jolly good. Best to wait until he's six months old for that. Until then, just keep him out of the sun."

The other mothers mumbled and nodded in agreement.

"He's got his parasol," I said, "and his hat."

I took off the bucket hat and dangled it in the air.

"God, he's like you, isn't he?" said Fiona. "Same shaped face."

Just the day before, I'd sent a picture of him to Alex and she'd replied telling me he looked like a space hopper . . . *He's a very cute space hopper, though* she sent, a few minutes later.

"Yes, just like me," I sighed, fantasising about running away but realising that Tom and the tank pram meant it wouldn't be that simple.

"Doesn't he look *anything* like your hubby?" asked Karen.

"Oh, no. I'm not married."

"Well, you know what I mean, your other half. Does he look like him?"

"No, not really."

I'd worried about it a lot when I was pregnant, wondering

if I was going to give birth to a miniature version of the man who wanted nothing to do with him. Someone had told me that newborn babies looked more like their fathers, an evolutionary trick to make them less inclined to do a runner, which would have been too late for us, anyway. Tom didn't look anything like him though, apart from perhaps his eyebrows, which swung out of the side of his temples like wings. And blue eyes, which I had too, and most newborn babies had. I'd come to the relieved conclusion that skinny and stubbly with long hair just didn't translate very well to baby. Tom might grow up to look more like his father, but for now, he was round and blonde, like me.

"Ooh, other halves," said June. "That reminds me! Next week we've got a very special visitor coming in. She's a marriage guidance counsellor and she's going to talk to us about how the arrival of Baby can affect our relationships."

"Oh, perfect!" boomed Karen. "I hope she's got all bloody day!"

"Tell me about it," said Fiona. "I might drag Dave here with me!"

"What about you, Emily, will you be coming?" asked June.

"I don't think so," I said, rolling the balls of Tom's feet between my fingers and thumbs.

"Oh, come on, we've not scared you off, have we?" said Fiona.

"No it's not that—"

"Just come, then!"

"Yeah, come on, it'll be a laugh!" said Karen.

"Hubby will thank you," laughed Fiona.

"I'm not married. Like I said."

"Oh, alright, then: partner, boyfriend, live-in lover, whatever you call him."

"I don't have one of those, either," I said, feeling some kind of rebellious rush as I decided to just fuck it and be upfront.

"Well where did he come from then?" Fiona screeched. "He wasn't the bloody Immaculate Conception, was he?!"

She guffawed at her own joke and Karen joined in. It took a few seconds for them to notice June's glare and realise they needed to shut up.

"Sorry!" Fiona said. "How was I supposed to know?"

I didn't say anything as I lay Tom in the pram and kicked off the brake.

"Ooh, it's a big old thing, that, isn't it?" Karen said, nodding at the pram. "Would you like some help getting out?"

"No, you're alright," I said, slamming the hefty fire door open with my arse.

When I had made it far enough down the road, I mopped up my tears with the bucket hat.

"Sorry," I said, plonking it back on Tom's head. "It'll soon dry in this heat."

He smiled at me, a bubble of spit popping on his lips. I smiled back, put my earphones in and pounded the tarmac in time to songs I used to dance to. I kept going until he was asleep and I was at the aviary. I leaned against the mesh and clung to it, like a cartoon prisoner at the bars of a cell.

"Hello?"

The Scouse parrot came flitting out of its house straight away, a majestic flicker of red and green. I had a hundred things to tell it. And it listened to them all.

Thirty-four

THE PARROT WAS a good listener and Tom's comedy smiles were endlessly entertaining, but I missed people. Adult ones, anyway. Friends from Manchester came to visit bearing gifts for us both, and I'd be proud and ecstatic for the day, but miserable when they left again. The highlight of my week became a trip to my brilliant counsellor, a free service provided by the local Surestart Centre. For one hour, Tom got to lie on the floor and play with a trove of crinkly, jingling toys, while I wondered out loud where the hell his father was, if I would realistically ever return to uni, or whether I would ever have sex again. An excellent charity, Homestart, also provided me with an amazing volunteer, who would come and visit once a week and take Tom and me out for walks or trips to the shops.

Still, everyone thought I should be hanging out with the other mothers. Even my counsellor, who up until that point, I'd thought was on my side.

"You'll have so much in common with the other mums," she said.

"No I won't. I won't have anything in common with them apart from the fact we have all given birth, and I didn't even manage to make a proper job of that."

"You don't know that unless you try."

She was normally so patient with me, but I could feel her getting annoyed with my point-blank refusal.

"The last mother and baby group scarred me for life," I said.

"Well, you can't form an opinion on all mother-and-baby groups based on that one. Just give another one a try, please?"

I agreed because I liked her

"We're going to baby yoga tomorrow," I told Mum.

"Ooh lovely, sounds right up your street. You love yoga, don't you? I bought you a video once."

"Mum, that was about five years ago. Back when I was young and supple."

"You're still young. And anyway you're a vegetarian! Everyone knows vegetarians like yoga. Hopefully the mums will be your type."

"It's Tom who does the yoga, not me. And those mums intimidate me more than the yummy ones. They're all co-sleeping and breastfeeding and being sanctimonious."

"Make your bloody mind up," Mum said.

When I wrestled my tank pram into the community centre the following morning, the circle of women in front of me turned and looked at me like I'd just farted at a wedding.

"Sorry," I said, "should I have left my pram outside?"

"Well, it is *rather large*," said the woman who looked like she was in charge.

"I know. Look, I'll put it with the others. Where are they?"

"Most of us *wear* our babies," said one woman.

"Right."

"And the rest of us just come in the car," said another.

"OK, well I'm sorry I'm late; I thought I was on time, to be honest."

"We try to arrive at least ten minutes early, to prepare. It helps if we can all centre before we begin," said the instructor.

"Right. I just went off the time on the leaflet."

"If you'd just like to sit down and lie your baby on a mat in front of you, we can carry on."

"OK, yeah."

I muscled in between another mother and baby and the instructor, who was demonstrating on a floppy, manic-looking doll. When I laid Tom down, he smiled at it.

"Ha, look, he's smiling at the doll. He thinks it's another person!" I said.

Nothing.

Baby yoga should be called baby origami. Eventually, when it gets really good, you can make your baby into a crane or a whale or a frog.

Babies are remarkably flexible for such fat things. If ever you're bored and you have the opportunity, you should try poking a baby in the nostril with its own big toe. "Can You Touch Your Nose With Your Toes?" was one of our favourite games.

"I could probably do with yoga more than him," I said, as I rolled Tom's bottom off the mat and curled it back down again.

"I'm sorry," sighed the woman next to me, without a hint of remorse, "but it's so boring when women complain about their baby weight and do nothing about it. I've got no sympathy. Don't eat for two and if you already have, do something about it. I put on three stone with my first, so I got a personal trainer. It's not rocket science.

A personal trainer.

"That might sound harsh, but I speak the truth."

"Right."

Just what I needed: another woman who prided herself on her brutal honesty.

After class, I committed the cardinal sin of asking to go to the kitchen so I could heat up a bottle for Tom, while everyone else just breastfed. By the time I reentered the circle, Tom was hysterical.

"This is why breastfeeding is just *so much easier*."

"Actually, I do breastfeed: in the morning and last thing at night."

"I don't understand." Another of the mothers was shaking her head slowly and narrowing her eyes. "Why don't you breastfeed him all the time?"

"We had a lot of problems and in the end that's how things worked out."

"What sort of problems?" asked the instructor, whose name I hadn't even been told.

"He just didn't want to do it, so in the end I wasn't producing enough milk."

"You do *know* that the more they feed, the more milk you produce, don't you?"

Jesus.

"Yes, but he wouldn't do it."

"Hmm, it can be hard in the beginning. You really do have to *persevere* though. If you really *want* to breastfeed, that is. I found it very difficult, but I just kept going."

There followed a conversation about siblings, waiting lists for primary schools, maternity leave, nappies, weaning, routine, slings, sick bugs and chicken pox.

"My hubby's just getting so sick of the crying at night when he has to be up for work in the morning, but he says we should try for Number Three soon, get it all out of the way in one go. That way I won't have to go back to work for long."

"Yes, my hubby says we'll just have one more and that'll be it."

"What about you?" One of the mums turned to me. "Do you think you'll try for another one?"

"Oh, I doubt it," I said, unable to even begin to imagine going through it all again, even if it were an option, "one's enough for me."

"You might change your mind in a year or so. What does your hubby say?" asked the personal trainer woman.

"Oh, I'm not married."

I'm almost certain she'd checked out my ring finger already and knew damn well I didn't have a hubby.

"Oh, sorry, your boyfriend, then?"

Here we go again.

"Well, I don't have one. So I can't have a baby anytime soon. So I guess that decision's been made for me."

"Oh *dear*," the woman said, cocking her head to one side in an attempt to look sympathetic.

There was an awkward silence, broken by the instructor.

"So! Who do we think is going to get a little toothy peg first?"

"Ooh, could it be Flora, or do we think Benjamin will pip her to the post?"

"I think we should have a boy winner and a girl winner."

Apparently, there was a race to see who could successfully cultivate a tooth in their baby's gums first.

"I'm not looking forward to him teething," I said.

"Oh, it's not too bad," said the instructor. "There's Calpol and Bonjela and those teething salts are meant to be very good."

"Teething salts?"

"Yes. It's like a little packet of white powder. You just put it on to the tip of your finger and rub it on to their gums."

"Oh, like cocaine?"

That's what I said, without thinking, in the baby yoga circle.

Silence, save for the sound of suckling babies and a couple of gasps.

"Well, it's like dentists, isn't it? They used to use cocaine, didn't they? To numb people's gums."

I threw out a nervous laugh, hoping someone would catch it.

Come on, guys.

But it just floated away, leaving me sitting there like an idiot who compares baby medicine to Class A drugs in front of people whose sense of humour got incinerated with their placenta. Assuming they didn't eat it, that is.

"I'll pretend I didn't hear that," hissed the instructor.

And that was the last time I went to baby yoga.

Namaste.

Thirty-five

ONE EVENING, ALMOST exactly a year to the day I found out I was pregnant, I did something really bad.

Hannah had come home from university for the summer to work her holiday job in a clothes shop. Tom had been sleeping in her room, but her arrival meant the cot crossing the landing and him coming back in with me. That wasn't the problem, though: it was more Hannah's presence and the tension it caused. Hannah had done nothing wrong and clearly loved Tom, but we were typical sisters in that there was always a degree of rivalry between us. She resented me for hanging round the house all day while she and Mum went out to work. I resented her for choosing to live with us when she could have been living the life of freedom I craved at her student flat in Leeds.

I was feeling trapped, and my mood dipped even more when I received a letter from the Child Support Agency: Tom's father had been located, but he was claiming benefits, meaning the maximum amount he was legally obliged to pay was five pounds per week. My plan to yank his head out of the sand had backfired. As I read the letter and re-read it again, I realised that there was no way he was ever going to get in touch, demand a DNA test, or ask to see Tom when he could forget the whole thing had ever happened for the bargain price of a fiver a week.

The hope that had hovered in front of me as I'd pushed

the pram in endless figures-of-eight around the park had vanished. I imagined the fivers, equally spaced apart, hung out on a washing line that stretched ahead like bunting, ending only when Tom reached eighteen. They would all add up, if I put them in a savings account for him, but they wouldn't buy him a dad.

Something about the time of year, too, was drawing emotions to the surface. It was humid, like it had been twelve months earlier, when I was free and daft, before I could have imagined living at Mum's and being a mother myself. The wholeness of the year made me reflect on everything that had happened, and not in a celebratory way.

That afternoon, Mum and Hannah came home from a shopping trip. Hannah walked into the kitchen and said an *Ohmygod* that made it sound as though she had found a dead body. What she'd actually found was the evidence of my day: a washing machine spewing damp baby-wear, rows of foggy bottles awaiting sterilisation and my failed attempt at making a healthy smoothie, splattered all over the hob and the kitchen worktops.

"I'm sorry," I pleaded, wishing I'd tidied it up instead of joining Tom for his afternoon nap.

Angry Mum I could handle, but Angry Mum and Angry Hannah together were a force to be reckoned with.

"You're lazy," she snapped, buzzing around the kitchen, picking things up, "and this is disgusting."

"I let you move in here rent-free, Emily, *rent-free!*" Mum joined in.

"I'm sorry," I said, grabbing a spoon off the worktop and wondering where to put it.

"Where's Tom?"

"He's upstairs. Having his afternoon nap."

"Well, why haven't you woken him? It's teatime. He'll never go to sleep tonight now. I keep telling you, Emily: that baby needs a *routine*."

I swore at them both as I threw the spoon across the kitchen. It landed on the fridge door, denting it and cutting a gash in the photograph of Nan that was stuck there, right on her neck. It ricocheted off the fridge and landed somewhere on Hannah, making her scream. Mum ran over to her like a shot, asking her if she was OK.

Then I walked out. I never would have done it were it not for the fact my mother was there to look after Tom, but that doesn't make it any better. In fact, it probably makes it worse, given that I'd just trashed her kitchen. I grabbed my purse from my bag on the way out, and went to the corner shop where I bought a packet of cigarettes and a lighter, then I went to the park and I told the Scouse parrot everything, then I sat at a picnic bench, chain-smoking and being devoured by midges and tried not to look at the snogging teenagers on the next bench, until it was dusk and the park keeper threw me out and I had nowhere to go apart from the pub, which I knew, deep down, wasn't a good idea.

When I got home, Mum and Hannah were in the living room.

"Don't worry," Hannah called, "we fed your baby."

". . . and put him to bed," said Mum.

I leaned on the door frame, facing Mum but not Hannah, who was conveniently on the sofa out of my line of vision.

"I'm really, really sorry," I said.

"Don't you ever, ever do that again," said Mum, not looking up from the telly.

"I won't."

"And never leave my kitchen in that state again, either."

"I won't."

I went upstairs to my room and sat down cross-legged next to the cot, where Tom was sleeping. The window was open and I could hear the high-pitched hum of insects overhead. I wanted to protect him from their bites, from the heat, from everything. Through the wooden bars, I stroked his fat-roll wrists and whispered that I was sorry. I was sorry for walking out, sorry for being a bad mother, and so, so sorry that his father didn't want to know.

Thirty-six

THE FOLLOWING DAY, it was almost evening before Tom and I were ready to leave the house and it was clean enough not to annoy Hannah and Mum, who were due home from work.

After a bus and a train, we arrived at our destination just in time for the sunset. I pushed the pram quickly along the avenue of gargantuan mansions, my eye on the orange horizon. When the tarmac gave way to sand dunes, I tried to keep pushing the pram, but it sank, getting stuck on tussocks of sea grass. I kicked off my shoes, lifted Tom out of the pram and wrapped him in a blanket.

"There they are, Mister," I whispered into his ear. "*The Iron Men.*"

The Iron Men was the locals' name for *Another Place*, an art installation by Antony Gormley on Crosby Beach. One hundred cast-iron sculptures of the artist himself, naked, are spaced out along the sand, staring out across the Irish Sea.

The first time I'd encountered *The Iron Men* was the day before I got pregnant, when we'd been to visit Nan in the nursing home. Mum, Hannah and I had extracted Nan from the stuffy chaos and brought her down to the seafront for ice cream. Only a few of the statues were in situ that sunny day, with the rest piled like corpses in the car park. While Hannah helped Nan eat her ice cream, I walked down to the ones that were already standing. Some of them were wearing seaweed wigs, one was sporting a cricket shirt, families were posing with them. I took my camera out and began to photograph them.

I loved the fact they were not in a gallery, not roped off from the public. Anyone could touch them, take pictures of them, interact with them. Scores of people who would never have gone to see an art exhibition were enjoying one, on a beach on the outskirts of Liverpool, on a perfect midsummer day.

"There's outcry in the local press, you know," Mum said. "People think it's a waste of public money."

"I'd tell them to come down here and look at this," I said, watching small children chase each other, weaving in and out of the sculptures.

I made up my mind then that I would write my dissertation about *Another Place* and the controversy surrounding it.

"Why don't you stay at mine tonight like Hannah?" Mum said, as we left the nursing home. "We could have some tea in Liverpool."

"I need to go back to Manchester," I said. "I'm meeting someone."

"Oh yeah, who? You've not stopped looking at your phone all afternoon."

"Just a friend," I said. "No one."

I hadn't been back to the beach since that day; I didn't fancy fighting against the wild sea winds when I was pregnant and it was winter. And I hadn't wanted to think about the significance of it all: that place, that day, how pivotal it was.

It was hard work walking up the steep dune with nothing to pull myself up; the sand was runny and my feet kept sinking into the cool, beige grains. I clutched Tom to my hip, where he fitted perfectly, clinging to me like a monkey. When I was pregnant, I worried I wouldn't know how to hold him, but when he was born, I just did. I had always been confident in handling Tom, from the delicate warmth of his newborn form, to then, when he was a big chunky thing, capable of lifting his head and looking all around.

"Here we are," I huffed, when we finally made it to the top, like we'd just scaled Mount Everest.

The statues had changed since the last time I'd seen them: some of them were up to their knees in sand, some were head-and-shoulders above the sea, most were caked in barnacles. I half-walked-half-slid down the other side of the dune on to the wet sand below. It had been a hot day, but the shallow pools of sea water were icy on my bare feet. The tide was low, and the sand lay in watery patterns that looked like the skin on my stretch-marked stomach.

"Here, look," I said, holding Tom face-to-rusty-face with one of the Gormleys.

He jutted out his bottom lip, looked absolutely devastated, and began to wail. On reflection, it probably was a bit much to expect of him to be enamoured by a featureless, rusty face when the only inanimate creatures he was familiar with were soft toys.

"Oh shit, no," I said, "don't be scared of him. He's a goody. They all are – I'm going to write about them."

Of course, Tom didn't understand a word, but he looked at me like he was really listening, blinking at the sea breeze with his ridiculously long lashes.

"That's Liverpool over there," I said. "That's where Uncle Paul and your great-nan are from. And those are the wind turbines. People don't like them, but I think they look quite good.

And that line there, where the sea meets the sky, is called the horizon, and it's as far as you can see. People used to think it was the end of the world and they'd drop off the edge, then they realized they could keep going, further and further, and they wouldn't fall off because the world isn't flat, it's round. People got brave and they kept going and they found out they'd be fine, and they got to loads of exciting new places."

Tom responded with a round of glorious babble. I loved it when he spoke to me; he must have wanted to say *something*, he just didn't have the words yet. I couldn't wait for him to speak actual words to me, and constantly wondered what he would say. Mum said I was wishing his babyhood away, but I wanted to have a conversation with him. One day, I would be able to talk to my son about wind turbines and the sea and the fact that people used to think the world was flat and he would be fascinated.

"Look at the sunset," I said, perching him on my forearm.

The sky looked bruised, with puddles of disparate colours merging into each other: orange, neon pink, purple. Against it all, the statues were black silhouettes, facing forwards, as though in contemplation.

Returning to university had seemed like a distant possibility at best; an unachievable, wild dream at worst, but I knew then that I had to do it. Mum had held back on bollocking me for being an absolute idiot, kept quiet when I held her hand so tight I crushed her knuckles, and hadn't complained when she had to be up for work at six and there'd been a newborn crying in the next room. If Mum hadn't offered Tom and me a home, I don't know how we would have coped, but it was time to think about moving on, and I could only do that if I finished university and got myself a job.

"In a few weeks, I am going back to university," I told Tom. "That means we won't be together so much. But it'll be good for you to hang out with someone who isn't me all the time. I promise I'll find someone kind to look after you. And one day, we'll have a house of our own, in Manchester. There's so much to do there. We'll go to the museums and art galleries and parks and I think you'll love it."

I never used a baby voice when I spoke to Tom, always just chatted to him like another human being. He was a human being, and most of the time he was the only one I had to talk to.

"Come on then, Mister," I said, when only a sliver of sun was left behind the horizon, "let's get you home."

I wriggled my toes, which had numbed in the chilly shallows, and dragged us both back up the dune. At the top, I looked back at the beach, now shrouded in dusk. In the distance, Liverpool had lit up for the night. There were still shards of fluorescent colour in the sky, but most of it, including the sea, was navy blue. Squinting, I could make out the black figures of a few of the sculptures, and the line where the water ended and the sky stopped but the world carried on.

Thirty-seven

O N T H E DAY I got my degree results, Mum had to fish my dissertation out of the kitchen bin.

I'd spent much of the previous year on boneshaker Northern Rail trains, shuttling between Manchester and Southport, trying desperately to avoid using the stinking onboard toilets.

The first day back had been exciting, once I got used to not having Tom with me. He waved, joyfully, when I left him with the childminder, a warm, welcoming woman with a husband, doting daughters, a cat and a dog, who lived just a couple of streets away from us - the perfect set-up for Tom. The walk to the bus stop was a challenge, because I felt like I was going to fall flat on my face. Turns out that when you've been pushing a pram for five months solid, it becomes a sort of zimmer frame.

Getting off the train at Oxford Road was like stepping into Manhattan. The tower of the Palace Hotel, the billboards outside the theatre, the Sainsbury's where I used to do my shopping when I worked at the call centre - all of it felt like home, but there was a sense of disbelief, as though I'd managed to blag a backstage ticket, because I don't think I'd ever really believed I'd be back there again. As I stood in awe on the corner of Oxford Street and Whitworth Street West, I realised that I didn't feel a speck of guilt for leaving Tom behind and picking up where I'd left off. Some of the women on

Motherboard had been inconsolable after the first time they left their babies in childcare. I felt suddenly very guilty for not feeling guilty, so I rang the childminder, who reassured me that Tom was absolutely fine and having a right old time discovering all the new toys. I cried, went into the old, familiar Cornerhouse to clean myself up and walked to uni, full of the gleeful freshness of a new academic year.

I put everything into my final year because I wanted to prove to everyone that I could have a baby and finish my degree. Most of all, I wanted to prove it to myself. Despite the inadequate, uncomfortable and often smelly trains, the journey to university was always exciting, my head swimming with ideas as I read books and made notes for my dissertation. The journey home, too, was always a joy (apart from the time a man inappropriately propositioned me at Wigan Wallgate). At rush hour, there was barely room to move and I often had to squeeze on to the train with centimetres to spare, getting up close and personal with not-so-fragrant strangers. On a Friday night, Mum sometimes collected Tom from the childminder's house so that I could stay out for a drink after university and pretend to be a proper student. It was always a wrench, leaving the buzz of Friday-evening Manchester behind, and the last train was always full of noisy drunks, the floor of the carriage often wet with spilt lager, but once I was on it, I was happy, because I knew I was on my way to see Tom. Hundreds of journeys on those awful trains, but all of them happy, because no matter which direction I was travelling in, I was always on my way to one of the two things that mattered the most.

By the time autumn turned to winter, I was in the swing of things. Tom's first Christmas happened; I bought him a rocking lion, which he sat atop and laughed. For New Year's

Eve, I went to visit Alex, who was living back in London, and listened to the world celebrate outside as Tom soundly slept. On New Year's Day, we walked along the Thames and took him to Tate Modern, where he made a couple in the café laugh because they thought he looked like Winston Churchill. I was comfortable being a mother, comfortable being a student, proud of my ability to somehow ace both.

Then Tom got sick. It was nothing serious, thank goodness, but his nose was running constantly and he kept vomiting. I was sitting up in bed, working on my dissertation, but he kept needing me. Every time I bathed him and changed him and put new sheets on his cot, he did it again. By this point, he was eating solid food, so the vomit was a much bigger deal than it had been when he was small. It came as a great shock to him, making him cry and the house smell and me arrange an appointment at the doctor's.

Tom sat on my knee, his breath sounding like purring, tugging at the doctor's stethoscope and grinning at her. He had a beautiful smile, with one dimple on the right-hand side, and he flashed it all the time. One of my favourite games was to sit with him on public transport and see how long it took Tom to break the miserable strangers who tried to avoid eye contact with him. It was never long before they were looking at him and grinning back.

"Look," I said, "he's happy. I just thought I'd bring him to be on the safe side really."

"When was the last time he vomited?"

"This morning," I said.

It had been disgusting, trying to avoid touching the stuff as I peeled off his clothes, running a bath and stripping the cot as he squirmed in my arm and screamed. Out of shit, snot and vomit, vomit was definitely my least favourite.

"It's probably gastroenteritis," said the doctor. "I'll prescribe antibiotics and rehydration salts."

"Thank you."

"Does he go to nursery?"

"No, a childminder."

"Right, well you'll have to keep him away from there until at least forty-eight hours after the last vomiting episode."

"I can't do that. He has to go there tomorrow, I've got a meeting with my dissertation supervisor."

The doctor dipped her head and looked at me over the top rim of her glasses.

"Emily," she said, "what's the priority here?"

I managed to reschedule the meeting for a few weeks later, on a day when the childminder ended up being sick. So I took Tom to uni with me and sat him on my knee, feeding him cold baby food out of a jar while I talked to my lecturer about historic controversies in public art.

Around Tom's first birthday, the conversation around *Another Place* got louder, as it was announced that the statues might be allowed to stay at Crosby permanently, rather than being moved to New York in November 2007, as was the original plan. The suggestion caused outrage, and it was decided that councillors would debate the issues and vote. I phoned the Town Hall and found out that there was nothing to stop me going along to the meeting. So I did. Mum looked after Tom for me and I caught the train and sat in the old, panelled room at Bootle Town Hall and listened to people argue, some of them quite passionately, about why they felt the statues had to go: they were dangerous, people might ignore the warning signs about quicksand and walk further on to the beach to get closer to the art and perish, and it would all be the council's fault. I scribbled furiously in my notebook, which was resting on my quivering thigh, no idea what the outcome would be. We were in a courtroom, and it felt like I was at a court case, rooting for the statues. After testimonies for and against, the councillors voted. It was decided that the statues would stay. I grinned as relief washed over me, not least because it gave me a neat ending for my dissertation. On the way out, I bumped into David, the man who'd been my boss on my work experience placement. It felt good to see him when I was so far over the other side. We had a brief catch-up about our sons, then out of the corner of my eye, I saw Antony Gormley himself and without thinking about what I was going to do or say, bounded up to him.

"Congratulations this is such good news I am writing my dissertation about controversy in public art based on this thank you so much I love *Another Place* it means a lot to me," I blurted, to the man whose naked form I'd been studying for months.

"Thank you," he smiled. "Good luck with the dissertation."

As the deadline for my dissertation got closer, I was re-minded of the fact that I work better in the night, when there are no distractions and I can keep going, through the gloaming, to dawn. Powered by tarry instant coffees that made my stomach spasm, I stayed up all night, hammering out the words on Mum's huge, slow PC. At 6 or 7 am, the time when I would have usually called it a night, put on a blindfold and slipped into bed, I'd hear a question spoken with a clarity that never failed to shock me and flood me with warmth:

"Mummy?"

Then I'd click 'save' and get to changing the nappy and

mashing a banana and Weetabix in milk, powering through, ragged with tiredness, until Tom was ready for a nap.

My dissertation was late, but I handed it in, proud of the hours I'd put in and the fact I had finished it at all. Until I got my results, that is.

"All that hard work," Mum was saying, waving the bright red binder in my face, "and now there's bloody baked bean juice all over it." Right on cue, a baked bean slid down the front cover and landed on the kitchen floor with a plop.

"All that hard work and I got a 2:2 – it's useless!"

"It is *not* useless," said Mum, "it is a degree."

"Dee-gee!" shouted Tom, who was sitting in his highchair, patting a puddle of beans and smearing his hair, with splayed, sticky palms.

"Everyone else got a first," I said, "or a 2:1, at least."

"*Everyone else* did not have a baby two-thirds of the way through their degree."

Mum had a point, but it did nothing to quell my disappointment in myself.

"Well, I'm not going to my graduation," I said. "You have to pay to hire the gown. What if I don't want to wear the stupid gown? Why should I pay to wear something that I don't even want to wear?"

"Because you'd look even more of a weirdo turning up to a graduation ceremony in your civvies than you would in one of the gowns."

"Which is why I just don't want to go."

"You better had. I want to see you graduate, because I am proud of you. Your sister's going to hers and I want both of your graduation pictures up in my living room, not just one."

"It's a load of rubbish," I said, pulling Tom out of his

highchair. "The whole 'Bachelor' thing is nonsense too. I am a woman."

"Not going to your graduation ceremony is like not going to the birth of your child."

"That is one of the most ridiculous things you've ever said, Mum."

"No, it isn't. You worked bloody hard for that degree. If you don't go to your graduation and have your picture taken, you'll regret it. Just think about how you feel about your first photo with Tom."

Mum was right. I had vetoed all photographs of me and Tom immediately after the birth, because I knew I wouldn't be one of those radiant new mums; I knew I'd look awful. What I didn't realise was how much I was going to love being a mother, and that I'd wish I had a permanent image of what I looked like the moment it began. The morning after he was born, before selfie was even a word, I took a selfie of me with my new baby. It took loads of attempts to get an angle that got us both in the frame. It's poor quality, pale and grainy, and it's not even of the very first time I held Tom. My eyes are wide and frightened and ringed by blue-black circles that make me look like I've been in a fight. I still regret not having a photograph of the first time I held Tom, but looking at that image reminds me how much I was dreading motherhood, and how very wrong I was.

A couple of days before the graduation ceremony, I decided I should probably go. I knew I had given my final year everything I could, but that nothing was going to undo the abysmal results I'd achieved in my second year. University hadn't mattered to me back then, only my social life and my job. When I returned as a mother, it was with a renewed vigour, a focus and a reason to work my arse off. It was too little, too late, but I still had a degree, which was more than I would have believed possible two years earlier.

I spent the night before my graduation at Jen's flat in Didsbury. My friends from my second year at uni had left by the time I resumed the course, and Jen had become my closest friend there. We'd studied together, delivered presentations together, drunk and been to gigs together. Time spent with Jen had been the antidote to the mother and baby groups in Southport, a reminder that I wasn't only a mother, but a single woman in my twenties. The graduation ceremony was a celebration of all that, as well as the academic stuff. Plus Jen had managed to come out of it all with a first.

My graduation outfit was a sixties dress I'd won on eBay, featuring lime green and turquoise flowers with cutwork around the neck, defiant against the white shirt and black skirt that had been suggested. When I arrived at The Bridgewater Hall and saw everyone else in their gowns, stalking the foyer like vultures, I felt more ridiculous than them, just like Mum had predicted. Even Jen had hired a gown. Thankfully, Mum arrived from Southport with Tom in his buggy, and paid for me to loan the gown of a no-show.

Poor Mum didn't get to see me graduate, after all her effort. She was too busy chasing Tom around in the foyer of the Bridgewater Hall; he had just learnt to walk and decided that trying out his new skills was way more fun than sitting still watching hundreds of identikit people walk on to a stage and off again (who could blame him?). In a way, it was perfect: without Mum to help me out with Tom, I never would have finished my degree, and without her to look after him that day, I wouldn't have been able to collect it.

My graduation photograph is up in Mum's living room. Hannah's is in the left alcove, next to the chimney breast, and mine is on the right. Hannah's is professional, glossy, posed. Mine is not. I might have managed to blag a gown at the last minute, but I'd missed my slot with the professional photographer. In my photo, there's no misty grey backdrop, no fake scroll, no official mount embossed in gold. In my photo, I'm standing in front of a lift in the Bridgewater Hall. Tom is in my arms, trying to grab the mortarboard off my head. He has a scrape on his chin from a recent fall. I look like I've got a stray tooth in my mouth, but it's actually a nervously-chewed lump of gum. We are both laughing. We both have triple chins. I don't have a scroll in my hand, but I do have a son.

Thirty-eight

"Poo!" exclaimed Tom.
  "Yes, poo, very good."
"I can't be late, I can't be late."
"Late. Poo."

I'd been using "my baby filled his nappy on the way out of the door" as a useful excuse for being late for most things for the previous seventeen months. Thankfully, it rarely actually happened. It did that day though, of course it bloody did.

I gathered towels and stripped off Tom and glugged half a bottle of Matey into the bath. I had to catch two buses. If I missed the first one, I would certainly miss the second one. And I had no money for a taxi.

"Spash, spash," said Tom, bashing the surface of the water with splayed palms.

Suddenly, I was wearing suds on my eyelashes.

Other than emergency vehicles, farm animals and trippy TV shows, there are few things more exciting to a one-and-a-half-year-old than baths. I wiped the suds away from my eyes, looked at my fingers and saw that I'd swiped off my mascara, too.

"Oh, shit."
"Oh sit!"
"Oh, dear, oh dear, I meant oh dear."

It's really hard not to swear around toddlers, but you have

to stop, because they copy you. The trouble is that living with very small children necessitates use of the word 'shit' at least twenty-five times per day. And that's a normal day, when you're not up to your elbows in poo and Matey and running late for your interview for an MA course.

"What time is your bus?" asked Hannah, sounding like she was full of a cold.

I turned around and saw her standing in the doorway, holding her nose with her finger and thumb. She adored Tom and loved babysitting, but she would only look after him on the proviso he had done a poo that day and was unlikely to need another one on her watch.

"Ten past."

"Right, well you've got no chance, have you?"

"Don't say that."

"Well you haven't. Sorry."

"I've got to be on time for this. Lateness is not an option."

"Well it's a bit late for that."

I scrubbed Tom's wet back with the duck-shaped sponge. "Poo!"

"I suppose I could take you," said Hannah.

"Pardon?"

"I said, I'll give you a lift. But I want the petrol money. And you have to be ready to leave the house in ten minutes."

"Oh my God, thank you so much!"

"Just hurry up."

Not long after that, we were careering down country lanes in Hannah's little purple car. Of course she had passed her driving test, when I'd failed twice and been too skint/afraid to try again. White noise hissed out of the stereo, with an occasional breakthrough from Radio 1. The squeaky wipers couldn't keep up with the fat splats of rain that pelted the windscreen.

The university was in Ormskirk, which was also home to the hospital where Tom had been born. I realised I hadn't been along the same twisty roads since then.

"That's the garage of pain," I said, as we passed a petrol station.

"What are you on about, Emily?"

"The garage of pain. I just remember getting a massive contraction as Mum and I went past that garage on the way to the hospital."

"Right," Hannah said, sounding like she couldn't be less interested.

"Thanks so much for taking me, I would have got drenched in this."

"How long will you be in there for?"

"I don't know."

"Well what am I supposed to do with Tom?"

"Just sit with him in the car? He'll be fine."

I flipped down the sunshade, trying to fix my smudged mascara in the cracked mirror.

"No, he will not be fine. He goes to sleep when the car is moving and when it stops, he wants to get out. That's what he does. You know that."

"Maybe you could take him to the park?"

"That's right, Emily. I could take your baby to the park in the torrential rain."

"Well OK, I don't know. Maybe you could go to a café or something?"

"I'll wait in here," Hannah said, as she pulled over in the car park. "Just don't be ages."

"OK, thanks. There's a sticker book on the back seat. Do I look alright?"

"Fine."

I ran quickly through puddles to the building, which looked like a lawn-fronted, American University from a film. I waited in the reception, wiping the silt splashes from my tights, nervously reading and re-reading a prospectus.

There is little I remember about the interview itself, apart from walking to it down dark, panelled hallways. I inhaled the scent of old books and wood and thought 'this is where I need to be'. I had absolutely no idea how the interview would go, though: I had a 2:2 degree in History of Art and I was trying to get on a Masters in Creative Writing.

"Tell me, the piece you submitted with your application – is it autobiographical?"

The course leader kicked things off with a tough question and I panicked, acutely aware of the fact that I hadn't thoroughly checked my dress for stray baby shit.

"Did you *think* it was autobiographical?"

I told myself to shut up, because you're not the one who's supposed to ask questions when you're being interviewed. Not unless they ask you whether you've got any questions at the end.

"Well, *is* it autobiographical?"

I'd been hoping it wasn't too obvious. Some authors advise disguising reality in fiction, but I was clearly too unsubtle to manage that.

"Well, yeah. But I'm not sure I wanted you to know that. Yet."

"So the young woman who finds herself in this . . . predicament, that's you?"

"Yes, it's me. Two years ago. I had a son and he's great. He's just outside in the car, actually."

I thought of him, screaming in his car seat. And Hannah, cursing me as she tried to placate him with the sticker book.

"I mean, he's with my sister, in the car. I didn't leave him out there on his own."

"Right."

"The thing is that I have always wanted to write." I took my eyes off the parquet floor and look straight at the lecturer. "I know everyone says that, but I really have. I won a certificate for writing excellent stories when I was five, Mum's still got it somewhere, and I won a poetry competition when I was about eight and got to plant a tree in a park as a prize and the tree's still there. And I got an A* in English Literature and an A in English Language and my English teacher always said she thought I could be a writer. It was good back then because I had assignments to complete. After that I felt like I knew I would write a book one day, but I never knew what it would be *about*."

"Go on . . ."

"Well, my son has given me something to write about. Sorry, am I waffling?"

"No, go on . . ."

I sighed, relieved to find the words I needed to say just flowing out of my mouth.

"When I was pregnant, all I wanted was to read an account of having a baby that was realistic and honest, and didn't involve a heroic man coming in at the end, because women have been left holding the baby since the beginning of time, and single parents are evil personified, according to some of the papers and really, most of us are just making the best of a difficult situation. So as well as giving me something to write about, my son has given me a reason *to* write. Maybe I won't just write about him; maybe I'll write short stories and maybe one day I'll write a novel, but I will write something, because I want to be a writer. For me but also for him. If I can be a mother, I can be a writer. I think that's what I am trying to say."

I stopped before my ranting got any more out of control, before I burst into tears.

The rest of the interview was more general: what books did I read? What was I reading at the time? What did I hope to go on to do after my MA? I don't remember much of it, really, only what the professor said at the end:

"Based on your enthusiasm and your ideas, I'm willing to offer you a place on the course."

"Unconditionally?"

"Yes, unconditionally."

I thanked him and thanked him and thanked him and put on my coat and thanked him and picked up my umbrella and thanked him again. I flew down the corridor to the toilet. I needed to check the mirror, to see whether it really was me who had just been offered a place on a Creative Writing MA. And it was. I had mascara streaks under both of my eyes, but it was definitely me.

I ran back across the car park, not caring about the rain, which smudged my mascara even more and dislodged one of my contact lenses.

"I'm sorry, I'm sorry," I said, as I climbed clumsily into the car, squinting into the cracked mirror, trying to slide my contact lens back in to place.

Hannah was sitting on the back seat next to Tom, who was howling, real tears slipping down his red cheeks.

"Oh, Tom, I'm sorry. Didn't he like the sticker book?"

"The sticker book didn't have any bloody stickers in it."

"Shit. Sorry."

I leaned over and kissed Tom's hot cheek.

"Dickers!" he said, breaking down in heartbroken sobs, "dickers!"

"Alright, love, we'll get you home. There are loads of dickers at home."

"Can I have my petrol money first please?" asked Hannah.

"Well, I need to go to a cash machine and I haven't got my bank card on me. Sorry, we left in such a hurry—"

"Typical."

When Tom had snuffled himself to sleep, we stopped at a red light and Hannah spoke.

"How did it go, then?"

"I did it. I got offered a place. I'm going to be a writer."

"Well done," said Hannah, putting the car into gear as the lights flicked to amber. "I knew you'd do it."

Thirty-nine

G ETTING ON TO the MA boosted my confidence and made me feel excited about the future, but soon afterwards, I hit a dip.

As a full-time student, I'd received invaluable funding from the Local Education Authority towards Tom's childcare costs. When I graduated, I didn't need the childminder anymore, and because the LEA funding stopped, I certainly couldn't afford to pay her. As much as she and her family loved Tom, she needed an income and was going to have to advertise the vacancy he'd left behind. Once the space was filled, I'd have to find a new childcare provider, and I already knew that there were none within walking distance of Mum's house.

I needed a job urgently, so that I could afford to pay the bills and Tom could keep going to the childminder's house. The Masters was part-time, with lectures in the evening, so although I knew I would have a lot of writing and studying to do, I also knew that I would be available to work in the day.

Still in love with Manchester and knowing there was a serious lack of employment in the arts and cultural sector in Southport, I applied for jobs in my beloved city. My ultimate aim was to earn enough money to be able to move there with Tom, to claim housing benefit initially, but to get a job and pay my own rent as quickly as I could after that. I also knew that I was going to find it much easier to get a job in Manchester, and commute to it, if I actually lived in Manchester.

What I hadn't realised was that finding accommodation when you're a single parent is incredibly difficult. Almost every agency and every advert bans 'DSS', meaning doors are slammed in your face before you even get to the viewing stage. At one point, I placed my own ad on a website, begging landlords to consider us, with my mum as our guarantor. One kind man got in touch and offered to let us look around his house. It was small and sweet, and as we sat at the cramped kitchen table talking contracts, I looked over his shoulder at the neat back garden and imagined Tom playing out there. He agreed we could move in, but only if I could show him an official document from the council to prove how much housing benefit I'd be entitled to. I filled in the form and sent it off to the council, but before it came back, the landlord emailed me to tell me, apologetically, that a couple had come along who could afford the rent and his partner had persuaded him that the sensible thing to do was to let them move in instead of me.

Not long after that, Rebecca announced that she was moving out of her flat in Withington to go on another far-flung adventure. It was a basement flat, dank and dingy, and the kitchen was a toddler-unfriendly square of lino in the corner of the living room, but we hatched a plan. Rebecca suggested I call the letting agent and offer to take it on straight after her, so they wouldn't need to advertise or leave it standing empty. We came up with the plan on a Saturday night, and I spent Sunday trying to decide which bedroom would be mine and which would be Tom's, and wondering whether Rebecca would let us keep the giant cheese plant in the bay window. On Sunday night, I hardly slept, and on Monday morning, I called the agency as soon as it opened.

"Sorry, love, that landlord doesn't accept children. A lot of landlords won't have little ones in flats, it's an insurance thing. High floors, open windows, you know."

"It's a basement flat."

"He still won't have kiddies in there, love, I know he won't."

"Can't you at least ring him and ask him?"

"Sorry, love, it's a definite no. Have you thought about trying for a council flat?"

Manchester City Council wouldn't house me because I had no family or job connection to the city.

My lowest point was when a student landlord, who advertised through the university, laughed at me.

"This is a family flat," he said.

"I know," I said, "it said that on the advert, that's why I'm calling."

"How many people in the family?"

"Two."

"Two children?"

"No, two people."

"Two people in the family?"

"Yes. Me and my son."

"But this is a student flat, for people who are studying at university."

"I know, that's why I called. I am a student, studying at university."

"But you have a baby. Come on now, how can you be studying at university if you have *a baby*?"

He laughed at me, actual cackles into the phone, as though I was some sort of deluded liar who'd decided to make up the fact I was a student in an attempt to persuade him to let me live in his flat.

"Sorry, my flat is not for you."

After all that, I realised I was going to have to put my plans to move out on the backburner for a little longer, to focus on getting a job and enough money to appease the landlords. Living in Southport and working in Manchester wouldn't be easy, but after my final year at university, I wasn't fazed by the long commute.

Day after day, I squeezed myself into an ill-fitting trouser suit and a pair of heels I could hardly walk in, paid the child-minder out of my overdraft and got the train to Manchester. There, I shook sweaty palms with dozens of panels and re-cruitment agents, only to be told that I hadn't been successful because the standard of other candidates was exceptionally high.

It took me too long to realise what a huge and ridiculous mistake I was making by boasting about Tom in interviews. As far as I was concerned, baby and degree under my belt, I was invincible. So, I told my potential employers everything. Well, not quite everything, but enough for them to know they didn't want to employ me. When they asked me if living back at home in Southport was a temporary arrangement, I told them that yes, it was, because I had a baby, and I hoped that, in time, the two of us would be able to move to Manchester. I was sure that the fact I had given birth, returned to university, got my degree (even if it was a 2:2) and been accepted on to an MA course made me highly tenacious and employable. What I didn't realise was that, even in the 21st century, no one wants to take on the mother of a baby, especially if she's single, but because of the law, they can always find another excuse for not giving you the job. I had clearly learned nothing from what happened at the call centre.

Eventually, I resigned myself to the fact that I was going to have to look for work closer to Mum's. At least that way I wouldn't have to trek back from Manchester once a week for my MA lectures. There was no way I'd ever be able to save up for a deposit on a Manchester house if I was forking out a fortune in train fares and extra childcare, and that was if anyone there would even offer me job.

At the Job Centre, an advisor told me: "most girls like you would just sign on, love", which made me even more determined to find a job. All they could offer me there though were jobs as a catering assistant or a care assistant, neither of which I thought I'd be much good at.

"Well, that was a complete waste of time," I said, when Tom and I got home.

"What did they say?"

"That I shouldn't bother, basically. Save myself the effort. And them."

"Come on, Em, there must be something you could do. Here." Mum threw the local paper across the room. It spun like a propeller and almost got me clean in the eye. "You could always go back to delivering that," she said. "How much did you earn?"

"£3.54 a week, for delivering 158 papers. Extra if they came with leaflets."

"When you weren't hiding the whole lot in the loft, that is."

"That was only once. I had a lot of school work on that week. It would have been a genius plan if you hadn't opened the hatch the next day. That was really unfortunate."

"Unfortunate for me when 158 newspapers nearly came crashing down on my head."

"Yeah, sorry about that. We are going back ten years though, Mum, and I'm pretty sure I apologised at the time. After you'd grounded me."

I flipped open the jobs section. As predicted: care assistant, care worker, care assistant, cook, chef, waiting staff, chef, care assistant and then there, at the bottom . . . "Travel agent," I said.

"Apply!" Mum shouted, immediately, "You could do it standing on your head."

I didn't want to be a travel agent forever. And I didn't want to live in Southport for much longer, but Mum was right: there wasn't much I didn't know about selling holidays, and two days later I was being interviewed for the job.

"Well, you've certainly got a lot of experience in travel."

The agency was a small, exclusive shop in an affluent village a few miles away from Mum's. I was sitting in the owner's conservatory, on a cane chair, surrounded by replicas of classical sculptures.

"Yes," I said, "I love the industry."

That much was true: I adored finding out about new places and talking to people about them – I just couldn't let this man know that it wasn't my long-term career choice.

"So, you've got this degree in . . . History of Art. Shouldn't you be applying for a job in an art gallery or something?"

"Good point. But I love the travel industry and it's what I know best. And the two aren't that unrelated. I studied a lot of landmarks for my architecture module. Ask me anything about the legacy of the Medici family, the Blue Mosque, The Dome of the Rock."

"Alright, alright. I think our customers are more interested in beaches than anything else. You might get the odd cruise, but it's mostly beaches."

"Oh, well that's what I'm used to anyway. I know my Caribbean islands and my Spanish Costas off by heart. And airport codes. You can test me on those, if you like."

"What I want to know is why you've moved back to Southport. This is a permanent job you know, not just a stop-gap."

"I know. I *need* a permanent job."

"So, you'll have to excuse me here, I'm just playing devil's advocate." He leant back in his chair and chewed his pen. "You've decided you want to go back to the travel industry, who can blame you? It's great – but why Southport? There are loads of travel companies in Manchester, the place is teeming with them. Why not just go back to your old place? I'm sure they'd snap you up."

There was an awkward pause while I thought about what to say, before I just gave in to honesty.

"Well, I'm living with my mum because I've got a baby. He's one and a half. I moved in with Mum nearly two years ago and I commuted to Manchester for the final year of my degree."

"Right." He sat up and slapped my application form down on the glass table. "Now we're getting somewhere. So, you live with Mum? And it's just you and the baby?"

"That's right. Just us two. I went back to university when he was five months old."

"And does your mum look after the baby?"

"No, the childminder does. Mum goes to work herself."

"Love, I'm sorry, I can't afford to take you on."

He shook his head, slid my application form over the table towards me and held up his hands in surrender.

"Why not?"

"You're a cracking travel agent, I'm sure you are, but the bottom line is that your baby comes first. Say he gets sick. Who stays home and looks after him? You. And who loses money? Me. It's that simple. Sorry."

And there it was: the thing that all the other employers were thinking, but were far too sensible to say.

Forty

" SOMEONE WILL BE very lucky to get you, Emily."
In the end, I put myself in the hands of a recruitment consultant. Beggars can't be choosers and after months of fruitless interviews and the brutal honesty of the travel man, I had finally realised that in the jobs market, I was a beggar.

The lucky person was the boss of Centaur, a call centre on a bleak industrial estate on the tired outskirts of town.

"Hi, my name's Emily and I'm calling from Centaur. We offer unique advertising opportunities in convenience facilities at some of the UK's busiest motorway service providers." (Translation: would you like to buy an advert on the door of a bog?)

Telesales. Not taking phone calls from excited people who wanted to book holidays, but badgering business owners, trying to convince them to pay for something that they didn't really need. In my case, this was animated advertising on the toilet doors of motorway service stations. Even worse, it was a pilot project for the company, so no one knew if it would work, and I was stationed at a lone desk, at the far end of the call centre, away from the other workers, who all seemed to be selling something far more successful and having a right laugh while they did it.

Lunchtimes were spent in the dark communal kitchen, heating tinned soups in a filthy microwave. On a Friday, after work, the entire workforce headed to the pub. Unlike my university days, I did not beg Mum to collect Tom from the childminder's so I could join them.

Most people will tell you that they have endured a terrible call centre job in their lives. Few professions are as soul-destroyingly miserable. Your job is to annoy people, to pester them, to stalk them. It's why I never get mad with PPI callers, even though I want to, because I know they would rather be doing anything other than the thing they are doing. Nobody wants to work in telesales; it is a last resort, when there really is no other choice.

That was why I kept a photograph of Tom taped to the desk, underneath the telephone. Every time someone laughed at me, hung up or told me to fuck off, I lifted up the phone and remembered why I was there.

One afternoon, on the way home from work, beaten by hours of answering machines and verbal abuse, I checked my phone and found a voicemail from the HR department of a museum. I'd applied for the job there weeks ago and forgotten about it, assuming I must not have even made the shortlist. They wanted me to go to an interview, but it clashed with a compulsory training session at Centaur. I called them straight away and asked if they could rearrange it. Amazingly, they could. As I confirmed the date and time, I looked back at the grubby building that housed Centaur and hoped I wouldn't have to go there for very much longer.

Forty-one

TWO HOURS BEFORE my job interview at the museum, I was ready. As I fed Tom his porridge and banana mash, I was careful not to let any splash on my suit.

I'd got up an hour before Tom woke, showered, blow-dried my hair, straightened it, researched the museum online (again), rehearsed my story (I had moved in with my Mum after university because I was skint, but as soon as I could, I would be moving out again. Absolutely no mention of a baby). Everything I needed to make a success of the interview was in place. Everything except a babysitter.

The childminder couldn't do it because she had a hospital appointment, Mum couldn't do it because she was at work, Hannah couldn't do it because she was also at work, Uncle Paul: another hospital appointment, Anna: at work, Jane: at work. Everyone else: at university. There was absolutely no one to look after Tom. Including his own father. I rarely thought about him, but when things got difficult, that ugly fact was patent again.

I got ready anyway, in the thin hope that one of the many people I'd begged to babysit might get in touch to say their plans had changed and they could do it. They didn't though, and an hour before the interview was due to happen, I put Tom in his playpen with a load of toys and stepped into the hall to call the museum.

"Can I speak to the HR Manager, please?"

"Sorry, she's in interviews."

Of course she was.

"OK. I wonder if you can help. I've got an interview this morning and I really want to come but I can't make it because of . . . unforeseen circumstances."

"Sorry, but today is the last day of interviews."

"OK, well, could you ask her to ring me please, just in case? I'd really love to come in, but I just can't get there today." I was shouting, to drown out the tinkling noise of Tom's toy crab. Watching him through a slim gap where the door joined the frame, I willed him to play with something quieter.

"As I said, today is the last day for interviews."

"But I—" Just then, Tom lamped himself on the head with the toy crab, which was solid plastic and fairly hefty.

"Hello?"

Five seconds of silence, that's how long I got when Tom had really hurt himself, before his face would crumple up and a great big growl would come out of his mouth.

"Hello?"

And there was the growl, straight into the phone, because by then, I had rushed into the living room and scooped up Tom and his sad, downturned mouth was right next to the receiver, which I was resting under my chin.

"Hello?"

"Sorry," I shouted, "please tell your manager to call me back. I really want the job but there's no one to look after my baby today."

Of course, she never called back.

Forty-two

NAN'S ALZHEIMER'S HAD been getting progressively worse, but it was pneumonia that got her in the end. I wasn't shocked when Mum called me to tell me early one morning, but I was very sad. I felt guilty, too, because I hadn't seen enough of her in her last two years.

I had seen her though, and she had met Tom. Occasionally, she'd yell suddenly, "*Whose* baby? *Your* baby?" but mostly she was happy in Tom's company, even if she did think he was called Yom. ("YOM! What kind of a ridiculous name is that?") "What a lovely little face," she'd say, "what a sweet little thing she is," forgetting from one minute to the next whether Tom was a boy or a girl. It was comforting to know that Tom had reached through to the lucid parts of Nan, that he had made her smile when she was so ill. And it was comforting, in the saddest way, that she no longer had to suffer that confusion and pain.

The morning of Nan's funeral was hectic. I'd taken Tom to Liverpool the day before, to catch the last day of an exhibition at the Tate. Not wanting to be outdone by Hannah, who I knew would be impeccably turned out, I had decided that I'd better buy an outfit for the occasion. I chose a pretty grey and black dress, which looked like a photocopy of a much brighter, floral frock, and a big, floppy, grey felt hat that I hoped would disguise my black roots and matching tears. All that would have been fine, were it not for the fact the shop assistant had left the security tag on the dress.

"Shit, shit, shit," I said, rifling through the kitchen drawers, looking for something to remove it with, then remembering that it was probably full of indelible ink that would spray out if I managed to get it open.

Mum was already in Liverpool with Uncle Paul, and Jane was on her way over from Manchester to drive us to the funeral. There was no time for me to travel into Liverpool city centre to have the tag removed; I'd have to forget the dress. I was just about to change into a baggy, bobbly black thing that I'd worn when I was pregnant, when I had a brainwave . . .

The woman at the supermarket probably shouldn't have agreed to use her tag remover to take a tag off a dress from another shop, but when I phoned up and told her, between sobs, that I needed it for my Nan's funeral, she agreed.

We were on the way to the funeral, via the supermarket, when my sister suddenly shrieked from the back seat. I turned round to see Tom regurgitating his breakfast.

"Oh God, no," I said.

Tom promptly began wailing.

"Don't worry," Jane said, in a sing-song voice, calm as ever. "We'll clean him up."

"I didn't bring any spare clothes!"

"Well, it's a good job we're about to stop at the supermarket," said Jane.

While I was in the shop getting the tag removed from the funeral dress and choosing some new clothes for Tom, Jane was expertly mopping up the mess with baby wipes and the old towels she just happened to have in the boot.

"See?" she said, when I arrived back, wearing the dress. "All sorted."

Jane's calmness was infectious, which was a good job

considering we were now running late for my grandmother's funeral. Somehow, thankfully, we arrived on time.

Uncle Paul had put together a slideshow of photos from Nan's life, which was to play on a big screen at the beginning and end of the service. When Mum told me about it, I was worried it might be cheesy, but I needn't have been concerned: it was beautiful. What really got me were not the photographs of Nan from my lifetime, but the ones prior to it, like the picture of her beaming on her wedding day in 1953, wearing the most stylish dress I have ever seen. Nan always told us that her wedding dress was blue because fabric was still expensive after the war and it was all she could get her hands on, but Mum told a different story: Nan's sister had got pregnant out of wedlock and had to have a shotgun wedding instead of the white one she'd always dreamed of. Nan knew her sister had been gutted about this, so kept things low-key when it was her turn. As the coffin was carried into the church, the photos continued: Nan stepping out with her WAF friends in the war, all slim and smart in their pencil skirts and wide belts; Nan clutching Mum and Paul as babies, her face etched with the joy of motherhood that I now knew. Those were the photos that caught me, the ones that reminded me that Nan wasn't always an old lady, that she had been young, in love, a new mum.

I don't know how Mum made it through her brilliant speech, but she did, hardly faltering. She ended by talking about the joy that Tom had brought to Nan in her last few months, the times her fractured, disjointed sentences suddenly made sense again, as she admired her first great-grandchild. Jane had offered to come to the church so she could take Tom outside if he got noisy during the service, but there was no need: apart from the odd outburst of gobbledygook, he sat happily in his buggy, amazingly content for someone who'd recently thrown up.

After the crematorium, it was back to Nan's house for the wake. A three-floored, Victorian end-terrace, it had always felt old and cold. Fifties bark-cloth curtains still hung in the front room and there was a huge clothes maiden on a pulley above the gas fire in the kitchen. A wake in the house where Mum and Paul had grown up and where Hannah and I had spent so much of our childhood was always going to be difficult. Black-clothed adults gathered around the dining table, picking at the buffet like crows. The stone mantelpiece and every one of the dark, mahogany surfaces were covered in silvery sympathy cards. On the sideboard, tiny piles of orange pollen had fallen from the waxy lilies, crowded in a crystal vase.

The mood at the wake didn't stay sombre for long though, thanks to the entertainment. After surreptitiously helping himself to far too many crackers from the buffet, Tom made everyone laugh with his animal noises, dances and songs.

"What a lovely little boy."

"He's so happy."

"Well done, Emily, he's gorgeous."

"You must be so proud."

And I was. As I watched Tom clamber on to a stool and plink-plonk a load of nonsense on the out-of-tune piano, I realised that, even if Nan had been able to understand what was going on, she would have come round to the idea of me having Tom, once she was over the shock. Just like I had.

Forty-three

I TOOK THE day off Centaur for Nan's funeral and I never went back. It was the only time in my life that I have ever left a job without giving notice, but I couldn't stand the thought of picking up the phone and harassing people to buy toilet advertising ever again.

Jane told me that a lot of our old colleagues at the call centre had been made redundant, but that some of them had been recruited by a home-working firm. I knew that home-working was big news in the travel industry; I'd looked into it when I thought I might be jobless when I was pregnant, but I also knew it wasn't without its pitfalls. Working from home meant no basic salary: the only money you made was from commission, so essentially you worked for yourself, giving a percentage of the money you made to the company who routed the phone calls to you. The main advantage was that you got to choose your own hours and didn't have to worry about things like taking time off because your baby was being sick. As long as I was living at Mum's, I was secure. With my MA well underway, I was feeling far happier than when Tom was smaller and I was scared I'd never leave the house again. I decided it was worth the risk; if it was as lucrative as the company claimed, I might be able to afford to move back to Manchester in a few months. In the meantime, the arrangements would be far from ideal: Hannah had moved back home after university, so Tom slept in my bedroom, but the only place I could work without being disturbed in the evenings, when my phone would be the busiest, was my bedroom, so poor Tom's cot got carried downstairs, where it floated incongruously in the middle of the dining room. Mum hung an old throw from two mug hooks in attempt to stop him from waking when she crept through to the kitchen in the mornings before work, and the two of us put a rickety book case filled with soft toys in front of the gas fire in an attempt to make the room feel more like a nursery. It was messy, in every sense of the word, but it would have to do – and it made me even more determined to earn enough money to move out.

I'd forgotten how easy I found selling holidays, and how much I loved it. There, from the corner of my damp little bedroom, surrounded by hillocks of bibs and vests and tiny pairs of jeans, I sent people all over the world. Between calls, I worked on stories and assignments for my MA, but there was no time for that late at night. The calls were directed to agents in order of who'd been waiting the longest, and sometimes the days were agonisingly slow, but in the evenings, my phone didn't stop. I worked out that most of the other home workers logged off at 10:pm, so after that, I was one of the few agents customers could reach. After a long day shopping around for holidays, people are bored, despondent and impatient to get something booked, which meant between the hours of ten and midnight, I sometimes made enough money to last me the week.

Often, customers needed to sleep on it, which was understandable. Invariably, they would call me back first thing in the morning, when I was still asleep. The phone would ring three times, then go to answerphone, and I'd hear the loud voice of someone saying something like, "Hi Emily, we spoke last

night, I'm calling back to book that holiday you found us—"
And I'd leap up, grab the phone and make some money, in my
pyjamas, before Tom was awake and either of us had even had
breakfast. I was hardly a millionaire, but I was successful. My
customers liked me and, grateful for my honest advice, they
passed my number on to friends, who also recommended me,
and who wrote me postcards from their happy holidays and
told their fellow holidaymakers about me. Before I knew it,
my bedroom empire was enough to live off and I was well on
my way to saving a deposit to rent a house.

One night, when I'd just hung up from the last of my calls
and I was sick of scouring the internet for houses to rent in
Manchester, something occurred to me: Mum had told me
that Nan had left a thousand pounds each to me and Hannah.
I had planned to use the money to get Tom and me set up
in our own place, but I knew that the income I was making
from my business would cover that. I probably should have put
Nan's money in a savings account, or done something equally
sensible with it, but there was something I needed to do with
it, a kind of unfinished business: something monumental;
an idea that, once it had entered my head, was never going
to leave. It was outrageous, but I knew I'd feel invincible if I
could pull it off, so, in a very roundabout way, it *was* a sensible
way to spend the money Nan had left to me.

The autumn night had chilled my room, but it was still
early in the year and there's no way Mum would have let me
put the heating on, so I huddled under a blanket at my desk. I
called Alex, who was living back in Australia with John (who
was now her fiancé), because it was daytime in the Southern
Hemisphere and also because I really needed to talk to her. I
gave her some dates and she said they suited her and I called

my friend Claire who lived in central Sydney and they also suited her and that was that: I was finally going to Australia. And I was taking my baby with me.

Forty-four

"OH GOD, YOU'RE not actually *going*, are you?" said Uncle Paul, when I phoned him to ask for a lift to the airport.

I was actually going: on a thirty-six-hour, four-plane flight to the other side of the world, with a twenty-month-old toddler and all of his necessary paraphernalia in tow.

As it happened, Paul couldn't do it, so it was Mum who drove Tom and me and the luggage to Manchester Airport, Mum who parked in the extortionate multi-storey car park, and Mum who helped us into the terminal and didn't let us go until she absolutely had to because we'd reached the security gate.

"Good luck!" she wept, as though she was sending us off into battle. "Keep him safe!"

As I grappled with a pushchair, a car seat, two passports, boarding cards, a changing bag, an enormous rucksack and a hefty child, I had to admit to myself that taking my toddler to Australia probably wasn't the most sensible plan I'd ever had. Still, I grinned through gritted teeth as I awkwardly hugged Mum, the changing bag repeatedly swinging round from my back and slapping her in the side.

I'd initially booked tickets to Sydney, via London and Seoul, but since then, John had got a new job, meaning he and Alex would be moving to North Queensland the day before Tom and I were due to arrive (excellent timing). This added an extra

2,000 kilometres (and a two-and-a-half hour flight) to the itinerary, but it was nothing, really, given the enormity of the whole journey. Altogether, we would be travelling (and waiting) for 36 hours, which was the same amount of time I'd been in labour.

The flight to Heathrow was swift and full of men in suits. One of them, sitting next to me, asked me where we were off to.

"We're going to Australia," I said, proudly, like a kid who's boasting they're off to Disney World.

"Right," said the suit, raising his eyebrows. "I've got a daughter his age. Good luck."

At Heathrow, we needed to move to a different terminal, so I took a kind member of airport staff up on his offer to wheel our luggage there on his trolley. Only when he offloaded our crap at the other end did I notice the sign strapped to the front of the trolley with cable ties: £8. I had no cash, but he happily escorted me to the ATM to get some.

The flight to Seoul would take eleven hours, so I armed myself with multiple sticker books, mini boxes of raisins and numerous new toys. As a child, family holidays were spent in the UK, and invariably involved long train journeys and numerous changes. The night before we set off, Mum would pack Hannah's and my swimming bags, and in each one she would sneak a selection of little surprises: colouring books, cardboard dressing dolls and plastic puzzles. I remember the utter excitement of unfolding a face cloth to find a new pen, or digging into the side pocket and drawing out a new book. Tom wasn't quite old enough to rifle through his own bag of surprises, but I took Mum's lead by making sure I had something cheap, amusing and new to whip out every time boredom arose.

One of the reasons why I'd decided to take Tom to Australia before he was two was the fact that I wouldn't have to pay for a seat for him; as long as we travelled before his second birthday, he would be classed as an infant and could be officially carried in my arms. He was a very big infant though, and when it came to actually booking my tickets, the thought of him squirming and trying to sleep in my lap for more than twenty hours hit home. I found a two-for-one deal on tickets with Korean Air and booked that, and ordered an aviation-approved car seat with wheels from America. The idea was that I could wheel Tom round the airport and then strap him in when we were on the plane, and sell the thing on eBay when we got back.

My biggest fear was Tom disturbing those around me; I'd been stuck on enough flights with screaming children to know that I'd be the enemy of my fellow passengers if that was to happen. What I hadn't accounted for were the seat back TV screens, which turned out to be a game changer: when he was awake, Tom chuckled at Korean cartoons and pressed the buttons, saying "puter, puter" over and over again. For around half of the journey, though, he slept, leaving me to watch films, contemplate the adventure ahead and scrawl in the thick travel journal Mum had bought me especially for the trip. I tried to sleep, but it was impossible; I've always struggled to sleep on planes, but Tom's presence and potential neediness meant any naps I did manage were short-lived and thin.

Over Russia and Mongolia, the plane jolted and wobbled, an announcement about turbulence was made, and the seat-belt signs glowed. I've never been frightened by turbulence; if anything, it rocks me into a kind of tranquillity. It's a break from the overall stillness of air travel, a reminder that you're defying gravity, tens of thousands of feet in the air, that you're going somewhere. I fastened my seatbelt and put my index finger in Tom's soft palm, rubbing his chubby wrist with my thumb. I closed my eyes then and let the sky rock me, not to sleep, but to definite contentment.

I'd been looking forward to exploring Seoul on our change-over, but there wouldn't be time to travel into the city and back again before our connection to Sydney.

"Ah, don't worry about that," said the burly man sitting in front of us, an Australian who'd been visiting family in London. "It's a terrible place. The food's disgusting and nobody speaks English." And he went back to watching *This is England* on his seatback TV.

"Make the most of the entertainment, by the way," he said. "All you get on the Seoul to Sydney leg is one TV at the front of the cabin playing flaming karaoke."

In Seoul, the airport, Incheon, was glossy and futuristic. My phone wouldn't work on Korean networks, so I changed some money into Korean Won and found a payphone. I wanted to let Mum know that we'd made it almost half way, to tell her how Tom had slept for most of the flight and it really hadn't been anywhere near as terrible as I'd been expecting. Mum and I had been arguing a lot, getting under each other's feet, but there, so very far away and incapable of calling her, I realised I'd grown used to her being my main companion and confidante, and that I was going to miss her terribly while we were away. I grappled with the phone, but I couldn't read the instructions on the booth, nor understand the verbal ones that chattered out of the receiver. It was easy for me to work out fragments of Spanish and French, and I had a B at German GCSE, but when it came to languages with totally different alphabets, I had to hold my hands up like a typical Brit and admit confused defeat. I abandoned the payphone, parked Tom next to a bank of computers and hired one to send Mum an email, a task that was tricky in itself thanks to a wildly different keyboard.

When I was done trying to send messages home, I pushed Tom around the terminal until I came across a soft play area and nearly cried. I hate soft play areas: they are full of screaming and sparring sugar-loaded children clambering over grubby-looking obstacles and battering each other, and they stink, and if you ever have a child, you'll be hard-pushed to avoid spending time in them. This soft play area was different though; it was heaven-sent. I unleashed Tom from the straps of his car seat and turned him loose, watching as he ran around, fell, got up, bounced, slid, fell, got up and laughed and bounced again. It was the perfect way to run off eleven hours of sitting still – ahead of the next ten and half hours of the same. Tom made friends with a Chinese boy, an Indian boy and a Korean girl, hugging them all before they parted. I tried to piece together conversations with the other parents, but we all struggled. In the end, it was easiest to smile, sit back and watch our children, for whom language was no barrier, play happily together.

Forty-five

THE MAN WHO'D been sitting in front of us on the way to Seoul had been right about one thing: there was indeed only one tiny TV at the front of the cabin on the next flight, and it was playing what looked to be some sort of talent show. This time I was going to have to get more creative with my in-flight entertainment. As the plane took off and Tom grumbled, I fed him some noodle snacks I'd bought at Incheon and willed the next ten and a half hours to whizz by.

"Cuckoo!"

I looked up and saw a boy of about twelve poking his head through the gap between the seats in front.

"Cuckoo!"

Another boy peeped round the end of the aisle seat and Tom began to smile.

"Cuckoo!"

By the time a third boy was waving at Tom through the gap by the window, he was creased up with contagious chuckles.

Cuckoo, it seemed, was South Korea's answer to peepo.

The boys were on a school trip to Australia. There were many of them in the seats around us, as well as a few teachers. Tom quickly became the centre of attention for the whole group, who passed him around and took turns to have their photo taken with him, throwing up the peace sign with their free hands. At one point, I looked around and couldn't see Tom, but he was grinning, about six rows back, being handed from one kid to the next like the parcel in Pass the Parcel. One boy whispered to his teacher for a translation before handing me a pencil case in the shape of a Converse Allstar.

"Kencil pace," he said. "Present for cute baby." It still had the tags on; he'd bought it at the airport.

"Honestly, no," I said, trying to hand it back to the teacher. "He doesn't have to do that."

It was decided, though: the pencil case was Tom's, as was a Korean Air ballpoint pen and three bags of the noodle snacks he had a new penchant for.

Before long, passengers were flocking down the aisles from the front of the plane, keen to grab a glance of the 'angel baby' that was rumoured to be sitting at the back. Tom got cuddled and fussed by elderly women, young women, children and men. And he loved every minute. I didn't need to worry about providing him with in-flight entertainment; he *was* the in-flight entertainment. For the entire Seoul to Sydney leg of our journey, Tom was either asleep or being showered with attention by strangers, which suited him (and me) just fine.

As we edged into Australian airspace, we passed sunrise, a long slice of fluorescent orange visible through the windows on the opposite side of the plane. It reminded me of the front cover of the Australia brochure that I'd stared at when I was working in the Southport travel agency: a beautiful shot of Uluru glowing bright with silhouettes of kangaroos hopping in front of it. I used to keep a copy in the drawer under my desk, torturing myself by frequently flipping through it. The stunning photographs in that brochure showed me what I could have had if I hadn't got pregnant and had to cancel my trip to Sydney. Now I was sitting next to my baby somewhere over Australia and we were really, nearly there.

When the captain announced that we were about to begin our descent into Sydney, Tom was wide awake. "We're here, baby," I said, my voice wobbling as triumph and ecstasy rose in my torso. "We're in Aussie!"

"OZZY!" he said, beaming and clapping his hands.

I took a photograph of him surrounded by toys, dishevelled and covered in bits of crispy noodle, his smile wide and glad. He didn't know exactly what was happening, of course he didn't, but he did know that his mother was extremely happy. Every time I look at that picture, I remember the feeling of having done it, of it all being worth it, the wild sense of invincibility.

Forty-six

THE FINAL FLIGHT of our journey was a three-hour domestic connection to Townsville. On its own, a three-hour journey with a baby would be a stressful mission, but after what we'd just done, it felt like a taxi home after a night out. I had barely slept in more than two days, but the tiredness didn't touch me because I was high on achievement and our proximity to Alex. Tom, unfortunately, felt differently. He had had enough, which was fair enough, really. He wasn't allowed his own seat on the plane, and had to sit on my knee with a belly belt for take-off. This was not on, as far as he was concerned, especially given the fact there was a perfectly empty seat right next to us. The difficulty with toddlers is that they want to do a lot of things that they physically can, but you can't explain to them why they're not allowed. When they don't understand why they are not allowed to do the thing that they want to do (usually for their own safety), they go into meltdown.

And so, finally, on the runway at Sydney, the meltdown arrived. Tom arched his back, kicked his legs, strained to get into that tantalisingly empty seat next to us. The whole time, I tried to calm him and reason with him, explaining that he could probably have that seat once the seatbelt signs were off, but that for now, he'd have to just sit still on my knee for a bit. He strained against the thick webbing, his T-shirt riding up so that the belt dug into the soft flesh of his belly; he slid down my knee and I yanked him back up again; he clawed at my hair and face, making hard, angry growling sounds that I had never heard him make before. As Tom repeatedly booted the seat in front, the person sitting in it tutted and shuffled and sighed.

"Jeez," said the flight attendant, "he sounds like a Tazzy devil."

When the seatbelt signs eventually switched off, I released the Tasmanian devil and let him lie across the next seat. He folded himself in half, hot and scarlet and cross, and sobbed himself to sleep. Every now and then, he remembered why he was angry again and the growling returned, but each time it quietened and weakened until there was one final outburst and he was fast asleep. Carefully, I shifted him so that his head was resting on my lap and his legs were outstretched on the seat. Now I was exhausted and ready to sleep, but I knew I had to keep going for this the final push. I stroked Tom's hot forehead, twisting my fingers in the clammy curls at the nape of his neck. And I noticed something moving.

The night before we set off for Australia, I went to university. In the middle of a workshop, when people were trying to read out their poetry, my phone kept ringing. It was in vibrate mode, which, because of its location in my coat pocket next to my keys, made more of a racket than if I'd just had it set to loud. When it rang a fourth time and people were clearing their throats and rolling their eyes, I whispered sorry and left the room.

Four missed calls from Mum. I tried to ring her back from the toilets down the corridor, but there was barely any signal and her words were disjointed.

"It's . . ." she shouted, "it's . . ."

"It's what, Mum?"

Then the line died. I ran downstairs and out of the front

of the building and called her from there, shivering in the November evening.

"Tom's got nits," she said.

"What do you mean he's got nits?" I said. "He's hardly got any hair."

"I know, but the childminder says he has. Apparently one of the other kids she looks after has got them. She says he's riddled and she can't believe you haven't noticed."

"Shit," I said. "Are people allowed on planes when they're riddled with nits? They're definitely not if they've got chicken pox."

"I don't know!"

"Bollocks."

"Maybe she's wrong," Mum said. "I've looked and I can't see anything."

An hour later, I was crouched down on the dining-room carpet, next to the cot, brandishing a torch and a magnifying glass from a Christmas cracker. The childminder was right: Tom's sparse, downy hair was indeed absolutely riddled and I don't know how I hadn't noticed. What followed was an itchy, panicky drive to the all-night pharmacy, and a bottle of the mildest possible head lice treatment, suitable for children under two. So mild, it seemed, that it didn't fucking work.

Not only had Tom's head lice survived a mild chemical treatment, they had hitched a ride to the other side of the world. What's more, upon studying the louse I had just plucked out of the hair behind his ear, I discovered that it was actually two lice, stuck together, engaged in an act that I did not want them to be engaged in on my son's head. I thought about how nearly every single lovely passenger on that flight from Seoul to Sydney was probably beginning their time in

Australia in the nearest pharmacy, enduring a humiliating and difficult struggle over the language barrier.

I spent the rest of the flight like a chimpanzee, pulling parasites out of Tom's hair and crushing them between my forefinger and thumb. It was the first of many sessions like it in the years to come. You get warned about the nappies and the sleepless nights and the tantrums, but nobody tells you about the nits.

The thick heat of Townsville thwacked us the moment we disembarked the plane. This was tropical North Queensland, and both Tom and I were going to have to acclimatise to the humidity, as well as the time difference. The closeness in the air only seemed to add to the fug in my mind. As I stood staring at the squeaky baggage carousel, waiting for our stuff to appear, I couldn't even begin to contemplate how many days I'd been awake, or what time it was in the UK. The disorientation wasn't all that dissimilar to how I'd felt in the first few days after having Tom.

It took a while for me to get all our belongings off the conveyor belt. While I was busy hauling one thing off, the next would go all the way round again. Eventually, everything was at my feet and I set about arranging it in the way I had learned: the main backpack, which was far bigger than Tom and almost as big as me, got its own seat in the form of Tom's buggy, whilst Tom got strapped into the car-seat-on-wheels. I looped the nappy changing bag over the buggy handles and shrugged my small rucksack on to my back. I then set off, weaving through the bustle, pushing the backpack in front of me and dragging Tom behind.

"Excuse me," said a kind stranger, "do you need some help?"

"I'm fine, thanks," I said. "I've got a system and it works."

Forty-seven

"DON'T HUG ME, I've probably got nits," I said, as Alex greeted me with her arms outstretched.

She was standing right in front of me, my wonderfully calm, practical friend from student halls in Manchester, waiting at the airport in this far corner of Australia.

"Actually, fuck it," I said, falling into her arms, "but keep your hair away from mine."

Townsville had felt like the end of our journey, but we were still ninety kilometres from Ayr, the small, sugar-cane farming town on the banks of the Burdekin River, where John was about to start his new job. On the hour-long drive there, I needed to sleep, but the scenery was too stimulating for that. We passed sun-scorched plains and eucalyptus forests, banana plantations and enormous trees dripping with ripe mangoes. Much of the vegetation was recognisable from my holidays in India and Jamaica, whilst lots of it was like nothing I'd ever seen before. Tom slept soundly in his car seat, but I was wide awake, staring out of the car window at a brand new world.

Alex and John's accommodation was a 'unit': a breeze-block bungalow with tiled floors that offered a welcome retreat from the stifling heat outside. It was as new to them as it was to us, given the fact they'd only just moved in. Most of their furniture was on the back of a truck, which was on the long drive up the country's east coast, and wouldn't be arriving until the following day at the earliest. Alex showed Tom and me to our new rooms, which were bare but for the mattresses on the floor. She and John went to the shop for food, whilst Tom and I settled down for some much-needed sleep.

Tom didn't need sleep like I did, though, and as exhaustion and jet lagged conspired to pull me under, he was wide awake and inquisitive about his new surroundings.

"What's dat?" he said, pointing at the ceiling fan overhead.

"What?"

"What's dat?" his voice was croaky from hours spent inhaling recycled air.

"It's a fan," I grumbled.

"FAN!"

"Yes, fan. It keeps us cool, so we can go to sleep. Let's go to sleep, love."

I drew him close to me, wrapping an arm around him in a restraint disguised as a cuddle. He was having none of it and was soon up and about, his little feet padding around on the ceramic floor. I knew I had to stay awake to keep him safe, that there was no way it was OK for my toddler to have free run of a house with hard floors and electrical sockets and only a fly screen between him and the great outdoors and all the dangerous creatures that Australia is famous for, but the jet lag was relentless and strong and it sucked me down like quicksand until—

"What's dat?"

I was awake again. Time had passed, but I had no idea how much. Shadows flickered past my closed eyes as the ceiling fan rotated. I opened my eyes. Tom was kneeling next to my head, holding something over my face.

"What's dat?"

I focussed, my slow, knackered brain taking a moment to register what my baby had in his hand.

It was a cockroach: burgundy with mustard markings, at least three inches long, plus its antennae, which were lightly brushing my cheek.

That woke me up.

After a shower and a bedtime story, I settled Tom on his mattress and he went to sleep, begrudgingly. Several hours later, he toddled into my room and started chatting to me. It was pitch black by this time, and Alex and John were fast asleep. It was ten pm in Ayr, but in Southport it was noon, and as far as Tom's little body clock was concerned, it was time to eat and be awake and have fun.

After a midnight feast on the food John and Alex had bought from the supermarket, I strapped Tom into his buggy, gave him a bottle of hot milk and began pushing him in figure-of-eight loops around the empty living room. It reminded me of the repetition of the route I had taken so many times around the park near Mum's, only slightly less scenic. The scenery, or lack of it, didn't bother Tom, though – as long as he was moving, he was relatively happy and calm. And so I continued on autopilot, long into the night, round and around the living room, listening to the strange sounds of insects and goodness knows what else outside, until eventually, dizzy and knackered and bored, I was able to settle Tom on to his mattress and melt into mine.

He was up again at dawn, though, naturally. This time, with light on our side, I wanted to explore further than the living room, so I loaded him into his buggy and we ventured outside. The street was long and flat and lined by identikit units like Alex and John's. At the end of it, the tarmac gave way to a rugged track and I found myself pushing the buggy through farmland. It was like the pathways that cut between the crops behind Mum's house, except this wasn't wheat or cabbage or sprouts. Ahead of me, the sky glowed orange, but not with sunrise. Thick, black smoke rolled into the sky and, as we got closer, ashy fronds snowed down around us. Alex and John had told me about the sugar-cane burning on our journey from the airport: in the Burdekin area, sugar cane grows in abundance because of all the water. The excess crop is set alight and burnt away to make the harvest easier and quicker. Apparently, the sight and sound of a field ablaze is a spectacular sight, but I wasn't about to head towards the smoke to see it, not with Tom in tow, anyway. Instead, I turned the buggy back and trundled along the quiet streets until we came to a park, its entrance flanked by an enormous mosaic sculpture of a snake.

Walking in the park in Australia, I quickly discovered, was very different to walking in the park in Southport. The last time we'd been in our local park, it had been between banks of fallen yellow leaves, both of us in wellies and hats and gloves; in the tropics, there was no such thing as autumn. There was no aviary in Plantation Park, but the trees were alive with the big, bright, noisy relatives of my beloved talking parrot. Whereas pigeons and mallards stalked the paths of the parks in England, in Ayr one of the most common birds was the ibis, with its long, curved beak. There were picnic benches, like at home, but there were also lots of public barbecues. Tall palm trees swayed in the breeze, encircled by nets to prevent damage from falling coconuts. Further into the park, I saw a tree I recognised from my travels: the flamboyant tree, or royal poinciana, bears fiery flowers and black seed pods that look like giant, flat vanilla pods. In Jamaica, I remembered a tour guide telling me that they are often given to babies to use as rattles. I found one on the floor and handed it to Tom and he shook it happily until he started trying to eat it and I had to confiscate it.

We spent a good hour in that park, crossing a milky tributary of the Burdekin and venturing into the Aboriginal Walk, which was like a miniature, accessible jungle with colourful sculptures tucked in the trees. Afterwards, we went to church, which would have pleased my mother.

I knew that life in Australia was very outdoorsy, but I hadn't expected to come across an open-air church in the middle of the park. God's Cathedral, as it was called, comprised a huge wooden cross, a mosaic altar, a nave defined by two long, tropical flower beds, and rows of stone benches. There was no service, but we had arrived just in time for the sprinkler system, which showered the flowers and spiky grass with water. It was early morning, but already very hot, so I took Tom out of his buggy and let him run and play in the spray. He'd always loved water, and I don't think I'd ever seen him look as happy as he did getting drenched that day. When I'd finished taking photographs and put my camera safely away, I joined him, surrendering to the cool arcs, my hair plastered to my face, my clothes to my body, chasing rainbows and Tom, laughing, watching his nappy growing bulbous with the water and not caring one bit.

Forty-eight

JOHN AND ALEX'S furniture arrived in Ayr the day after us. Much of it had come from John's mum, who lived near Brisbane, and she had sent a cot for Tom. It was vintage, white wood adorned with transfers of blue and pink bunnies, and I loved it. Alex, ever-practical, pointed out that the sides were low and that Tom would probably be able to climb out of it, so we dragged it into my room and wedged it between my bed and the fitted wardrobes.

While we were waiting for the furniture to be delivered, John drove us all to Alva, the nearest beach. We climbed to the top of a high dune, looking out across the flat, azure waters and the spit of creamy sand that reached out into the ocean. It was tempting to go for a paddle, but signs everywhere warned about the presence of stingers. In Queensland, 'stinger season' was in full swing and the risk of an encounter with a deadly box jellyfish was high. Of course, Tom had absolutely no idea why he couldn't just run into the water and splash around and kept straining towards the shoreline. I picked him up and walked with him, dodging needle-sharp cuttlefish and hairy husks of coconuts, the reality of where we were slowly kicking in.

After an afternoon helping John and Alex unpack, assemble and shift furniture, it was time to treat Tom and me for the head lice. I used a tea tree treatment we'd been recommended by the local pharmacist, and it was so noxious that it stung the eyes of everybody in the house, including Tom. When he'd forgiven me and we'd eaten tea, we went to bed. I was sure that after our early morning adventures, the sea air and the tea tree oil trauma, Tom was bound to sleep through the night. After writing about our day in my journal, I turned off the lamp and fell into a deep sleep, which lasted until Tom woke me a couple of hours later.

"Oh dear!" he said. This was followed by a dull thud next to my head and a ping of mattress springs. I turned on the light and saw a wet nappy next to where my head had been and Tom standing proudly in his cot, looking very pleased with himself. Oh dear, indeed.

I wanted to take him out for another walk, but the yard was full of poisonous cane toads and I had no idea what lay beyond that, so I strapped him in his buggy again and wheeled him around the living room, this time in a route more complicated than a figure of eight, because it weaved around two sofas and a coffee table.

We spent the following few days settling into Ayr. The town centre was an intriguing place that reminded me of a fifties town in an American film set, maybe Hill Valley in *Back to the Future*. Most of the buildings were single-storey and pastel-coloured, and tinny music played continuously out of speakers along the high street. There was a bowling alley, a couple of cafés, a theatre and several shops; the most interesting of which sold magazines and greetings cards. So far, so normal, apart from the mannequins wearing sequinned dresses and clown wigs that gestured towards the various goods for sale. Outside the front, two of them 'staffed' a table of jarred preserves for sale.

Ayr was surreal, but we grew to love it, especially the

outdoor municipal swimming pool. Back in Southport, Tom had been having baby swimming lessons since he was five months old. Our weekly trip to the pool was one of my favourite times with him, and watching him dive under the water and swim towards me, Nevermind-style, was amazing. Here, he held on to my back as he had learnt in our lessons as I swam endless, contented lengths.

When we weren't swimming or relaxing in the back yard, Alex and I were planning a great adventure. She hadn't got round to fixing up internet in the unit, so we spent hours in the local cyber café, Tom beside us in the buggy, as we booked hire cars and picked out the best places to stay.

The day before we set off, Alex headed home to make tea and I took Tom to the only internet café that was open in the evenings, tucked inside the bowling alley. I emailed Mum and Anna and my other friends and shared our first few Australia photos on some new 'social media' website called Facebook. Then I found myself hunting for flats in Southport, deciding that a view of the elusive sea could be inspiring. I was missing Mum, but every time I spoke to her over the phone, she complained about the piles of clean clothes in my bedroom, or the unopened bills on the windowsill by the front door, or the sharp increase in her gas bill, which was down to me putting the heating on too much. She loved Tom and me dearly, and I knew I'd be eternally grateful to her for giving us a roof over our heads, but I also knew that the arrangement was coming to an end. Sitting in a bowling alley in a small farming town in Australia, with Tom asleep next to me in his buggy, I felt capable of moving out and managing on my own.

After a futile hour of looking at flats I couldn't afford and/ or didn't actually want to move into, I headed back to Alex and John's. Outside, darkness had descended, bats flitted and swooped low and the air was heavy with the promise of rain. It sprayed us with a fine, dusty mist that clung to my glasses, and by the time I reached the unit, it began to slap down. The smell of wet earth lingered in the air and the back yard was full of even more cane toads than normal.

It had taken a week for Tom to get the hang of the new time zone, and that night, he finally fell asleep in the evening. But I couldn't. As I listened to the thunder and heavy rain outside, I contemplated the road trip ahead. Queensland had so much to offer; I wanted to see the ancient rainforests, the Great Barrier Reef, the incredible wildlife. And Alex, awesome as ever, had offered to drive us to it all. Flying to Australia had been a monumental journey, and we were about to go on another.

Forty-nine

WE TOOK A coach from Ayr to Townsville, where we picked up the cheapest hire car we'd been able to find online. It was tiny, but there was enough space for us and our luggage, good air conditioning and a radio.

Alex drove us along the Bruce Highway, also known as the A1: a long road that travels up the east coast. The journey to Mission Beach, our first overnight stop, would take about three hours, if we did it in one go, but we knew there'd be short breaks along the way, especially as Alex had to do all the driving herself. True to form, Tom slept for most of the time we were on the move and woke when we were stationary. Alex and I chatted about life in general and the plans we had for the coming days, but the whole time, my eyes were on my surroundings. Every time we passed a eucalyptus forest, I squinted, desperate for the blur of grey bark to slow down so I could glimpse a koala, even though I knew they wouldn't be that close to the main road. After an hour, we stopped at the Frosty Mango, a legendary roadside café, for delicious ice cream and stretched legs. Then it was onwards to Cardwell, where the road touched the coast and we got out of the car again. The tide was in, but there was still a thin strip of beach for us to stroll on. From there, we could see across to Hinchinbrook Island. Cardwell Beach was picture-perfect tropical, with palm trees leaning towards the sea and peach and yellow frangipani blooms raining down on to the sand.

We collected handfuls and took them back to the car, and I decorated the dashboard ready for the drive further north. Not long after that, the skies darkened ahead and heavy rain rushed down. Alex was steadfast and kept on driving through the storm, the wipers on our little car working hard, the vivid flowers glowing against the gloom.

As we drove on, the rain lessened and the landscape became more tropical. We were surrounded by lush greenery: ancient, twisty trees with vines hanging from them like ropes. Ahead of us, broad, tree-clad hills rose from the horizon, thick clouds shrouding their peaks. The forest at the side of the road was threadbare in places, because of the huge cyclone that had torn through the area and destroyed swathes of it a year earlier. In those patches, greenery was sparse and tall spikes of snapped trees scratched the sky. We knew Mission Beach was nearby when we started to see large yellow road signs warning us to be "Casso-wary".

The cyclone had stolen acres of habitat from cassowaries and driven many of them into Mission Beach, where they were at risk of being hit by cars - and humans were at risk of being attacked by protective parents. Before I went to Australia, I didn't really know much about cassowaries, but Alex had told me about them and I'd been reading up on them in advance. They are mysterious, flightless birds like something Roald Dahl would write about. Once a female cassowary has laid her eggs, she wanders off into the jungle and leaves the father to sit on them until they hatch, then raise the chicks, training them to survive life in the forest. Cassowaries are as tall as human beings, with red and blue rubbery wattles, horns on their head and thick dagger claws that can tear through human flesh with one swipe. And Mission Beach was a popular haunt with the displaced ones, apparently. I was all at once terrified and intrigued.

Our base in Mission Beach was a backpackers' hostel made of Portakabins surrounding a swimming pool. It was bright and cheerful and most of the people staying there were gap-year types. A wooden veranda jutted out of the front of the rooms, providing a place to sit and talk with Alex, and to write when she had gone to bed. The room itself was tiny, with space for a double bed and nothing else. Tom's bed for the night would have to be his buggy, wedged inside the pokey bathroom so that Alex and I would have to step over him every time we used the loo.

Before bed, I went to the communal kitchen to clean and sterilise a bottle for Tom and fix him up with some formula. In there, a loud group of British people a bit younger than me were washing pots and giving me odd looks. I don't think anyone expects to share their backpacker's hostel with a baby; they were probably worried that they were going to be kept awake all night by crying. I did wonder how exactly I was going to convince Tom to go to sleep for a full night strapped into his buggy, which didn't even lay down completely flat, but given the lack of space, it was his only option.

When I came back with Tom's bedtime bottle, Alex had taken him into the pool.

"Best to use up all that energy," she said. "He has spent most of the day sitting in the car."

"You're a genius," I said. I put the bottle on the veranda and walked over to the pool, dipping my toes in the water.

"A bedtime swim," I said. "Wish we could do that at home."

"Look at the moon," Alex said, pointing it out to Tom. It was almost full and particularly bright.

"MOON!" Tom exclaimed, gazing up at it, his eyes excited and wide.

Soon, clouds sidled in front of the moon until it was completely obscured, and dollops of rain fell from the sky, punching holes in the surface of the pool water. Tom laughed and splashed and tilted his open mouth skywards, thrilled by the luxury of water on water. I knew that Australia might never be a memory for him, but he had swum by moonlight and in the rain, and I'd always be able to tell him about it.

The storm was over as swiftly as it started. Tom toddled along the bright, wooden veranda in front of our room, talking to the hostel's resident cat and offering it a leaf.

"Come on," I said, "time for bed." I scooped him up in a towel, sat down on one of the plastic patio chairs on the veranda and plonked him on my lap. "That was probably the most exciting swim you've ever had," I said. "Possibly the most exciting swim you'll ever have. Sorry, son, you've peaked at one."

I hoped that Australia wouldn't be my last adventure with Tom. He had proved to be an exemplary travelling companion and he couldn't even speak yet. Once again, I imagined the conversations we'd have about the world when he could begin to understand it. Travelling so far away from home may be once in a lifetime, but I knew there would be plenty more opportunities for exploration, discovery, and adventure – even if they were just to the local park.

As I dried Tom off, rocking him on my knees, I overheard the group of travellers I'd seen in the kitchen. They were gathered around a table on a veranda round the other side of the pool.

"OK, OK, I have never . . ." one of them began, "I have

never . . . had a threesome." Cue jeers and cheers and laughter.

I Have Never: a drinking game I recognised from my student days. I wasn't a fan of it, or drinking games, full stop, but I knew that that group of people, also in their early twenties like me, were having a very different type of trip to the one I was having. And even though in a former life I never would have believed it, that was fine by me.

Fifty

WE SPENT TWO nights in Mission Beach before
moving on to Kuranda, a rainforest village close to
Cairns. The drive was more than two hours, but it went
quickly. As we drove further north, crossing countless creeks
with British names, the scenery became more impressive and
dramatic.

Our home in Kuranda was a rainforest lodge: a great
wooden barn with rooms off a central, communal table. There
were no cots, but Tom had slept for two nights in his buggy
in Mission Beach, so we knew he would be fine in it again.
Once he'd fallen asleep, Alex and I sat outside the room at the
large, wooden table, talking to fellow travellers and drinking
wine.

In Kuranda, the moisture in the air was palpable. At night,
our lodge was surrounded by a cacophony of mysterious calls
and cries. We could have stayed in a hostel in Cairns itself,
but I'd wanted to see as much of the rainforest as I could, so
we'd made the decision to stay in the very thick of it – and we
were glad we had. In the communal area, giant, golden bugs
knocked noisily against the florescent lights overhead. I learnt
that they were called Christmas beetles, not because of their
impressive shininess, but because of the time of year they can
be seen in Australia and Papau New Guinea. It was nearly
Christmas; I wasn't looking forward to returning to the cold
and the dinginess, but I was intrigued to see whether Tom

would understand something exciting was happening, and hoped he'd appreciate his presents.

Tom and I took the Kuranda Railway through the jungle, and rode a glass cable car over the treetops. It stopped at several stations, each one on a different level of the canopy, where elevated wooden boardwalks snaked between the trees.

"Well, this makes a change from Southport Pier," I said to Tom, pushing him along the shady paths, past the trunks of ancient trees, leaves as big as him, and spiders' webs so huge they made me shiver (and insist that the people at the cable car stations checked my hair and body for stray spiders before I boarded the next ride).

One of my favourite photographs from that particular excursion was taken by a stranger: me, backpack on, just casually pushing my baby through the rainforest in his buggy.

I was so grateful to Alex: for having us, for being our driver, for understanding why the adventure was so important to me. The fact she was more unfazed by babies than I was made the whole trip more pleasant for everyone concerned. When I said I'd like to try diving on the Great Barrier Reef, Alex offered to look after Tom while I did it, and said she'd drive me to the port to catch my boat. As she negotiated the zig-zag roads in our hire car, Tom threw up his breakfast. I wanted to stay ashore and help Alex clean up the mess, but she insisted that I didn't miss my boat out to the reef. While I saw breathtaking coral and tropical fish, Alex cleaned up my baby's puke and took him to a seafront paddling pool for a splash.

On our way back from Cairns, Alex took us on an inland detour over the Atherton Tablelands, a longer route than the Bruce Highway, but more scenic, that would allow us to see the edge of Red Dirt Country. There, at the side of the road, we saw phenomenal termite mounds the size of houses. We stopped to take photographs next to them and saw our first wild kangaroo in the form of shattered bones spread across the ground.

I was tired that day, thanks to a combination of the oppressive humidity and staying up late the night before, talking to travellers, writing and listening to the wonderful jungle noises that I never wanted to forget. There had been no time for coffee before we left Kuranda, and we planned to stop at a coffee plantation en route, but until then, without the daily caffeine kick I'd come to rely on since becoming a mum, I was useless. Despite the breathtaking beauty outside our hire car windows, just like Tom, I closed my eyes and let the motion of the car lull me to sleep.

"Emily," Alex said, with all the sternness she used when it was my turn to wash the dishes in our student flat, "wake up, you're not missing this." She had parked up at Millaa Millaa Falls, one of those beauty spots that always looks amazing and deserted in the guidebooks but is overrun with tourists in reality (and you can't really get annoyed about tourists when you are one). "Come on," Alex said, again, unfastening Tom from the back of the car. "I don't care how knackered you are; you have to see this."

We were lucky: it was relatively early in the day and the hoards of coach trippers were yet to arrive. Instead, we found a deserted, jade-green pool with a strip of frothy water cascading into it from high above. (Later, we found out that it had been used in a shampoo advert; that was the kind of place it was.) It was just us, a few dragonflies the size of sparrows, turtles basking on the rocks and an inquisitive brush-turkey. Tucked deep in the jungle, surrounded by overflowing basket ferns and enormous, bright blooms, it was so ridiculously beautiful, even beating the temple in India (the memory of which is now permanently ruined: every time I look at a photograph of it, I remember labour). I liked to think that Nan would have approved of me spending her money on that moment; it might not have been the most sensible investment or a tangible thing, but I knew that the memory would be up there with the best I'd ever had, and that has to be good value for money.

As dreamy as it would have been to take Tom for a dip at Millaa Millaa, swimming was forbidden, so I slipped my sandals off and dipped my toes in the water, sitting Tom on my knee. "It's amazing!" I whispered into his ear.

"'mazing," he copied.

I didn't notice Alex getting my camera out of my bag and photographing us sitting at the edge of the water, or her zooming in on us and clicking the shutter just as Tom said, "Wow!" his little lips poking out like a daffodil's trumpet. The sun cream I'd managed to smear across the lens gave the picture an accidental soft focus, which was apt; the moment felt like a dream, a culmination, a beginning and an end.

Fifty-one

TOM AND I had a few more days left in Ayr before we'd be moving on to Sydney. We visited a wildlife sanctuary and finally met the elusive cassowary, which was every bit as strange and majestic as we'd imagined. We fed wallabies by hand, Tom giggling at the feel of their muzzles on his palm and amazed by babies peeping out of their mothers' pouches. When we had our photograph taken with a koala, Tom patted its wiry hair and said, "Ah, nice teddy," and I didn't know who was cuter, the koala or him.

On our penultimate day in Ayr, we went to a Christmas fair and queued up for Tom to meet the world's worst Father Christmas, who, as well as a beard that looked like it was made from cotton wool, was also wearing a pair of those joke glasses with a big plastic nose stuck to the front. In Tom's first photo with Santa, he is clutching me tightly, screaming, a look of sheer terror on his face. At the fair, I bought John and Alex herbs and plants for their garden, along with a frangipani tree to remind Alex of our road trip. I wasn't sure what I could possibly buy that would sufficiently thank them for welcoming us into their new home when they didn't even have furniture and we were riddled with nits, and Alex for driving us miles and mopping up my kid's vomit while I disappeared on a boat, but it was the best I could do.

When I said goodbye to Alex at the airport, we were both weeping. It would be months or even years before she'd next be coming to England and I didn't know how I would cope without her. My sadness was temporarily curbed in Sydney, our last port of call before heading home, where Tom and I had a whirlwind couple of days exploring the sights. Claire lived right in the centre of the city, making it easy for us to get around. Tom was an instant hit with her friends, joining us at the dining table for tea and lapping up the attention they lavished on him. We visited the Harbour Bridge and the Opera House, where I chased him up and down the tall steps outside. At Bondi Beach, Tom toddled off along the soft sand at speed, throwing his arms around unsuspecting sunbathers. I caught up with him, breathless and apologetic, but thankfully, everyone he'd preyed upon seemed to be delighted by the experience.

Claire and I stayed up late on the balcony of her high-rise apartment, drinking wine and putting the world to rights. On the second night, I decided we'd have to stay longer, and Claire said we'd be welcome, but when I tried to ring Korean Air to find out how much it would cost to change our tickets, I couldn't get through, and that was probably for the best. Just before we left for Sydney Airport, I rang my mum. I'd been trying to get hold of Jane, who'd offered to meet Tom and me at Manchester Airport, but her phone was switched off.

"Look," Mum said, sighing, "she told me not to tell you in case you worried, but Jane's in hospital. "

"Why?!"

"We don't know at the moment. She's having tests. But she's awake and sitting up."

"I want to go and see her," I said.

Jane was like family and the reason I hadn't totally lost the plot when I was pregnant. Ever since she'd reacted so calmly to my news in her car that night after work, she'd been a source of confidence, practical help and love. I couldn't stand to think of her ill. I wanted to be back in Manchester with her straightaway, but I had to get through three flights and three days before I'd be home.

"Let's just get you back in the country first, shall we? I'll collect you from the airport."

"Thanks, Mum."

I must have looked glum when we were waiting to board the flight from Sydney to Seoul.

"Excuse me, are you travelling on your own with him?" The woman next to me nodded at Tom, who was playing at my feet.

"Yeah."

"Bloody hell, you're brave."

"Or mad. One of the two."

"I'm Nicola," she said, "let me give you a hand."

Nicola was my age, on her way back from visiting friends in Australia, equally nervous about her return to reality. She swapped seats with somebody so she could sit near me and Tom, giving us comfort and company for the journey from Sydney to Seoul. We only had twenty-four hours in South Korea, and I'd wanted to explore, but our flight was delayed, meaning we couldn't venture beyond the sleek airport hotel we'd been allocated. So Nicola, Tom and I had dinner together, paid for by the airline, in the hotel's fancy Italian restaurant. It wasn't what I'd expected to be eating in Seoul, but it was delicious nonetheless. Tanned and handsome after his month in the tropics, Tom sat resplendent in his high chair, smearing tomato sauce all over his face, whilst Nicola and I chinked glasses of cold white wine. Inevitably, the question of how I'd ended up travelling on my own with Tom came up, and after it, the one about his father, who I'd hardly thought of in Australia.

"You're a great mum," Nicola said. "You're doing an amazing job, and all on your own."

"Thanks," I said, "I'm trying my best." I didn't want to tell her that I felt like a fraud when people said things like that, that I wasn't truly doing things on my own because I had my mum. I wanted to know what it was like to have a household that was just mine and Tom's, to be responsible for the bills, to have to remember for myself when it was time to replenish my stock of nappies. I wanted to know what it was like, but I was terrified of how I'd cope.

When you travel, you sometimes meet people who you might never see again, transients, who can touch your life and help you in small ways that makes them unforgettable. The same thing had happened on my journey to becoming a mother: the woman in New Zealand who'd reassured me, via an internet messageboard, that I'd survive what lay ahead; the taxi driver who didn't judge me; the midwife, Beth, who'd made me excited by the prospect of motherhood. That night, Nicola bathed Tom while I sorted out our bags for the next leg of the journey. As I folded clothes and counted nappies, I listened to her voice echoing against the gloss of the en-suite bathroom, telling Tom he was cute and good, and I was so glad that she had been next to us in the boarding queue.

"To more adventures," Nicola said on the plane back to London.

"Yeah, more adventures," I said, tapping my plastic cup of warm white wine against hers.

On the flight, Nicola got talking to a group of people a

few rows in front who were taking full advantage of the free in-flight drinks. She kept going back and forth between me and Tom and them and ordering more wine.

"Go and sit with them," I said.

"Are you sure?"

"It's an order," I said. "Enjoy the last bit of your holiday."

Later, when Nicola and her new friends had been thoroughly ticked off by the cabin crew and told that they were forbidden from ordering any more alcohol, one of them came swaying down the aisle towards my seat.

"Excuse me," he said, "my mate's just been sick. I don't suppose you've got a baby wipe we could borrow, have you?"

"I've got hundreds," I said, feeling way more organised and grown-up than I was, "but I don't want them back when you're done, thanks."

Somewhere between Seoul and London, I was queuing for the toilet with Tom in my arms, when the man in the nearest seat began shouting at us in Korean and gesticulating wildly. I smiled awkwardly, hoping the queue would move on quickly. The man kept shouting, though, and I soon realised that he was pointing at the floor, where something brown and round was rolling in the aisle. I patted my head for my glasses, but realised I'd left them back at my seat. We'd recently had dinner, so I thanked the man for pointing out that someone had dropped some food on the floor and bent down to pick it up. It wasn't a bread roll at all though. It was a turd. A turd that had somehow made its way out of Tom's nappy and down the leg of his pyjama bottoms and on to the aircraft floor. The thing that the man had been shouting at me was clearly Korean for "your baby's shit is on the floor of the plane and you had better clean it up now before someone stands in it." As I grabbed baby wipes and nappy sacks and apologised profusely, Tom toddled off to the plane's door, where he reached for the chunky, bright yellow and red emergency door handle, which must have looked to him like something made by Little Tikes. I bagged the turd like a dog owner in the park, wrestled Tom into the toilet cubicle and attempted, in the limited space available, to clean him up. Except he kept pressing the 'help' button, because that was as interesting as the emergency-exit lever, so I had to keep fielding the concerned flight attendants who were rapping on the door to make sure we were OK. I had known the journey home wouldn't be as fun as the outbound one, but I didn't expect to be scrabbling around on the floor picking up poo. And it was about to get worse.

I waved goodbye to Nicola at Heathrow. She looked pallid and knackered, huddled under the airline blanket she'd managed to sneak off the plane.

"I just want my mum. And a bath."

"Me too," I said.

Nicola and I stayed in touch and a year or so later, she emailed me to tell me she was pregnant, and that the father didn't want anything to do with it. I told her not to worry, that she'd be a brilliant mum. Despite everything that had happened to me, and my confidence that Nicola would be fine, the suddenness of her imminent transition from backpacker to mother was a shock. A few months later, she had a beautiful daughter who looked just like her; from her emails and photographs, she seemed right at home in motherhood, just as she had with Tom in Seoul.

Only one more flight to go, the shortest of them all, and Tom and I would be almost home. All I could think about was getting back to Manchester and seeing Jane. Tiredness stung my eyes and I felt translucent, but I knew that we'd nearly made it. But our final flight was delayed because of strong winds. The airline staff couldn't tell me exactly when it would be safe to take off, and advised me to stay close to the boarding gate to await information. I phoned Mum and told her I didn't know what time we'd be arriving back in Manchester, but that I'd keep her posted. Exhausted and unable to find a seat, I wheeled Tom, who was sleeping, into the corner of a corridor and curled up there on the cold, hard floor. It was difficult to sleep with heels clip-clopping and suitcases rumbling right past my head, and the draught that stung the small of my back, but there was little else to do but try.

Finally, an announcement spouted out of the PA, telling us to queue for boarding. I bought a scalding, overpriced black coffee and pushed Tom over to the gate.

"You can't take that on the plane," said the airline woman, when she saw the car-seat-on-wheels.

"I needed somewhere for him to sleep while we waited," I said.

"Well it'll have to go in the hold now."

"Look, are there any spare seats on this flight? He's asleep and if there are, he can just go straight into the seat like this and I won't have to wake him."

"There might be spare seats on the plane, madam, but that car seat is not approved for aviation use."

"It is! It's *designed* for aviation use. I've just flown across the world with it, for God's sake." As anger rose in my voice, the air hostess got more patronising. I still remember the lipstick streaking her teeth.

"It might very well be alright for whichever airline you flew across the world with, madam, but it is not approved by us.

You can't just bring any car seat you like on to a plane, you know, there are *regulations*. I don't make them up, you know, it's for your child's safety."

It felt like I was being told off for being a very silly girl, like when the anaesthetist wouldn't let me have an epidural because she didn't think I'd done my research. "I know about the regulations," I said, lifting Tom's legs, trying to find the Civil Aviation Authority sticker that was somewhere on the thing. "It's CAA-approved. If there are no spare seats on the flight, I'll put him on my lap, but if there are, please just let him have one."

"I tell you what I'm going to do," she said. "I'm going to board the plane and see if there are any seats left. If there are, you can take him on board in that." She looked at the seat in disgust.

"Thank you."

"But if there aren't, it goes in the hold and he goes on your knee." The airline woman looked at me with as much disdain as she did the car seat. I couldn't help but wonder whether she'd have spoken to me in the same way if I'd had a husband with me.

I watched as the other passengers filed on to the plane. It was the Friday-night commuter flight from London to Manchester and most of them were in smart business dress. When everyone had boarded, the woman turned to me and said, tersely: "There is a spare seat. You can take your baby on in that seat, but it had better be aviation-approved, because I haven't authorised it."

"Thanks," I said.

The car seat wouldn't fit down the thin aisle of the smaller plane, so a flight attendant helped me lift it to the back of the plane, where we'd been allocated seats. As we passed the other passengers, they heralded our entrance with a slow round of applause. "Why are they clapping?" I asked the attendant, clutching the front of Tom's car seat and shuffling backwards down the plane.

"Don't worry about that, madam, just concentrate on getting to your seat so we can take off as quickly as possible."

The clapping continued, though, and with it came tuts and headshakes and dirty looks. Not realising that I'd been told to board the plane last, the other passengers clearly thought that I was just running late and delaying the flight even more. All the way down the plane, I was surrounded by mumbles and judgements and that slow, sarcastic clapping. So I broke, and I took everything out on them: the lack of proper sleep, the reality I was about to face, the shit British weather, my fears about Jane.

"They told me to get on last," I blurted out, breaking into a cry, "because of my car seat. That's not my fault! Can't you see that? It's not my fault?! Why are you clapping?"

We'd arrived at our seats now, and the flight attendant and I had lowered Tom into his. I wasn't sitting down, though, I was standing in the aisle, sobbing. "You don't understand. None of you understand. The woman told me to get on the plane last. I'm knackered and I am travelling with my baby and why do people have to be so . . . so . . . *horrible?*"

The flight attendant, clearly terrified at the prospect of an air-rage incident, tried his best to sit me down.

"Look, madam, we really need to take off now. If you don't sit down and put your belt on, we might miss our slot with air traffic control and then we'll be even later."

"It's not my fault," I said, sitting down and grappling with the seatbelt. "I've been travelling for hours, I'm knackered, it's not my fault."

"I know," he said, offering me a tissue and looking at me like I was a madwoman. "You'll be home soon."

Home. All I could think about was seeing Mum's face when we got through customs, of telling her about our adventures as she drove us back to Southport.

Mum always had my back, no matter what. She's the most non-confrontational person I know, but in the hospital, when the anaesthetist was refusing to give me the epidural I begged her for, Mum left the room because she said she had an over-whelming urge to punch her. She would have stuck up for me when the horrible people were shaming me as I boarded the plane with my baby. At the back of my mind was the frightening knowledge that I was going to have to move out of her house in the not too distant future, but for now, all I could think about was seeing her and that first, soothing hug.

In the chaos of getting on to the plane, I'd forgotten to send Mum a message to let her know it was finally due to take off. I tried to, once Tom and I were settled in our seats, but the flight attendant told me off and I had to put my phone away.

The wind buffeted the plane all the way back to Manchester. It was an uncomfortable ride, but quicker than usual, and Tom slept all the way. After passport control and the baggage carousel, I set up my luggage system for one last time and cut through the bustle towards customs. Despite my exhaustion, I practically sprinted down the 'nothing to declare' corridor, desperate to see Mum's face when the doors slid open. When they did, Mum wasn't there.

"Where are you?!" I whinged, tears and snot leaking down my face. "I thought you'd be waiting for us."

"Well, I haven't set off yet," she said. "I was waiting for the nod from you."

"Sorry," I said. "I had a nightmare getting on that flight at Heathrow and they wouldn't let me use my phone when I did."

"Well I didn't know that, did I?"

I could feel a familiar tension edging between us.

"Couldn't you have checked the departures online?" I said, knowing that we had at least another hour and a half of more airport-waiting ahead.

"I'm sorry, love, but it's a windy night. I didn't want to set off in the car until I knew you were definitely on your way."

"Hang on," I said, pushing Tom into a toilet cubicle, "I need the loo. Tom, speak to your nanny for a bit." I passed Tom the phone and wrestled the luggage into the cramped room. As I grappled with the lock, I heard a plop followed by Tom saying "Oh dear".

My phone was down the toilet.

"Oh, God," I said, wincing and reaching in to pick it up.

Despite its fast retrieval and several blasts under the hand dryer, it was completely dead. I had to change Australian dollars into pounds using the crap airport exchange rate, then buy a sandwich for Tom and use the change to call Mum from a payphone.

"I'm leaving now," she said.

"Don't come to the airport," I said, "I'm going to Rosie's." Rosie had moved into my old room when I had moved out to have Tom and we had become friends. Now, she lived in a different house-share in Didsbury. I couldn't stand the thought of hanging out in an airport any longer, so I got a taxi there.

Predictably, it was raining hard in Manchester. I was still wearing my sandals and when I got out of the taxi, I stepped right into an icy puddle. In Rosie's house, Tom toddled around, asking "What's dat?" about everything, from paintings to ashtrays.

"He's wide awake," she said.

"He's on Australia time," I said. "I've no idea how long it's going to take him to readjust."

Mum took forever to arrive. When she did, I fell into her arms and told her I was sorry for shouting at her, that I'd just been desperate to see her when those doors parted.

"It's alright," she said. "Anyway, why don't I take Tom home tonight, and all your dirty washing, and you can stay here with Rosie and visit Jane in the hospital tomorrow?"

I really didn't know how I was going to manage without my mum.

Fifty-two

THE NEXT DAY, I had to fight my way out of bed to catch the bus to the hospital for visiting time. Rosie lent me a pair of winter boots and a coat and I set off to Wythenshawe with a bunch of flowers. When I arrived, Jane was sitting up in bed, reading.

"Hi," I said.

"Oh my goodness! I didn't expect to see you here. Sit down, sit down."

"I had to come and see you," I said.

"I am so sorry I couldn't pick you up from the airport."

"Don't be ridiculous. Are you OK?"

"Yes, fine. There was a lump they were worried about, but it's only a cyst."

"That's such a relief."

"Yes. The worst thing about all this is that I've been diagnosed with diabetes. No more cakes for me."

"Gutted," I said.

"Anyway, enough about me – tell me about *Australia!*"

I perched myself on the edge of the bed and scrolled through the images on the screen on the back of the camera. Tiny pictures, all of them vivid, of everything we had just done.

"Well, I must admit," Jane said, "we all thought you were mad dragging Tom all the way to Australia, but it looks to me like you both had a wonderful time."

"We really did," I said.

"You were planning to go when you found out you were pregnant, weren't you?"

"Yep. I thought it was game over when I did that test in the call centre loos."

"Well, it wasn't."

"No, it definitely wasn't. Anyway, I feel ready to move out of Mum's now. If I can take Tom backpacking in Australia, I am pretty sure we can manage in our own place."

"Can you afford it?"

"If the travel business keeps going well," I said. "January's always busy and that's not far off."

"True," said Jane.

"Do you think we'll be OK?"

"I think you'll be fine," Jane said, "but I don't know how your poor mother will manage without you!"

"Oh, she'll miss Tom," I said, "but I think she'll cope without me."

I stayed at Rosie's again that night, and the jet lag roused me early the next morning. Everyone in the house was asleep, so I got dressed and went for a walk. It was past sunrise, but there was hardly any daylight, and the pavements were covered with the last few sopping leaves of autumn. I walked past countless To Let signs, making a mental note of the streets they were on. It would be expensive to live in Didsbury, and I had no idea whether I'd be able to find a landlord willing to take me on, but I wanted to be near our friends.

I kept walking until I was in Withington, on the old familiar walk from the bus stop that had become an angst-ridden waddle two years earlier. When I got to my old house, the curtains in my bedroom were closed. They were the same ones: lace in the bay window, chintz behind. I thought about how many sleepless nights I'd spent in that room, how many times I'd puked in the avocado toilet, how nearly every night I'd spent in that house had been fraught with worry and fear. I wished I could have seen what it was really going to be like; maybe then I could have been happy

I wrapped Rosie's coat tighter against the cold wind, and made my way back to her house. Breakfast, then the first train back to Southport, to be with my son.

Fifty-three

THIS IS THE still.

I close the Devil Book and slide it on to the wonky book case.

I asked Tom what book he wanted for his bedtime story, expecting *Peter Rabbit* or *The Gruffalo* or *Not Now Bernard*, and he asked for "The Devil Book". It terrified me, for a moment, until he got up out of his little bed, toddled over to the bookcase and took a board book off the shelf.

"The Devil Book," he said, handing it to me.

It was a souvenir from Australia, all about Tasmanian devils, a memory of the time a flight attendant told him he sounded like one.

"Oh, the Devil Book," I said, sighing with relief, glad that he wasn't hankering after anything Satanic.

We read through the pages together and looked at the pictures and spoke about what we saw. Tom can speak now, in full sentences, his consonants clear, his vocabulary wide, his voice still babyish and sweet. We have whole, long, full conversations about animals and books and the things we see in museums. I'm relearning all that's amazing about the world and it's even more amazing this time around. Caterpillars turn into butterflies, dinosaurs once roamed the earth, the seasons change the trees.

Tom is almost asleep now. His fat fingers are laced around the chewed tail of the stuffed monkey he's had since birth. His knuckles are dimples. At the nape of his neck, just above his stork bites, his hair gathers in blond ringlets. His eyelashes are two ample black crescents I wish I could steal. Under the glow of the beetle light next to his bed, his cherubic face is tinged with green.

His is a jungle bedroom, with a huge leaf canopy, a massive collection of stuffed animals and monkeys climbing the curtains. It's slim, L-shaped, cosy, and it's a reminder of our trip to the Australian jungle. Where we live now is very different to that.

Our home is a two-up-two-down, mid-terraced house, with a doorstep that leads straight out on to the Yorkshire-stone pavement. It's in Salford, just around the corner from Anna's house. There's a vast, permanent puddle in the back alley that we have to pass on our way to nursery. Tom loves splashing in puddles in his lion wellies and his matching sou'wester, but he always gives that one a wide berth because of the crocodile that lives in its oily depths. That's the closest thing to Australia around here. Whenever we take the bus into town, Tom tells me and everyone on board to look at the castle, straining in his buggy, pointing out of the window at the grey tower block that looms above Salford Shopping City. Our back yard is a small oblong of concrete, but we filled it with an inflatable paddling pool, a table and chairs and plants that Tom loves to water. Weeds grow out of the cracks in the path at the front of our house, but we leave them there because the flowers they bear are bright.

We love it here. Tom really likes nursery and brings home soggy paintings and diary entries about his days. I have two jobs: selling holidays from home and being a librarian. The fivers from Tom's father are sporadic and, eventually, I will let go and close the maintenance case.

For my MA dissertation, I'm writing a collection of short stories. When I have time, I write about being Tom's mum on the internet. Sometimes people read it and respond, and it makes me feel less alone in the hours when Tom is asleep.

"I love you," I whisper, as I lean in and kiss him.

"Love you," he murmurs, his eyes still closed.

I sit for a while and listen to his breathing soften and fall into the rhythm of sleep. I could stay here for hours, marvelling at him. Sometimes the fact he even exists hits me and I have to stop and run the months over in my head because I can't believe it. He's two now. The shock is fading now, but it's still there. Watching your child sleep is fascinating and satisfying: your work for the day is done, your child is happy and calm and there. I could stay here all night, not just because I am in awe of Tom, but because then I wouldn't have to do the housework.

I sigh and heave myself off the low bed, clicking off the beetle light and creeping to the door. In the bathroom, I listen to the quiet sizzle of bubbles dying in the bath. I pull out the plug and collect the nit comb and the various plastic sea creatures that are bobbing in the lukewarm water. The octopus has got black mould growing in the gaps between its suckers, I notice. I dig my old toothbrush out of the tampon basket, sit down on the toilet and begin to scrub at the mould. It spatters my face and smells like soil. It is an act of love. Twenty minutes later, the octopus is spotless, but the house is still a tip.

I gather the small, paint-stained clothes from the bathroom floor, take them into Tom's room and sit on his bed again. He's properly asleep now, his eyes moving freakishly fast beneath the thin skin of his eyelids. He feels me sit down, purses his lips, furrows his brow and chews the air.

I'm not thinking about the dirty washing, or the clean-but-damp washing, or the pans piled up to the taps. The psychedelic pat of Play-Doh that's melded to the living room floor melts away. The lumps of food under the table are gone, as are the yogurty fingerprints on the telly screen, and the raisins that are stuck to my socks. Never mind the flashing number seven on the answering machine, or the essay that's due in tomorrow, or the potty that needs emptying. Forget the fact it's bin night and there's a small mountain of full nappy sacks by the back door.

When I've been lying next to Tom for another ten minutes, I kiss his springy cheek again. Then I go downstairs, little clothes bundled in my arms, to face the incredible chaos we call home.

Epilogue

IT'S A SHARP, March day, just before Tom's ninth birthday, and we are rushing down Market Street. I had an eye test this afternoon and Tom sat through the whole thing without complaining. Afterwards, we tried on glasses and pulled daft faces in the mirrors.

"Mum, your feet are bleeding!" Tom said, behind me on an escalator in the Arndale.

"I know, it's just my shoes," I said.

The morning had been sunny, so I'd swapped my winter boots for summer pumps and they'd grated the skin off the backs of my ankles.

"Ouch."

"Yep, ouch. Let's just get home as quickly as we can."

We don't get home quickly though, because on our way to the train station, Tom remembers the new play area in Piccadilly Gardens. "*Please* can I go on it?"

"You're a bit big for it now, aren't you?" It seems absurd to think that my son is getting too big for children's play areas, but it is true.

"No, there are bigger kids than me on there!"

"Go on, then," I say, glad of a rest from the shoes. "Just five minutes."

I plonk myself down on the steps overlooking the play area, rubbing my throbbing ankles with my thumbs. Tom climbs a tall silver pole with a wheel at the top, clinging on with his legs, his body dangling upside down, his coat flapping around his ears. "Mum!" he shouts, his hair swaying wildly in the cold breeze, "look at me!"

"Very impressive!"

I watch as Tom and the other children begin playing together, taking turns to hang from the wheel and spin each other as fast as they can. Two of them are chattering in Arabic, the language barrier broken by the ever-universal rules of play.

"Come on," I say, "I'm freezing here!"

"Two more minutes?"

"Go on, then, but you have to stick to it if you want film night tonight. I'm timing you."

Over the years, Tom and I have danced at festivals, camped on beaches and hunted for buried treasure, amongst other unforgettable things, but one of our favourite things to do is film night. The two of us, curled up on the sofa with blankets and the cat, watching a film, scoffing popcorn and chocolate. I know I haven't got long left before my son's desire to stay in and watch films with his mother is a thing of the past, so I want to squeeze in as many film nights as I can.

"Is that Queen Victoria?" Tom says, bounding over to me.

I look over my shoulder at the familiar statue looming above.

"Yep, that's her."

"She's huge!"

"I know," I say. "It's her dress! Imagine wearing something that heavy all the time." I grab Tom's hand. "Sit down with me for a minute," I tell him.

"I thought you wanted to catch the train."

"Just sit here with me."

"Why?"

"Because this is a very important statue."

"Mum! I thought you weren't interested in the royal family."

"I'm not," I say, his assertion making me laugh.

"You know when I found out I was pregnant with you, it was a big shock?"

"Yes."

"Well I was really sad and scared and I came and sat right here under Queen Victoria."

"I bet she was saying *I am not amused*," he said, adopting his best posh-lady voice.

"Why?!" I'm laughing again.

"You know, she probably wouldn't have been amused with you because of, you know, the *sex* thing. She probably wouldn't have approved."

"You're absolutely right. She wouldn't have done. But how do you know that's what she used to say? The 'not amused' thing?"

"I dunno." He shrugs. "I think I saw it on *Horrible Histories*. Tell me the rest of the story, anyway."

"Well, after that day when I was really upset, I came back and I sat on Queen Victoria's steps again and I decided that things were going to be OK, because they'd have to be. But I didn't like the way Queen Victoria was looking at me."

"Was she not amused again?"

"*Definitely* not amused."

"So where did you move to?"

"I moved round the back of Queen Victoria."

"So she couldn't see you?"

"So she couldn't see me. Except I wasn't round the back of Queen Victoria."

Tom's brow furrows and he looks, for a flash, like he did when he was a newborn baby. "Where were you, then?"

"Well, I did go round the back of Queen Victoria, to the steps around the other side, but it turns out you can't see the back of her, because there's another statue there. I didn't notice it until five years later."

"What's that statue then?"

"Let's go and have a look," I say, leading him around the steps.

"It's a lady with some babies," Tom says. "Who is she?"

"I don't know."

"It looks like Mary and Jesus, but she's holding two babies."

"I know. Holding two babies and feeding one."

"I like the mosaic behind her too. It's a lovely statue. What's her name?"

"Well, she hasn't got a name, but the statue is called Maternity, which means having babies."

"I know what *maternity* means, Mum."

"Of course you do."

"Hang on, what does that say, underneath the lady?" Tom reads the carved words out loud: "*Let me but bear your love, I'll bear your cares.* That's nice."

"Yes. It's from Shakespeare, *Henry IV*, think."

"Didn't you know she was there when you sat underneath her, then?"

"No," I say. "I was looking right in front of me, at children playing in the fountains."

"You never let *me* play in the fountains."

"No I do not, there's all kinds of horrible crap in that bloody water."

"Weren't you worried about the children playing there that day?"

"No. I was too busy worrying about *you* and what the heck I'd do with you when you arrived."

"But you didn't need to worry, Mum," Tom says, putting his arm around me, "it was only me."

"Yep. I'd have been excited if I'd have known all the fun we were going to have."

"Like film nights?"

"Exactly like film nights. Let's go."

And we walk quickly to catch our train, holding hands (but only when we cross the road), leaving Victoria behind.

Acknowledgements

M ASSIVE THANKS TO my mum, my sister, my uncle, Julie and anyone else who babysat while I wrote and edited this book, or who listened to me and encouraged me to write it. An extra thank you to Mum, for being a devoted and brilliant nan, and to my sister for being an excellent auntie. An enormous and heartfelt thank you to Emma Jane Unsworth for unerring friendship, for reading and re-reading the many different guises this book took on its road to readiness, for copious wine and advice and late night discussions, and for kicking my ass when I almost chickened out. Thank you to Matt, for much-needed and appreciated support, motivation and love. Thanks to Natalie O'Hara, Valerie O'Riordan and Richard Hirst for reading, for friendship and for feeding back. Thank you to all my wonderful family, friends and colleagues. Special thanks to Amy for being an extraordinary pal and auntie, and to Sophia for being the same (and for all those unforgettable Sunday walks). Ella, I will never forget that horrible cup of tea and the friendship and adventures it led to – muchas gracias. Thanks Sarah G for believing in me and being ace. Jude, you were and are awesome and I will always remember, thank you very much. Claire N, thank you for your understanding and positivity. Rachel, thanks for repeatedly popping back and making us both smile. Huge thanks to everyone who appears in the book, for whatever role you played. Thank you to the people who read and commented on my blog and gave me the confidence to keep writing. Thank you to Peter Francis and all the lovely staff at Gladstone's Library, where much of this book was written, to the Arvon Foundation for amazing opportunities and to Kate Clanchy for guidance. Thanks to Jen and Chris at Salt Publishing for your patience, support and genius.

Finally, a gargantuan and indescribable thank you to my son, who encouraged me to publish this book and understood why I wrote it, and who is ace. Thanks for giving me something magnificent to write about, and for making my twenties (and thirties) the best.

NEW BOOKS FROM SALT

XAN BROOKS
The Clocks in This House All Tell Different Times
(978-1-78463-093-5)

RON BUTLIN
Billionaires' Banquet (978-1-78463-100-0)

MICKEY J CORRIGAN
Project XX (978-1-78463-097-3)

MARIE GAMESON
The Giddy Career of Mr Gadd (deceased) (978-1-78463-118-5)

LESLEY GLAISTER
The Squeeze (978-1-78463-116-1)

NAOMI HAMILL
How To Be a Kosovan Bride (978-1-78463-095-9)

CHRISTINA JAMES
Fair of Face (978-1-78463-108-6)

SIMON KINCH
Two Sketches of Disjointed Happiness (978-1-78463-110-9)

This book has been typeset by
SALT PUBLISHING LIMITED
using Neacademia, a font designed by Sergei Egorov
for the Rosetta Type Foundry in the Czech Republic.
It is manufactured using Creamy 70gsm, a Forest
Stewardship Council™ certified paper from Stora Enso's
Anjala Mill in Finland. It was printed and bound by
Clays Limited in Bungay, Suffolk, Great Britain.

LONDON
GREAT BRITAIN
MMXVII